Anthropology and autobiography

Social anthropology, more than any other discipline in the humanities and the social sciences, has developed the practice of intensive fieldwork by a single individual. Clearly, the 'race', nationality, gender, age and personal history of the fieldworker affect the process, interaction and emergent material, yet the notion of autobiography within anthropology is regarded by some anthropologists as mere narcissism.

This volume challenges that view by presenting detailed autobiographical accounts in the context of fieldwork and relationships with the people encountered. From a cross-cultural perspective, the contributors examine their work among peoples in Africa, Japan, the Caribbean, Greece, Shetland, England, indigenous Australia, Indonesia and Sri Lanka, and provide unique insights into the fieldwork, autobiography and textual critique of anthropologists. The collection makes a stimulating contribution to current controversial debates about reflexivity and the political responsibility of the anthropologist who, as participant, has traditionally made only stylised appearances in the academic text. The contributors show that, like fieldwork, the process of writing and the creation of the final text involve a series of choices which depend on the selective interests of the ethnographer: monographs, often presented and read as definitive and timeless, are in fact selective and historically contingent.

Anthropology and autobiography will appeal to students and teachers in the social sciences, especially those interested in ethnographical approaches to the self, reflexivity, 'qualitative' methodology, and the production of texts.

ASA Monographs 29

Anthropology and autobiography

Edited by Judith Okely and
Helen Callaway

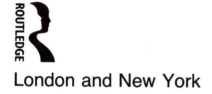

London and New York

First published in 1992
by Routledge
11 New Fetter Lane, London EC4P 4EE

Simultaneously published in the USA and Canada
by Routledge
a division of Routledge, Chapman and Hall Inc.
29 West 35th Street, New York, NY 10001

Filmset by J&L Composition Ltd, Filey, North Yorkshire
Printed and bound in Great Britain by
Biddles Ltd, Guildford and King's Lynn

British Library Cataloguing in Publication Data
A catalogue record for this book is available from the British Library.

Library of Congress Cataloging in Publication Data
Anthropology and autobiography/ edited by Judith Okely and Helen Callaway.
 p. cm. — (ASA monographs; 29)
 Includes bibliographical references and index.
 1. Ethnology—Biographical methods. 2. Autobiography. 3. Ethnology—
Authorship. 4. Ethnology—Fieldwork. I. Okely, Judith.
 II. Callaway, Helen. III. Series: ASA monographs; 29.
 GN346.6.A58 1992
 301'.072—dc20   91–32485
                                                                                         CIP

ISBN 0–415–05189–4

Contents

Illustrations

Contributors

Helen Callaway is Deputy Director of the Centre for Cross-Cultural Research on Women, Queen Elizabeth House, University of Oxford.

Pat Caplan is Professor of Social Anthropology, Goldsmiths' College, University of London.

Anthony P. Cohen is Professor of Social Anthropology, University of Edinburgh.

Malcolm Crick is Senior Lecturer in the Department of Social Anthropology and Sociology, Faculty of Social Services, Deakin University, Victoria, Australia.

John Davis is Professor of Social Anthropology at the Institute of Social and Cultural Anthropology, University of Oxford.

Kirsten Hastrup is Professor of Anthropology, University of Copenhagen, Denmark.

Joy Hendry is Reader in Social Anthropology, Scottish Centre for Japanese Studies, University of Stirling and Oxford Polytechnic.

Margaret E. Kenna is Lecturer in Social Anthropology, Department of Sociology and Social Anthropology, University of Swansea.

Roland Littlewood is Reader in Psychiatry and Anthropology, University College Centre for Medical Anthropology, University College, London.

Julie Marcus is Senior Curator in Social History at the National Museum of Australia, Canberra.

Judith Okely is Reader in Social Anthropology, University of Edinburgh.

Nigel Rapport is Lecturer in Social Anthropology, University of Manchester.

Paul Spencer is Reader in African Anthropology, School of Oriental and African Studies, University of London.

C. W. Watson is Lecturer, Centre of South-East Asian Studies, University of Kent.

Preface

Judith Okely and Helen Callaway

The chapters in this book emerge from the Association of Social Anthropologists' Annual Conference held at the University of York in 1989. The theme was the same as the ensuing title of the book; *Anthropology and autobiography*. Contributors were invited to consider one or more of the following themes:

1 the anthropologist as fieldworker;
2 the individual member of the specific culture;
3 the anthropologist as writer.

Social anthropology, more than any other discipline in the humanities and the social sciences, has developed the practice of intensive fieldwork by a single individual, sometimes in collaboration with a spouse. The implications of this unique experience have not been fully theorised. Yet the 'race', nationality, gender, age, and personal history of the fieldworker affect the process, interaction and emergent material. Contrary to the claim that reflexivity has been incorporated into the discipline, there are few published examples. Some have begun to appear in the US. Otherwise, autobiographical accounts have been split off into novels, secreted under pseudonyms or in diaries. Alternatively, accounts appear as imagined heroism or are popularised as comic yarns for a readership indifferent to ethnography.

Participant observation involves either close or superficial rapport with a variety of individuals. Their specificity is often lost or generalised in the standard monograph which tends to present the society through the overarching authority of the named author. Increasing interest in autobiographical narratives (or life histories often reprocessed as biographies) reveals the power of the individual voice.

In the construction of the final ethnography, not only are the voices of many others concealed, but also that of the author. The occasional 'I' inserted in the text gives, as has been suggested, authorial authority but masks the intellectual and experiential biography of the ethnographer. Like fieldwork, the process of writing and the creation of the final text involve a series of choices which depend on the selective interests of the ethnographer.

There are ways of making these more explicit to show how a monograph is created. Specialists in literary texts who have begun to re-examine ethnographies as texts ignore the experiential knowledge and practice of fieldwork. Their work, moreover, does not emerge from lived relationships in the cross-cultural encounter.

The themes overlapped and extended certain strands from previous ASA conferences, namely those producing *Semantic Anthropology* (Parkin 1982) and *Anthropology at Home* (Jackson 1987). The words by Edmund Leach at the 1987 ASA conference effectively launched the next but one when he declared:

> There can be no future for tribal ethnography of a purportedly objective kind. Ethnographers must admit the reflexivity of their activities; they must become autobiographical. But with this changed orientation, ethnographers should be able to contribute to the better understanding of historical ethnography. (1989: 45)

The papers and discussions pursued the social construction of subjectivity, identity, the fragility and intersubjective origins of material and the false line between poetics and politics. The sessions of paired papers brought out revealing juxtapositions and reciprocal insights. Many refractions of self emerged: the self as a resource for making sense of others; plural identities; gendered awareness; age and transitions when returning at later dates to the same place and people, themselves changed; bodily memory; dreams and reinterpretations; the personal as political and also as theoretical. Again, as is customary within the discipline, some anthropologists gave, in oral discussion, revealing autobiographical accounts which helped to locate their ethnographies. Although prepared to make these personalised interventions to an audience of over a hundred, they did not consider them relevant for academic publication.

Analysing relations with individuals encountered in fieldwork raised sensitive questions. What was an appropriate term for an assistant working with an anthropologist over a long period? The term 'informant' was inadequate. 'Friend' was problematic , as some of the essays in this volume reveal. Other words proved unsatisfactory or misleading. Participants recalled moments of misguided perceptions and mutual misunderstandings which themselves produced powerful insights. As this volume confirms, the necessity for hearing others' voices and other forms of autobiography is none the less through the mediation of the anthropologist as author.

Along with multiple selves and others, the topic of multiple texts emerged: diaries; fieldnotes; journals of informants; letters to and from the field; autobiographies and novels by individuals; local histories; and indigenous social science. The point was made that reflexivity was not carried through to the production of texts. Textual debates risked being too vaguely situated; poetics without politics and devoid of power relations. Monographs have too often been presented, then read as definitive and timeless, rather than selective and historically contingent. Ethnography requires a personal lens, its historicity made explicit.

Political dimensions of reflexivity took the forefront with questions of what changes occur when ethnographies are read by the people they portray and 'informants' take part in anthropological meetings. One participant suggested that the recognition of shared meanings during fieldwork needed to be extended to the production of texts; she had sent her monograph back to the people for possible revision before publication. Another partipant said that she wrote for a readership in the dominant racist society to expose their treatment of a persecuted minority.

If the chapters in this book attest to the vibrant cross-currents of discussion, they cannot convey the wit and laughter that enlivened the four days of the conference. There were also passionate disagreements. For some the notion of autobiography within the social sciences is still deeply threatening. Autobiography was also confused with self-aggrandisement, despite the evidence to the contrary from many of the papers. One participant commented afterwards that an ASA conference provides an unusual forum for debate and open disagreement because only one session is organised at a time. Those who disagree with a specific theme cannot avoid hearing the detailed analysis. Those with shared assumptions have to learn about the opposition.

Besides the usual publishers' displays, a photographic exhibition was mounted of anthropologists and their hosts in the field. We thank Pat Caplan, Joy Hendry, Margaret Kenna, Roland Littlewood and Paul Spencer for these. As is usual at these events, more papers were presented than those included here. Owing to publishers' constraints, there was not adequate space. Some of the papers included had to be rigorously pared down. Others were in any case withdrawn for publication elsewhere. We thank Anne Akeroyd, Haim Hazan, Tanya Luhrman, Ian Edgar, Judith Ennew and Alison James for their excellent and original contributions. We are grateful to those who chaired sessions: Peter Riviere, Parminder Bhachu, Rosemary Firth, Raymond Firth, Claire Wenger, Jerry Eades, Jonathan Webber, Valdo Pons and Shirley Ardener; and to discussants Elizabeth Croll, Ladislav Holy, Malcolm Young, Marilyn Strathern, Lidia Sciama, Nick Allen, Joke Schrijvers, Elizabeth Tonkin and Adam Kuper. Special thanks must go to David Parkin for highlighting key issues and integrating themes of self/lives/ and text (derived from the etymology of auto-bio-graphy).

Our warmest thanks are due to Anne Akeroyd who worked for many months as local organiser to provide congenial conditions for this lively meeting. Finally, we thank Heather Gibson for her encouraging and patient support for this project from its inception through to publication.

REFERENCES

Jackson, A. (ed.) (1987) *Anthropology at Home*. London: Tavistock.

Leach, E. (1989) Tribal Ethnography: Past, Present and Future. In E. Tonkin, M. McDonald and M. Chapman (eds) *History and Ethnicity*. London: Routledge.

Parkin, D. (ed.) (1982) *Semantic Anthropology*. London: Academic Press (ASA Monograph 22).

Chapter 1

Anthropology and autobiography

Participatory experience and embodied knowledge

Judith Okely

This collection is not concerned with the autobiographies of individual academics who *happen* to be anthropologists. It asks questions about the links between the anthropologist's experience of fieldwork, other cultures, other notions of autobiography and ultimately the written text. Autobiography for its own sake is increasingly recognised by the literary canon as a genre (Olney 1980) and, together with individual biographies, is being used within history (Bertaux 1981; Vincent 1981; Bland and John 1990). Doubtless anthropologists could make innovative contributions in those domains. Within the discipline of anthropology, there is further scope for its insertion. Here the anthropologist's past is relevant only in so far as it relates to the anthropological enterprise, which includes the choice of area and study, the experience of fieldwork, analysis and writing.

In the early 1970s, Scholte saw reflexivity as a critical, emancipatory exercise which liberated anthropology from any vestige of a value-free scientism:

> Fieldwork and subsequent analysis constitute a unified praxis ... the ethnographic situation is defined not only by the native society in question, but also by the ethnological tradition 'in the head' of the ethnographer. Once he is actually in the field, the native's pre-suppositions also became operative, and the entire situation turns into complex intercultural mediation and a dynamic interpersonal experience.
> (1974: 438)

Scholte did not specify how this 'interpersonal experience' should be written up, but his advocacy of a reflexive approach can be seen as a necessary preliminary to the inclusion of the anthropologist in the analysis. In this volume, Kirsten Hastrup draws attention to the peculiar reality in the field. 'It is not the unmediated world of the "others" but the world between ourselves and the others.'

While reflexivity or some autobiographical mode may have been incorporated within specific interest groups elsewhere, there is considerable reluctance to consider autobiography as a serious intellectual issue within

British anthropology. In a pioneering paper, David Pocock (1973) suggested a reflexive examination of anthropologists' texts in the light of their biography. He gave examples from his own work. The details remain unpublished, although the notion of a personal anthropology is used imaginatively in an introduction to the discipline (1975). Fifteen years since Pocock's paper, Ernest Gellner has written against a reflexivity of the mildest, least personal form found in Geertz's *Works and Lives* (1988):

> My own advice to anthropology departments is that this volume be kept in a locked cupboard, with the key in the possession of the head of department, and that students be lent it only when a strong case is made out by their tutors. (1988: 26)

A popular put down is that reflexivity or autobiography is 'mere navel gazing', as if anthropology could ever involve only the practitioner. The concern for an autobiographical element in anthropology is to work through the specificity of the anthropologist's self in order to contextualise and transcend it. In other instances autobiography or reflexivity in anthropology has been pejoratively labelled 'narcissism' (Llobera 1987: 118). This use of the classical Greek myth is even more confused. Self-adoration is quite different from self-awareness and a critical scrutiny of the self. Indeed those who protect the self from scrutiny could as well be labelled self-satisfied and arrogant in presuming their presence and relations with others to be unproblematic. Reflexivity is incorrectly confused with self-adoration (Babcock 1980).

A fundamental aspect of anthropology concerns the relationships between cultures or groups. The autobiography of the fieldworker anthropologist is neither in a cultural vacuum, nor confined to the anthropologist's own culture, but is instead placed in a cross-cultural encounter. Fieldwork practice is always concerned with relationships (cf. Campbell 1989). The anthropologist has to form long-term links with others across the cultural divide, however problematic. All of the contributors to this volume, in so far as they write of themselves, consider the self in terms of their relations with others. The autobiographical experience of fieldwork requires the deconstruction of those relationships with the rigour demanded elsewhere in the discipline. There have indeed been poor autobiographies by anthropologists who have perhaps believed that the genre is more exhibitory than exploratory, especially where 'the other' is used as a trigger for the writer's fantasies. Where the encounter is exoticised, the autobiographical account merely embodies at an individual level the discredited practice of fictionalising the other in order to affirm western dominance.

In promoting dialogical modes, Clifford retains a defensive and pejorative view of autobiography; the former 'are not in principle autobiographical; they need not lead to hyper self-consciousness or self-absorption' (1986a: 15). While recognising the validity of 'acute political and epistemological self-consciousness', he is obliged to reassure the reader that this is not 'self-absorption' (ibid.: 7). The 'armchair' anthropologist, as sedentary and solitary researcher, has tended to interpret anthropological autobiography in this way. By contrast, the autobiography of fieldwork is about lived interactions, participatory experience and embodied knowledge; whose aspects ethnographers have not fully theorised.

Recent developments of the 'production of texts by means of texts, rather than by means of fieldwork' (Fardon 1990: 5) and a near exclusive focus on the writing as activity risks diverting attention from fieldwork as experience. Geertz (1988) has, for example, reduced fieldwork to an instrumental account. As Carrithers has noted: 'on Geertz's showing, research seems only a frustrating and solipsistic appendage of the supreme act itself, writing' (1988: 20). The new emphasis on fieldwork as writing sees the encounter and experience as unproblematic. When Fabian (1988) cleverly distinguishes fieldwork as 'writing down' from the construction of a monograph as 'writing up', there is none the less a danger of simplification.

In an extreme stance, fieldwork has been downgraded to the mechanical collection of ethnography which is contrasted with the superior invention of theory (Friedman 1988). Anyone apparently, can *do* ethnography, it is for the desk-bound theoreticians to interpret it. This brahminical division assumes that the field experience is separable from theory, that the enterprise of inquiry is discontinuous from its results (Rabinow 1977). Participant observation textbooks which reduce fieldwork to a set of laboratory procedures rest on the same assumptions. Before the textual critics, field-work was also considered theoretically unproblematic by much of the academy. Its peculiarity, drama, fear and wonder were neither to be contemplated nor fully explored in print. Neophytes were simply to get on with the job with tight-lipped discipline (cf. Kenna). Veracity was confirmed by faith in what Fardon calls 'experiential positivism' (1990: 3). Here, positivism destroys the notion of experience which I wish to evoke. The experience of fieldwork is totalising and draws on the whole being. It has not been theorised because it has been trivialised as the 'collection of data' by a dehumanised machine. Autobiography dismantles the positivist machine.

An interest in the autobiographical dimension of the anthropological encounter has been conflated with a suggestion that ethnography has no other reality than a literary make-believe (e.g. Gellner 1988). Yet, as Smith argues, the autobiographical contract is not as fluid as that which binds the fiction writer and the reader:

In autobiography the reader recognises the inevitability of unreliability but suppresses the recognition in a tenacious effort to expect 'truth' of some kind. The nature of that truth is best understood as the struggle of a historical rather than a fictional person to come to terms with her own past. (1987: 46)

Another confusion is that between textual concerns and an apolitical dilletantism. Scholte came to regret a fusion between literary 'scholarly gentlemen' and reflexivity (1987). Yet a reflexivity which excludes the political is itself unreflective. A critique of the anthropologist as 'innocent' author can be extended to the anthropologist as participant, collaborator or, in some cases, activist (Huizer 1979). The existing and future personal narratives of anthropologists in the field can be examined not only for stylistic tropes and their final textual construction, but also as a record of the experience, the political encounter and its historical context (see Huizer and Mannheim 1979; Okely 1987). In this way the anthropologist as future author is made self-conscious, critical and reflexive about the encounter and its possible power relations (Street 1990).

Postmodernism which challenges master narratives and total systems has itself been understood as an extreme form of relativism where, in an atmosphere of valueless cynicism, anything goes. The disintegration of totalities, however, can be differentially interpreted as the unleashing of the full range of creative possibilities (Nicholson 1990). The cultural past can also be re-examined. Alternative paradigms have always existed at the margins; in this case, autobiographical texts which defied the master canon. Postmodernism may have created a climate where different autobiographies elicit new interest, but the former did not create the latter.

Hesitations about incorporating and expanding the idea of autobiography into anthropology rest on very western, ethnocentric traditions. Autobiography, as a genre, has come to be associated with a 'repertoire of conventions' (Dodd 1986: 3). The tradition has been constructed by 'inclusion, exclusion and transformation' (ibid.: 6). This is not to deny that autobiography can ever be more than a construction (Spencer, Kenna, Rapport, this volume), but the specific criteria for its acceptance within a genre has been confined to the Eurocentric and literary canon. The western origin of the form is St Augustine with other major examples from Rousseau and J. S. Mill. A 'Great Man' tradition which speaks of individual linear progress and power has defined what constitutes a meaningful life (Juhasz 1980: 221). While there will have been historical fluctuations in the tradition, western writers have worked within and against it. Dodd suggests:

> vocation ... is central not only to St Augustine's *Confessions*, but to Victorian autobiography ... the point of closure ... is vocation, the resolution of self-determination. (1986: 5)

Other forms of autobiography are marginalised or excluded. Working-class autobiographies have tended to be excluded from the literary genre and 'bequeathed to social historians' (Dodd 1986: 7). Autobiographies from seemingly vocationless women have been judged neither culturally nor aesthetically significant by earlier normative criteria (Smith 1987: 8). Women have 'internalised a picture of themselves that precluded the kind of self attention which would generate autobiography' as recognised by the canon (Kolodny 1980: 241). There is another non-literary category by politicians which is explicitly addressed to political historians, but is still a message of individual public success.

What has been labelled the 'confessional', as opposed to St Augustine's or even Rousseau's, is not included as part of the genre (ibid.: 240), and implies a series of indiscretions which give the lie to prevailing assumptions and dominant ideals. The confessional has also come to be regarded as concerned only with salacious indiscretions. Instead, in the context of anthropological fieldwork, it could be an attempt to analyse the actual research process in place of an idealised, scientised presentation. The confessional also implies loss of control. This again defies a carefully constructed tradition in which 'Omissions and deletions have constituted the very art of the form' (ibid.: 240) and where 'detachment' is 'a prescription that comes ... out of the entire accepted canon of western autobiographical writing' (ibid.: 239). A genre of autobiography has focused on a constructed public self with the private made separate and discussed in terms of its threat to the public persona. Alternatively, the private is confronted only to be highly controlled and rationalised, as for example Rousseau's confessions about auto-eroticism (Derrida 1967/76).

The linear public progress established within the dominant western tradition has emphasised the individual as all-powerful isolate. Edward Said has voiced regret over an increasing interest in autobiography precisely because the subject is presented as outside time and context (1982: 17). But as Dodd argues, Said has 'confused autobiographies and the Autobiography constructed by the Tradition' (1986: 11). Similarly, anthropologists who are reluctant to consider autobiography may be reacting to the carefully constructed tradition which sees autobiography as 'egoistic'. Raymond Firth's controlled, near invisible insertion of personal narrative as part of his 'background to anthropological work' in Tikopia is followed by an apology for a:

> somewhat egoistical recital not because I think that anthropology should be made light reading ... but because some account of the relations of the anthropologist to his people is relevant to the nature of the results. (1936/65: 10)

Firth thus has to overcome several western associations with autobiography – that it risks being 'light' or trivial and that it is self-inflating. The western tradition both defines autobiography as egoism and in turn demands it.

Anthropologists have inserted the 'I' only at key junctures in ethnographic monographs in order, it is argued, to give authority to the text (Clifford 1986b; Pratt 1986; Rosaldo 1986). Otherwise they produced accounts from which the self had been sanitised. To establish authority, it seems, requires only the briefest of appearances. The 'I' is the ego trip, and in 'arrival' accounts emerges not so much from the practice of fieldwork, but more from writing traditions in western culture (ibid.). That the anthropologist soon disappears from the text is, as I have argued above, consistent with the belief that autobiography is no more than the affirmation of individual power or confessional self-absorption.

The western tradition of autobiography has been most clearly articulated by Gusdorf, writing in the 1950s, and validated by Olney (1980: 8–9). Gusdorf either ignores non-western autobiographies or dismisses them as 'a cultural transplant' (Stanford Friedman 1988: 35). Autobiography is associated with western individualism and, according to Gusdorf:

> is not to be found outside of our cultural area; ... it expresses a concern peculiar to Western man, a concern that has been of good use in his systematic conquest of the universe. (1956/80: 29)

Gusdorf asserted that autobiography does not develop in cultures where the individual:

> does not feel himself to exist outside of others, and still less against others, but very much *with* others in an interdependent existence that asserts its rhythms everywhere in the community. (1956/80: 29–30)

Gusdorf's definitions of the genre, effectively the Great White Man tradition, drew upon pre-existing western assumptions both about autobiography and about other cultures. Despite their rejection of the monolithic stereotypes of non-western cultures, western anthropologists have not escaped these assumptions.

A corollary of the autobiographical tradition which emphasises individualistic and public linear development, is a clear demarcation between the autobiography and the diary. The latter is the place for the personal, if not the secret. A diary is also the 'classic articulation of dailiness' (Juhasz 1980: 334). Gender differences noted in women's autobiographies carry aspects otherwise consigned to diaries. Juhasz suggests that:

> women's stories show less a pattern of linear development towards some clear goal than one of repetitive cumulative, cyclical structure ... dailiness matters – by definition it is never a conclusion always a process ... The perspective of the diary is immersion not distance. (ibid.: 223–4)

It is that very dailiness and immersion, along with insights into the personal, which make Malinowski's *Diary* (1967) so informative about the experience of fieldwork, his relations with others, and the cultural encounter. In an earlier paper, I advocated that self-awareness of the anthropologist in the field be explored through such forms as the diary, which should be seen as integral to the anthropological endeavour. Malinowski did not treat his diary as such, but as a place where the self could be split from the would-be scientist which his official publications had aimed to present. The fieldwork practice recorded in the diary did not fit the methodological exhortations outlined in *The Argonauts* (1922).Thus for example, Malinowski mingled intimately with white men, while officially abjuring contact (Okely 1975). The posthumous publication of the diary surprised and scandalised many of his followers. Geertz's response diverted a discussion of the self to generic notions of the person (1974). In his postgraduate Malinowski course at Cambridge in 1970, Leach declared to us that it should never have been published. His later interest in autobiography (1984, 1989: 45) suggests a change of mind.

The anthropologist, imbued with western notions, is torn between the Tradition of Autobiography as public achievement by lone hero and its antithesis which undermines it. Once autobiography is set up as the celebration of power then its opposite always threatens, namely the loss of power, the loss of face. The confessional, belittled by the canon, then becomes what autobiography is defined to exclude – namely the loss of control. That in turn is invidiously confused with self-analysis. So long as the self is rigorously split off and secreted in diaries, then self-analysis in anthropological practice is perceived as loss of professional armour. Yet anthropologists, more than most, are in a position to question western definitions of autobiography, since they are made aware of cross-cultural alternatives.

In the Great White Man tradition, the lone achiever has felt compelled to construct and represent his uniqueness, seemingly in defiance of historical conditions, but actually in tune with the dominant power structures which have rewarded him. By contrast, those on the margins may first learn through an alternative personal experience their lack of fit with the dominant system. Their individual experience belies the public description at the centre. Out of their experience have arisen alternative forms on the margins. Autobiographies from the marginalised and the powerless – those of a subordinate race, religion, sex and class – have not inevitably been a celebration of uniqueness, let alone public achievement, but a record of questions and of subversion. The most personal, seemingly idiosyncratic, hitherto unwritten or unspoken, has paradoxically found resonance with others in a similar position. A solidarity is found through what seemed only an individual perspective. Stanford Friedman notes that:

> the individualist concept of the autobiographical self that pervades Gusdorf's work raises serious theoretical problems for critics who recognise that the self, self-creation and self-consciousness are profoundly different for women, minorities, and many non-western peoples. (1988: 34)

Contrary to the expectation that an autobiography which speaks of the personal and specific should thereby elaborate uniqueness, autobiographies may, as has been found among the marginalised, evoke common aspects. The reader is invited to recognise similarities, 'individualistic paradigms of the self ignore the role of collective and relational identities in the individuation process' (ibid.: 35). In a study of de Beauvoir's autobiography, I have argued that the *Mémoires* (1958) invite the woman reader to identify with common aspects of a young girl's childhood (Okely 1986: 22–50). Stanford Friedman explores how the autobiographies of women and members of minorities may expose historically generated differences from dominant groups, depending on sex and race:

> Isolate individualism is an illusion. It is also the privilege of power. A white man has the luxury of forgetting his skin color and sex. He can think of himself as an 'individual'. Women and minorities have no such luxury. (1988: 39)

Neither do anthropologists have such luxury when in another culture. But the specificity may be lost in the thinking and the writing.[1] Any autobiography by the anthropologist, while emerging from a unique and personal experience, evokes resonances of recognition among others. There are solidarities as well as contrasts to be examined, and systematised for the enrichment of the discipline. The autobiography is not a linear progress of the lone individual outside history, let alone outside cultures and the practice of anthropology. There are ways of breaking from the individualistic western paradigm both in the autobiography of the anthropologist and through autobiographical forms in other cultures. Other peoples have varying notions of self and ways of describing them through experiential narrative in both oral and written traditions. These await fuller exploration.

Whereas in literary studies a concern has been to move the analysis of others' autobiographies into the literary canon, if autobiography were fully incorporated into anthropology, it would be about the construction of both the anthropologists' autobiographies in the field and those of others. An anthropological perspective concerns reflexivity in the field and the process of autobiographical construction, not simply the critique of others' existing texts. Here social anthropology has characteristics especially apt in relation to any genre of autobiography. The practice of intensive fieldwork is unique among all other disciplines in the humanities and social sciences. The bounded periods of participant observation conducted by sociologists bear no comparison. Long-term immersion through fieldwork is generally a total experience, demanding all of the anthropologist's resources; intellectual, physical, emotional, political and intuitive. The experience involves so much of the self that it is impossible to reflect upon it fully by extracting that self. Under pressure to be 'scientifically objective', anthropologists have traditionally compartmentalised that fieldwork experience.

An example appears regrettably in the Marxist *Critique of Anthropology*. Kielstra regrets the confusion in status between anthropologists as specialised professionals and as general intellectuals:

Fieldwork is a strongly emotional experience. If a fieldworker has some creative talents that does not necessarily make them interesting from a scientific point of view ... People who are insecure about their academic positions and doubtful about their status as intellectuals may mix them up ... One should not be afraid to accept that anthropology ... is a partial activity, dealing with only part of human experience. (1987: 90)

The splitting of reasoned from emotional activity which Kielstra advocates is embedded in the European Enlightenment. He also confuses 'creative talents' with (denigrated) emotions. I would suggest the very opposite to Kielstra, that those who are most insecure about their identity as intellectuals may cling to a professional and instrumental facade. Moreover, a division of labour advocated in a Marxist journal which privileges professional activity, as opposed to intellectual and other work, goes against the spirit of Marx's celebrated passage in *The German Ideology*: (1846, 1960 edition: 22). Marx was arguing against a division of labour which separates critical thought from action, mental from manual labour and one intellectual pursuit from another.

In 'The Self and Scientism' (1975) I argued that the emotional and personal cannot be so easily separated from intellectual endeavour. Malinowski's response in moments of anger against the Trobrianders, recorded in his diary, cannot be seen as merely idiosyncratic and private, since it reveals the racist overtones of his European cultural heritage. In the 1970s, the Women's Liberation Movement argued that 'the personal is political'; I contend also that in an academic context 'the personal is theoretical'. This stands against an entrenched tradition which relegates the personal to the periphery and to the 'merely anecdotal': pejoratively contrasted in positivist social science with generalisable truth. Yet, anthropologists are steeped in the anecdotal.

The pressure to split off the self and the autobiography of fieldwork from its total practice owes a great deal to the positivist history of social anthropology which emphasised the neutral, impersonal and scientific nature of the enterprise. This involved a peculiar combination of intensive fieldwork by means of participant observation with the ideal of the objective observer. Dumont has noted the paradoxical consequences:

more 'empathetic involvement' was achieved in the field experience ... At the same time, the more that 'involved sympathy' emerged during the fieldwork experience, the more 'disciplined detachment' was found in the published reports under the pretext of objectivity. (1978: 7)

The self's engagement in fieldwork could not be naturally suppressed, but had to be self-consciously worked at. The autobiographical mode was highly controlled within mainstream ethnographies. But the self would leak out; in the oral culture of the academy, secreted in diaries, transformed as fiction or split into separate and hitherto marginalised accounts. In this volume, Helen Callaway examines in greater detail some of these earlier texts by women.

In the now classic *Return to Laughter* (1954) by Laura Bohannan, alias Smith Bowen, we see the transformation of autobiography into fiction under a pseudonym. In the preface, Bohannan describes the familiar split between the academic and the whole person, one of which others such as Kielstra might approve:

> When I write as a social anthropologist and within the canons of the discipline, I write under another name. Here I have written simply as a human being, and the truth I have tried to tell concerns the sea change in one's self that comes from immersion in another and alien world. (1954: xix)

Thus Bohannan's reading of 'the canons of the discipline' excluded autobiography and analysis. The self and its narrative of experience had to be split off into 'fiction'; a creative mode viewed with suspicion by social science.

Powdermaker's *Stranger and Friend* (1967), breaking from pseudonym and fiction, integrated autobiography with theories and methodologies in her varied fieldwork. Of an earlier generation than Bohannan, but writing at a later stage, she successfully analyses relevant aspects of her earlier life and her academic training under Malinowski to confront the implication of class, sex and ethnicity in her work. This happy integration of the anthropologist's self with fieldwork practices was rare and, significantly for academic orthodoxy, was written near her retirement. Later texts on participant observation either ignore the self (Wax 1971) and gender of the researcher (Freilich 1977), or tend to recognise gender in order to control for 'bias' (Whitehead and Conaway 1986). Now that so-called qualitative methodology is being increasingly institutionalised within the social sciences, it seems that social anthropologists have either abdicated responsibility in describing it or deferred to those (especially sociologists) who would routinise the practice in the form of simplistic flow charts. Yet there are ways of reflecting upon and theorising the total experience of fieldwork which cannot be reduced to a set of neo-positivistic techniques. And that would include autobiographical reflection.

From the 1960s, and especially the 1970s and 1980s, some anthropologists, mainly outside Britain, began to write separate semi-autobiographical accounts. Some gave chronological accounts of the fieldworkers' entry, immersion and departure using the 'I', but not necessarily showing reflexivity (Okely 1975). Some are explicitly addressed to a popular readership with no interest in the rest of anthropology (Barley 1983). They risk exploiting the very stereotypes about exotica and eccentric academics which anthropology would hope to dismantle. In a postmodern era when the orthodoxy of classical ethnographies has been more readily challenged within the academic canon, later autobiographical accounts have been unconvincingly hailed as innovative contributions (e.g. Rabinow 1977). Their acclaim within specific academic circles may be in part explained by patronage and peer group solidarity (Geertz 1988: 91). Others have remained on the margins. Caplan (1988) has echoed the outrage felt by many women anthropologists at Clifford's exclusion of women anthropologists (1986a) on the grounds that feminists had contributed nothing to his definitions of theory and experimental texts. In fact, many of the later autobiographical accounts lack the breadth and subtlety of Powdermaker or Bohannan who were experimental in an era when this quality was not judged relevant within the academic canon. Others have again been published under pseudonyms (e.g. Cesara 1982) and classified as a confessional; too embarrassingly uncontrolled or unedited for mainstream acceptance.

An outstanding contribution to the autobiographical mode integrated within a monograph about the people, the other culture and the fieldwork encounter is Dumont's *The Headman and I* (1978). This was in part a response to *Tristes Tropiques* (1955) which held the promise of an autobiographical account, but where Lévi-Strauss – 'remains outside . . . There is no back and forth movement between experience and consciousness' (Dumont 1978: 10). Given this absence of the self as problematic and personal, *Tristes Tropiques* was correctly read as part of the heroic questing tradition which western autobiography celebrates, and is confirmed in the collection title, *The Anthropologist as Hero* (Hayes and Hayes 1970). Consistent with this absence of self, Lévi-Strauss (1988) has rejected the specifically personal in any autobiographical mode.

In Britain questions of reflexivity and personal aspects of fieldwork were made most apparent during the 1985 ASA conference Anthropology at Home (Jackson 1987), because the anthropologists were obliged to be self-conscious about the similarities or contrasts in the context of fieldwork in their native country. Alongside political concerns of intrusion and partisanship, questions of national, ethnic origins were confronted and, in some cases, gender by women. Those who pursued these implications were in effect writing autobiographies, but in few of these cases had the anthropologists approached fieldwork at the outset with thoughts about having to analyse and write these details in an academic context. Reflexivity has rarely been seen as significant for the total project in the same way that pre-fieldwork acquaintance with 'the ethnographic literature' has been prescribed (Fardon 1990). We have rarely gone into the field with the self-consciousness of preparing an autobiographical account either within or in conjunction with a monograph. Some examples from European anthropology attempt to interlink the two, e.g. Favret-Saada (1977/80, 1981), Favret-Saada and Contreras (1981) and Loizos (1981).

Dumont, unlike for example Fardon (1990: 7–8), has suggested a significance in the fact that it was women who wrote the earlier accounts of fieldwork, as has Helen Callaway in this volume. Women were:

left with the task of conjuring the impurities of experience. They had to cope with the blood, sweat and tears aspect of fieldwork – feelings and sentiments included – while the men were exclusively doing 'the real thing'. (1978: 8)

Although an explanation which draws on expressive roles stereotypically associated with women is unconvincing, none the less there is a hint in Dumont of the contrast, described by women, between public presentation and lived practice. To describe the dailiness and minutiae of personal encounters in the field is to question the 'fine distinctions' between public and private which Kolodny (1980: 240) suggests have served as guides for the male autobiographer. The split between public and private self has been contested as gender specific. Theorists of sexual and textual difference have explored how men and women have acquired a differing sense of self and relationship to a master discourse. Given that both sexes, at least in dominant western cultures, have tended to have had a female adult as primary carer in infancy, Chodorow (1978) suggests that the resulting 'feminine' identity is marked by more flexible, permeable ego boundaries than those for a 'masculine' cultural identity (*pace* Bordo 1990). There are differing narratives of the self; the 'feminine' one being open to representing experience as interpersonal while the 'masculine' one privileges individualism and distance (Smith 1987: 12–13). Moreover, the girl/woman enters a world where the dominant paradigm is that of masculine experience. The differing formation and life experience of persons according to their sex/ gender have implications for theorising and for self-presentation. Women writing about anthropological fieldwork may show aspects similarly considered unacceptable in the literary canon of western autobiography. Significantly, earlier fieldwork texts were written by women whose professional position was relatively marginalised (Silverman 1989: 294).

When women have difficulty in seeing themselves as self-important and with less professional face to lose, it follows that the use of 'I' and its dailiness in the text are expressions of neither authorial authority nor of egoism. Rather, the I is the voice of individual scepticism from the margins; in many instances not only the I of *difference*, but one of subversive *diffidence* in the face of scientism. The individual 'I' is not making claim to generalisations within a dominant discourse (cf. Davis). The 'I' says 'but in my experience ...'. This, in the final analysis, cannot be falsified from the outside. It is knowingly but defiantly open to a critique of being non-representative. This specificity challenges also the orthodox canon of autobiography which demands that the supreme example be a 'representative' and 'eminent person' (Misch 1951). The woman ethnographer does not fit the norm of the generalised male. This is a different 'I' from an impersonalised authority. In the most creative sense it is a way of exploring an alternative identity and 'those previously, silent, unrecorded areas of experience' (Anderson 1986: 64). The master narrative both for autobiography and for ethnography is subverted.

The suggestions offered by Pratt (1986: 32–3) for overcoming the contradictions in ethnography between personal and scientific authority, the repression of the experiencing 'I', and the ensuing impoverishment of knowledge focus primarily on matters of style. The concern is more a matter of writing, especially the finished product, than also thinking about the content and experience of fieldwork. Both the style and the content are affected by the extent to which the anthropologist has privileged some aspects at an early stage and not others. While it is taken for granted the fieldworker writes extensive and personal notes in the field about the others, it is not considered necessary to analyse and take notes about his or her relationship with them (Okely 1975). We simply do not know how to explore the specificity of the fieldworker in those relationships, in order to theorise participation. Autobiographical accounts, when they do appear, are judged in terms of professional ethics, or as voyeurism or humanistic testimony. We are like pre-Freudians presented with the plain narratives of dreams whose significance we are not called upon to decipher. The personal narrative and encounter need to be confronted far earlier than the writing stage. The dilemma and internal struggle for example between self and positivist, noted by Pratt (ibid.), is there long before pen is placed on notepad.

The focus on culture and anthropology as written rather than experienced is consistent with Derrida's deconstruction theories (1967/76). Derrida suggests that in the west, speech is considered superior to the written and that the latter has been taken to be an unproblematic record of speech. Instead, Derrida argues that the written text is a construction in its own right. His insights have made us more self-conscious about the production of texts and, in this case, the production of ethnographies. These may be read as inevitably partial and historically specific. The author is also de-centred, since a text may have a life of its own in ways which the author did not intend (*pace* Davis, this volume). Derrida looks for contradictions with which the author may be consciously and unconsciously grappling. Similar observations can be found in Freud (1900, 1914/48).

The suggestion that the author is no longer in control of the text has been resolved for some by mechanistically interpreting Bakhtin's dialogical mode where a text might be envisaged as the product of multiple voices (1981). Whereas Freud offered forms of analysis to expose hidden conflicts and wish fulfilments, the move to multiple voices, or dialogue, presented like tape transcriptions, may avoid all authorial intervention. In so far as interpretation is left entirely to the vagaries of the reader, we are back to a pre-Freudian era where dreams and statements are considered plain tales and stories without underlying significance. As Hastrup reminds us in this volume, ethnography involves more than mere recording. The informants' voices, however many direct quotations are included, do not penetrate the ethnographer's discursive speech.

The 'arrival' stories where the anthropologist/author has been most visible, but is not yet in dialogue, are only the start of it. The anthropologists' opening descriptions focus predictably on the superficial, visible contrasts and first encounters. The account cannot by definition convey the responses and insights from the hosts. In the long run it is important to know how they viewed and related to the anthropologist as stranger, guest, then apprentice, perhaps friend and scribe. The key incidents, where the anthropologist is initially treated as outsider, rebuked for rule breaking and by varying degrees incorporated or rejected, all speak of the self-ascribed marks of one culture and its relations with representatives of others.

The relations with the anthropologist as outsider reveal both the specificity of that rapport and its potential generalities. The relationship between the anthropologist and hosts is ever changing, with continuing implications for mutual comprehension. While an anthropologist's gradual disappearance from the monograph is commented on with approval (Carrithers 1988: 20), what we do not learn is how the changing daily relationship and experience give sense to an accumulation of illustrations forming a coherent whole. Where the anthropologist continues to insert (or reflect upon) the particularities of her discussions through the length of the field experience, the material does more than describe the type of relations between the anthropologist and the people concerned. We are also able to see how the interrogator acts as a catalyst in eliciting defining aspects for specific members (Rabinow 1977: 119; Omvedt 1979). That continuing dialogue is worked out both between persons as representatives of differing cultures *and* between specific individuals. Here the 'race', sex (Golde 1986),[2] class origins, age and persona of the anthropologist are significant. All ethnographers are positioned subjects (Hastrup this volume).

An early exclusion of reflexivity has implications for the later texts. Since anthropological questions of autobiography or reflexivity were never raised in the academy before or during my fieldwork in the early 1970s, this absence therefore affects the subsequent writing. Some examples already exist (Okely 1975, 1983: ch. 3, 1984, 1987). There were several reasons why self-awareness was excluded and they are not personal, but consistent with the historical, political and academic context. When approaching the Gypsies, I found myself acting and thinking *against* the romantic tradition epitomised by George Borrow, Mérimée, Bizet and all the stereotypes which are significant in the dominant society's construction of Gypsies. Borrow and others were the equivalent of the exotic travel writers that anthropologists seek to distance themselves from (cf. Kenna), or the only equivalent to the ethnographic 'regional' literature with which the orthodox anthropologist has to engage (Fardon 1990). Like other anthropologists, I needed to establish my identity as a social *scientist* and maintained a sceptical distance from the folklorist literature; the 'orientalism' of Gypsies. Perhaps there was a fear of contamination, the exoticism could be overwhelming.

The need for distance was not merely a reading and library matter. Most non-Gypsies I spoke to, were themselves caught up in the romance. Their eyes lit up when they heard what I was doing. They projected their longings on to me, and were compelled to tell me about the Gypsies. I was treated as the silent therapist who triggered off their fantasies and monologues. This projection was continuous: I was typecast and given a fictive Gypsy identity, not among Gypsies but among Gorgios (non-Gypsies). This even happened at a university party for social anthropologists where I had dressed up for the festive occasion. It was not interpreted as my celebration of being away from the field and its constraints – including the necessary frumpy and controlled clothes required among Gypsy women. Instead my long velvet dress was labelled 'Gypsy' by one of the lecturers.

Forced into this stereotyping, I decided to push it to its limits, to test the Gorgios' reactions. At a suburban party, a few miles from the Gypsy camp, I was talking to a young solicitor. After some preliminaries, I informed him that I was of Gypsy descent. Tears came to his eyes; brimming with uncontrollable emotion. He seemed unable to reconcile the juxtaposition of my educated, middle-class talk with my alleged genetic origins. His reactions were unnerving and informative. Through this vicarious experience of being 'the other' to others, I was perforce led back to the stereotypes, which are part of the Gypsies' reality made by Gorgios. The Gypsies also, I learned through participatory experience, manipulate those stereotypes.

These glimpses into the non-Gypsies' need to project their fantasies on to Gypsies, despite of or because of the lack of day-to-day acquaintance with the people who actually live as Gypsies, help to explain something which has puzzled me for some time. Why is it that certain stories about my fieldwork, certain events have become my personal repertoire? I have indeed constructed a personal narrative through selected memories, selected stories which I repeat when asked by non-Gypsies, by students and friends about my fieldwork. Others have described how they have dined off a number of tales from the field (Kenna). The temptation is to respond to the demand for tales of 'the anthropologist as heroine'. I recall spontaneously telling a university interview committee for a research award how I had been drawn into some illegal activities in the field and that I had been a character witness for a Traveller at the Old Bailey. He had been charged with attempted murder by shooting and kidnapping, although found not guilty. I was uncontrollably recounting the sensational in a highly controlled academic encounter.

My stories about fieldwork with the Gypsies have been embellished through the telling, with exclusions and inclusions through oral delivery. Some evoke laughter and I ask why. In all cases my listeners are non-

Gypsies. Thus the fashioning of the oral autobiography, even before any written autobiography for specific readers, is affected by the listener's demands and shared meanings (cf. Spencer). The anthropologist as heroine, or 'honorary male', is only in fact a minor aspect. The major themes in the stories relate to the differences between Gorgio and Gypsy (Okely 1983: ch. 3, 1984). Listeners are intrigued, just as I am, with the predicaments of crossing class, ethnic, gender and cultural boundaries. These are all the more paradoxical because they take place within a shared geographical space which the listeners appear to inhabit with the Gypsies. I am speaking to a tradition of differences. As narrator, I become amusing through those differences. The listeners help to create the autobiographical account with its specific emphases. To prove this we must ask: could the stories be told to the others (the Gypsies) we have lived with and written about? What kind of autobiography of the anthropologist could be or is constructed and told to them? A quite different autobiography of the anthropologist would be created.

Reflexive knowledge of fieldwork is acquired not only from an examination of outside categories, but also from the more intangible inner experience (Turner and Bruner 1986). Anthropologists, immersed for extended periods in another culture or in their own as participant observer learn not only through the verbal, the transcript, but through all the senses, through movement, through their bodies and whole being in a total practice (cf. Jackson 1983, Littlewood, Kenna, this volume). We use this total knowledge to *make sense* literally of the recorded material. Writing up is more than the 'pure cerebration' it has sometimes (Fardon 1990: 3) been made out to be. Fieldnotes may be no more than a trigger for bodily and hitherto subconscious memories. We cannot write down the knowledge at the time of experiencing it, although we may retrospectively write of it in autobiographical modes. The specific ways in which we learned awaits the recounting (Okely 1978). Bourdieu notes how the body can be treated 'as a memory' (1977: 94), it cannot always be consciously controlled. Anthropologists acquire a different bodily memory in fieldwork experience as an adult in another culture. The commonplace analogy between the anthropologist and a child learning another culture is misleading since the anthropologist is already formed and shaped by history. He or she has to change or superimpose new experience upon past embodied knowledge (Mauss 1938), and come to terms with a changing self embodied in new contexts. In recent discussions, denigrated visualism has sometimes been replaced by another privileged sense; orality (Fardon 1990: 23). The more general physicality is not embraced.

One example of embodied knowledge is physical labour. Fieldwork is so often among groups where manual labour is a significant part of production, in contrast to the anthropologists' sedentary academic milieu. Participant-observation does not mean mere observation, but often shared labour (cf. Rapport). Fieldwork takes on its original meaning: work in fields. In both my major periods of research – among the Gypsies (Okely 1983) and among Normandy farmers (Okely 1991), participation in production brought a major breakthrough. I was perceived differently by the people and I learned through participation, however incompetent, in for example, potato picking, scrap metal dealing, harvesting and hand milking.

When I asked to learn how to hand milk cows in a small Normandy farm, the woman who has done this for forty years left the stable for a few minutes. She returned with a flash camera and took several photos of me. The unsolicited act reversed the usual relationship between anthropologist and 'informant'. My attempts at manual labour, which continued for several months, undermined for peasant farmers the stereotype of the metropolitan *professeur*. It gave embodied knowledge of a daily practice and created a shared experience for ever-unfolding discussions between us.

The fieldworker both consciously and unconsciously responds to certain rhythms and patterns as immersion proceeds. In a photograph of a Gypsy woman and myself taken by a stranger Gorgio, I have unknowingly imitated the Gypsy woman's defensive bodily posture. We are both standing with arms folded, looking away from the lens. In some more explicit instances the anthropologist is drawn by the hosts into performative ritual and shared embodied knowledge. At key moments both Smith Bowen (1954) and Powdermaker (1967) were called upon to participate in dancing. Ignorance or unfamiliarity with the group's rules or rhythms brings key crises. These are also informative. After noticing a young Gypsy woman in trousers, I gladly wore some to avoid the cold. But I was reprimanded and told that trousers were permitted so long as I wore a dress to cover the hips. With Gypsy values inscribed on my body, I was led to thinking about the body and female sexuality (Okely 1983). After ending long-term fieldwork, I would occasionally visit some families for the afternoon or evening. I had lost the unconscious rhythm of day-to-day experience. On one of these visits, I was truly conned of my gold earrings – I would not have been so gullible if I had still been sharing the rhythm of co-residence. For them I had become an ignorant and despised outsider again.

Many contributors to this volume, analysing their seemingly individual identities, reveal themselves as social categories in the cross-cultural encounter.

Paul Spencer places relevant aspects of his individual history as English and middle class in the broader context of British postwar history. The Suez crisis exposed 'the ugly side of ideas' with which his generation had grown up and his past gullibility. An earlier unquestioning acceptance of the supremacy of the British Empire, the sanctity of the family and the unambiguous truth of Christianity was replaced by an ambivalence about being English. By contrast, and because of this, he found among the

Plate 1.1 In this photograph of a Gypsy woman and Judith Okely (left), taken by a stranger, the author has unknowingly imitated the Gypsy woman's defensive posture. Southern England, 1970s

Samburu a completeness and a seemingly unchanging concept of tradition which the people themselves elaborated (cf. Riches on the Inuit 1990). Spencer's changing identity, whether as of young or subsequently older age category, is found to be a resource both in his relations with and for his interpretation of the Samburu *moran* and the Maasai elder. The careful connections made by Spencer between individual life history and cross-cultural encounter are neither narcissism nor the uncontrolled confessional which the profession so fears, but a demonstration of the profound resonances between the personal, political and theoretical.

Both Pat Caplan and Margaret Kenna examine the implications of age, outsider status and gender through the course of fieldwork periods which span over twenty years in the same locality.

Both went first as young unmarried women. Unlike a number of male contributors, their categorisation as unmarried appeared so crucial that it features extensively in their accounts.

The women's return field visits as wife and later mother changed the nature of the encounter. Their movement through individual life cycle, historical changes at home and in the field, and shifts in the discipline of anthropology also transformed their earlier enquiries.

Caplan switched allegiance from a specific male informant to his wife. Her changed identity as mature woman/mother elicited approval. Kenna, who, as a young woman, had passed time with older chaperoning women, moved subsequently as public expert to mixed gender events.

On their return, both were confronted with the naïveties and misinterpretations of their earlier fieldwork. For Kenna, sufficient trust had been generated, for the people to inform her about the past. She was to learn that her seemingly modest bodily posture was associated with that of a prostitute. As with Spencer, the women's categorisation and experience as either young or middle aged became specific resources for each period.

As young single woman outsider, Caplan, I suggest, was most suited as neutral, innocent confidante for projection by the self-styled Don Juan. On her subsequent trips, Caplan's greater interest in gender divisions reflected a political and academic momentum from feminism. Kenna's 'confessions' to an earlier political and historical naïvety revealed no idiosyncratic failure, but the limits of British anthropology at the time. The islanders on their migrations, rather than the academy, 'dragged' her to the city and towards the relevance of sociological material.

Kenna's earlier outspoken objection to injustice reflected her own political upbringing, but in the long run was useful for understanding the islanders' long-established strategies of caution in the face of political repression. Her return with her long-awaited child was celebrated in the people's idiom by a personal pilgrimage. Walking barefoot up a rocky path to make a thank offering at the Monastery, she was drawn to 'a greater understanding ... of the connections which the Greek Orthodox tradition perceives between outward form and inner meaning'. Thus the purely instrumental aspects of participant observation were transcended. Knowledge was experiential and through bodily action. Caplan's and Kenna's changing perspectives of the field area and people through several decades highlight the historical and individual specificity of each encounter and ethnography. These can never be total accounts, never definitive (see Watson) in time or space, but their specificity enriches rather than undermines the enterprise.

Both Roland Littlewood and Julie Marcus were explicitly confronted by their own identity as white in societies with a history scarred by racism, slavery and genocide. Littlewood's classification as White man was inescapable in a Trinidadian community, the Earth People, who were preparing for the return of the Black Nation. The charismatic leader, Mother Earth, used Littlewood's arrival to reconsider her opposition of negative science against positive nature. Littlewood arrived as their 'other'; male, White and a scientist. His biography as nonconformist in his own culture drew him to a millenarian community and empowered him to challenge their stereotypes. It was no great step as former 1960s radical to walk naked from his sea bathe into the unclothed community. Rather than undermining their classification, Littlewood's presence led to changing notions of Black and White; the Earth People later believed that Whites could be Black 'inside'.

Marcus uses her identity as White female anthropologist as a pivot between her discovery of a White woman anthropologist, active among Aborigines in the 1930s, and her own encounter with an Aboriginal woman. Like Olive Pink before her, Marcus's biography is situated in that of the White settler society. In exchanging confidences and comparing experiences, the Aboriginal Louisa Montgomery is astonished at the absence of police punishment for the delinquencies in Marcus's suburban childhood. Marcus's understanding of Olive Pink's life rests both on her present day knowledge and on her own autobiography. The Aboriginal woman is shown to be living under a terrorising surveillance which the White woman recorded fifty years earlier, in a different language.

Nigel Rapport is classified as offcomer in a rural English community but is perceived as originally French rather than Jewish. His childhood ambivalence about belonging is resolved at first by seeing fieldwork as a passage to 'genuine' Britishness. Within the field, he chooses another kind of conformity by minimising difference: avoiding tourists, and participating as manual labourer rather than as contemptible penpusher. Contrary to expectations, this does not turn out to be anthropology at home. Like Rapport, Malcolm Crick passed as another form of 'other'; an Australian, for fear that English was a marked colonial category in Sri Lanka. Dramatically, in response to another Sri Lankan categorisation, Crick changed his original research project from Buddhist notions of social action to tourism, when he was mistaken for a hippie by a novice monk. The subsequent parallels he makes between the tourist and the anthropologist arise in part from his clearly bounded relationship with Ali. For we learn through his candid account that he prefers not to meet Ali on his family territory in a context outside tourism.

Anthony Cohen, in resisting external categorisation by others, distinguishes between what is known *about* a person and what is known *by* the self. The self is used to study others. To argue that anthropology is informed by the anthropologist's self is not the same as any suggestion that the discipline should be 'about the anthropologist's self'. Using autobiographical experience and inspired by a discussion with a Whalsay islander, he contrasts others' external categorisation with the inner driven self. Far from worrying about any accusation of self-absorption, he uses knowledge acquired from his 'most solitary, Cartesian soliloquy' as a resource to comprehend others' resistance to simple archetypes.

Bill Watson confronts the question of unequal power. As soon as he introduced himself as an anthropologist in Indonesia, he was made aware of the vehemence among Indonesian intellectuals towards the inequality of academic exchange. Watson's previous observations in print had, he was informed, been pre-empted by Indonesians, but theirs had not been given comparable recognition. Like Cohen, Watson draws attention to the mistaken assumption that the other is undifferentiated, that for example the Javanese speak with one voice. Ways of letting others speak have been hampered by the pretension of a totalising ethnography. An alternative approach, midway between indigenous text and academic production, is through shared experience and the mutual exchange of personal knowledge through friendship; 'the rest will follow naturally'.

Such optimism appears to be belied by examples from other contributors, especially those of Crick and Hendry. However, Watson, starting from the lessons of autobiographical experience in Indonesia, proposes that friendship take precedence. For Hendry and Crick, friendships were always constrained by or subordinate to the conventions of the research project. Marcus's account of her relationship with Louisa Montgomery brings a certain realism, placing the encounter of two individuals in the context of contrasting histories and social categories from which neither could escape. Liking each other was a prerequisite, but not the central ingredient. Hope of a genuine 'friendship' was abandoned.

Joy Hendry's cautionary tale of a friendship, destabilised by collaborative research, is not a straight rebuttal of Watson's utopian solution. The example reveals the ingredients of 'studying up' (Nader 1969). Whereas Crick feared giving too much remuneration to his poorer collaborator, lest the anthropologist lose face and authentic knowledge, Hendry's wealthier Japanese friend and assistant soon resented payment, since she appeared to lose equal status. Sachiko had believed anthropology to be the study of people lower down the hierarchy and now found herself to be the object of study. Ultimately, the élite graduate was in a strong position to block the invasion of her privacy. Hendry's account has parallels with those of Caplan and Kenna in that she traced her experience over two decades, in her case, through a single relationship which shifted from friendship to professional collaboration and then to mutual mistrust. At the start, they shared identities across the cultural divide as university educated women, and later as married mothers. They had each lived in each others' home territories before the research. Differences emerged as their careers took different directions which were acted out in the research.

The detailed relationships selected and described here by the contributors are in the majority of cases between persons of the same sex (Spencer,

Marcus, Kenna, Hendry, Crick, Cohen, Callaway and Okely). Helen Callaway made brief life histories of three men and three women in Western Nigeria, then found herself drawn more fully into the women's lives. This, she contends, was not because of the stereotype of a 'natural empathy' nor shared physiological experience, but because she was intrigued by what seemed to her then the women's remarkable autonomy. I suggest that she was implicitly contrasting her own gendered and culturally specific experience with theirs. Caplan's shift from a male to a female informant reflects and creates a fundamental change in her ethnography. Littlewood's link with Mother Earth replicates that of the recruits, the majority of whom were young men. Rapport, unusually, gives equal space to his relationship with both a man and a woman.

Beyond the general categories within which the anthropologist and indigenous persons must negotiate, there were degrees of individual exchange and reciprocity. The texts show different ways of giving voice to others. The autobiography of the anthropologist runs alongside others' autobiographical interventions. The Maasai elder creates his current identity through narratives of his past whose embellishment, concealment, and selectivity reveal the values of his culture (Spencer). Littlewood records Mother Earth's biography as presented to him and where it resonates with others' personal experiences. Her life is the text for others' lives. Mohammed's diary is both individual confessional and culturally revealing text (Caplan). None the less its personal form cannot be independent of the ethnographer's appropriation – its very existence came about through her intervention. Having explored how other life histories have kept the researcher and the one-to-one encounter outside the frame, Callaway scrutinises Julianah's story. The material became a resource for abstract analysis. Callaway considers that she suppressed Julianah's voice and, two decades later, is conscious of the alternative texts that might have been generated. Other contributors, notably Marcus and Hastrup, argue that whatever form the dialogue might take, the text is the final construct and responsibility of the author. Even Rapport's scrupulous attention to how the others experienced *his* presence, is perforce his own textual construction.

In a number of instances the anthropologist's power of textual production was treated as a resource. Ali wanted to be named in Crick's text, in defiance of the anthropologist's espousal of professional ethics. Littlewood's arrival was predicted in a dream by Mother Earth who asked him to write their story. His identity as white doctor was seen as a vital protection against medical or police harassment. The dialogue between anthropologist and people continued through the writing. The response by a Whalsay fisherman to Cohen's manuscript was profoundly instructive. After reading and changing Marcus's text, Louisa Montgomery requested that her details be published. Kenna returned part of the islanders' history to them through her video, which in turn created debate.

The textual analysts' critique of the brief autobiographical insertions in classical monographs is contested by John Davis. They conflate *being* an authority and *having* authority, and assume that having authority is reprehensible. Davis defends not so much the autobiographical mode, but the device for demonstrating that the anthropologist was there. Unlike photographs, literary representations do not prove that the author was there. In addition, Davis questions the uniform interpretation of an authority-establishing introduction in the past tense. Against the deconstructionists, he contends that attention should be paid to what the writer intended. Evans-Pritchard's description of his 'Nuerosis' like others' brief insertions, could alternatively be read as a caveat. Perhaps Evans-Pritchard intended to convey a less secure authority than in the Azande monograph where the introductory passage is even briefer. This interpretation does not, however, appear to extend to the personal insertions scattered through the Azande text.

Both Davis and Hastrup address the question of tense. Davis catalogues the multiple and varied tenses to be found in ethnographies. It is misleading to describe anthropologists as using '*the* ethnographic present'; in English at least, there is a repertoire: participatory, observational and true, either by definition or by experience. He concedes that anthropologists might consider using the past tense more frequently. On the other hand, Hastrup contends that the ethnographic present, in its widest symbolic sense, is the only appropriate tense, because it speaks of an encounter fixed at a certain moment and created by the juxtaposition between the anthropologist and others. Rapport's essay depicts such an encounter in its most immediate form. Whereas Fabian (1983) argues that the ethnographic present denies history to 'the other', Hastrup points to a confusion between genre and epistemology, and one which implies that representation is taken for reality. The experiential nature of fieldwork cannot be excluded. Fieldwork is marked by a betweenness both for the anthropologist and the 'others'. What they recount in the ethnographic dialogue is spoken from a liminal space. Hence the notion of an informant of unmediated cultural truth evaporates.

Whatever the potential in mutual encounter, Hastrup argues, the ethnographic project involves a degree of symbolic violence. The anthropologist hardly respects the other's right to remain silent. Hastrup learned, through a unique personal experience, what becoming the subject of another's text entailed when her autobiography and fieldwork in Iceland were staged as a play. The performance reframed her in an alien discourse, and she sensed an appropriation when the theatre company departed on a world tour. Her experience was used to comprehend that of the 'other' in anthropological discourse, as in examples from her work elsewhere (Hastrup 1987).

The contributors explicitly or implicitly, although without consensus, address questions of unequal power relations or 'the systematic imbalance in the creation of knowledge' (Watson). With the possible exception of

Hendry, those who discussed the experience had done fieldwork among people with a history of colonial rule, or with vulnerable minority status, or subject to a greater metropolitan control. This political reality affected the nature of the encounter. In some instances people with power or relative privilege were incorporated or hovered around the text. Marcus argues that the politics of representation and texts be confronted by focusing on politics and the gaze of the state. Her account of racism and terror finds echoes in the results of the Australian Royal Commission in 1991 into deaths in custody of Aborigines. Her critique of earlier ethnographic omissions of the political persecution of Australian Aborigines is confirmed elsewhere (McKnight 1990).

Reflexivity may seem comfortably neutral for some. That depends how it is interpreted. In its fullest sense, reflexivity forces us to think through the consequences of our relations with others, whether it be conditions of reciprocity, asymmetry or potential exploitation. There are choices to be made in the field, within relationships and in the final text. If we insert the ethnographer's self as positioned subject into the text, we are obliged to confront the moral and political responsibility of our actions.

Generally, the notion of autobiography or reflexivity is seen as threatening to the canons of the discipline, not because it has been interpreted as having political consequences, but because of its explicit attack on positivism. The reflexive I of the ethnographer subverts the idea of the observer as impersonal machine. The autobiographical insertion is different from the stamp of author's authority: not simply 'I was there', but the self and category whom the others confronted, received and confided in. The people in the field relate to the ethnographer as both individual and cultural category, whether or not the ethnographer acknowledges this. Autobiographical accounts of fieldwork are not confined to self-understanding in a cultural vacuum. They show how others related to the anthropologist and convey the ethnographic context.

Theoretical links lie between the anthropologist's experiential, embodied knowledge, its continuing resonances and the ultimate printed text. The extent to which autobiography can be written into the ethnography is a matter for creative experimentation. There are ways of exploring new forms appropriate to the anthropological endeavour. The genre need be fixed neither in a Great Man, western tradition nor within established literary conventions. Other traditions have existed as sceptical testimony and as celebrations from the margins. There are alternative possibilities which anthropology might imagine.

NOTES

1 At the first conference of the European Association of Social Anthropologists (Coimbra, 1990) when the issue of gender was raised at the general meeting, an

eminent male anthropologist announced that he had never thought of himself as a man, only as a human being.

2 Consistent with the editors' cavalier attitude towards feminist anthropology in *Writing Culture* (Clifford and Marcus 1986), the sex/gender of the anthropologist is given short shrift for theoretical analysis by the contributors, whereas the political status, history and even ethnicity of the anthropologist are seen to have theoretical implications for the final text.

REFERENCES

Anderson, L. (1986) At the Threshold of the Self: Women and Autobiography. In M. Monteith (ed.) *Women's Writing: A Challenge to Theory*. Brighton: Harvester Press.

Babcock, B. (1980) Reflexivity: Definitions and Discriminations. *Semiotica* 30 (1/2): 1–14.

Bakhtin, M. (1981) *The Dialogical Imagination*, M. Holquist (ed.). Austin, Texas: University of Texas Press.

Barley, N. (1983) *The Innocent Anthropologist*. London: British Museum Publications.

Beauvoir, S. de (1958) *Mémoires d'une jeune fille rangée*. Paris: Gallimard.

Bertaux, D. (1981) *Biography and Society: The Life History Approach in the Social Sciences*. Beverly Hills, Calif.: Sage Publications.

Bland, L. and John, A. (1990) Special Issue on Autobiography and Biography. *Gender and History* 2 (1), Spring.

Bordo, S. (1990) Feminism, Postmodernism, and Gender-Scepticism. In L. Nicholson (ed.) *Feminism/Postmodernism*. London: Routledge.

Bourdieu, P. (1977) *Outline of a Theory of Practice*. Cambridge: Cambridge University Press.

Campbell, A. T. (1989) *To Square with Genesis*. Edinburgh: Edinburgh University Press/Polygon.

Caplan, P. (1988) Engendering Knowledge. *Anthropology Today* 4 (5), Oct.: 8–12.

Carrithers, M. (1988) The Anthropologist as Author. *Anthropology Today* 4 (4), Aug.: 19–22.

Cesara, M. (1982) *Reflections of a Woman Anthropologist*. London: Academic Press.

Chodorow, N. (1978) *The Reproduction of Mothering*. Berkeley, Calif.: University of California Press.

Clifford, J. (1986a) Introduction: Partial Truths. In J. Clifford and G. Marcus (eds) *Writing Culture*. Berkeley, Calif.: University of California Press.

—— (1986b) On Ethnographic Allegory. In J. Clifford and G. Marcus (eds) *Writing Culture*. Berkeley, Calif.: University of California Press.

Clifford, J. and Marcus, G. (eds) (1986) *Writing Culture*. Berkeley, Calif.: University of California Press.

Coimbra (1990) Unpublished statement by a speaker at the first meeting of the European Association of Social Anthropologists (EASA) in September at Coimbra, Portugal.

Derrida, J. (1967/76) *Of Grammatology*, trans. G. C. Spivak. Baltimore: Johns Hopkins University Press.

Dodd, P. (1986) Criticism and the Autobiographical Tradition. In P. Dodd (ed.) *Modern Selves*. London: Frank Cass and Company Ltd.

Dumont, J.-P. (1978) *The Headman and I*. Austin, Texas: University of Texas Press.

Fabian, J. (1983) *Time and the Other. How Anthropology Makes its Object*. New York: Columbia University Press.

—— (1988) Introduction to 'Twenty Years of Critical Anthropology' Conference, Amsterdam.

Fardon, R. (ed.) (1990) General Introduction. In *Localising Strategies*. Edinburgh: Scottish Academic Press; Washington: Smithsonian Institution Press.

Favret-Saada, F. (1977/1980 Catherine Cullen trans.) *Deadly Words*. Cambridge: Cambridge University Press.

—— and Contreras, J. (1981) *Corps pour Corps*. Paris: Gallimard.

Firth, R. (1936/1965) *We the Tikopia*. Boston, Mass.: Beacon Press.

Freilich, M. (ed.) (1977) *Marginal Natives at Work*. Cambridge, Mass: Schenkman Publishing Co. Inc.

Freud, S. (1900) *The Interpretation of Dreams* (1955). London: Hogarth Press.

—— (1914/1948) *Psychopathology of Everyday Life*. London: Ernest Benn.

Friedman, J. (1988) Paper and remarks at 'Twenty Years of Critical Anthropology' Conference, Amsterdam.

Geertz, C. (1974) From the Native's Point of View: On the Nature of Anthropological Understanding. In *The Bulletin* of the American Academy, October.

—— (1988) *Works and Lives*. Oxford: Polity Press.

Gellner, E. (1988) Conscious Confusion. Review of *Works and Lives*, by C. Geertz. *Times Higher Educational Supplement*, 22 April: 26.

Golde, P. (ed.) (1986) Women in the World. Berkeley, Calif.: University of California Press. First edn 1970.

Gusdorf, G. (1956/1980 trans.) Conditions and Limits of Autobiography. In J. Olney (ed.) *Autobiography: Essays Theoretical and Critical*. Princeton: Princeton University Press.

Hastrup, K. (1987) Fieldwork among Friends. Ethnographic Exchange Within the Northern Civilisation. In A. Jackson (ed.) *Anthropology at Home*. London: Tavistock.

Hayes, E. N. and Hayes, T. (eds) (1970) *Claude Lévi-Strauss: The Anthropologist as Hero*. Cambridge: MIT Press.

Huizer, G. (1979) Research-Through-Action: Some Practical Experiences with Peasant Organisation. In G. Huizer and B. Mannheim (eds) *The Politics of Anthropology*. The Hague: Mouton.

—— and Mannheim, B. (eds) (1979) *The Politics of Anthropology*. The Hague: Mouton.

Jackson, A. (ed.) (1987) *Anthropology at Home*. London: Tavistock.

Jackson, M. (1983) Knowledge of the Body, *Man* 18 (3): 327–45.

Juhasz, S. (1980) Towards a Theory of Form in Feminist Autobiography: Kate Millett's *Flying* and *Sita*; Maxine Hong Kingston's *The Woman Warrior*. In E. Jelinek (ed.) *Women's Autobiography*. London: Indiana University Press.

Kielstra, N. (1987) The Anthropology of Southwestern Europe. *Critique of Anthropology* **VII** (2), Autumn: 88–90.

Kolodny, A. (1980) The Lady's Not for Spurning: Kate Millett and the Critics. In E. Jelinek (ed.) *Women's Autobiography*. London: Indiana University Press.

Leach, E. (1984) Glimpses of the Unmentionable in the History of British Social Anthropology. *Annual Review of Anthropology* 13: 1–23.

—— (1989) Tribal Ethnography: Past, Present and Future. In E. Tonkin, M. McDonald and M. Chapman (eds) *History and Ethnicity*. London: Routledge.

Lévi-Strauss, C. (1955) *Tristes Tropiques*. Paris: Plon.

—— (1988) *De Près et de Loin*. Paris: Odile Jacob.

Llobera, J. (1987) Reply to Critics. *Critique of Anthropology* **VII** (2), Autumn: 101–18.

Loizos, P. (1981) *The Heart Grown Bitter*. Cambridge: Cambridge University Press.

McKnight, D. (1990) The Australian Aborigines in Anthropology. In R. Fardon (ed.) *Localising Strategies*. Edinburgh: Scottish Academic Press; Washington: Smithsonian Institution Press.

Malinowski, B. (1922) Argonauts of the Western Pacific. An Account of Native Enterprise and Adventures in the Archipelagos of Melanesian New Guinea (Studies in Economics and Political Science). London: Routledge & Kegan Paul.

—— (1967) *A Diary in the Strict Sense of the Term*. London: Routledge.

Marx, K. (1846/1960 edn) *The German Ideology*. New York: International Publishers.

Mauss, M. (1938) Les Techniques du Corps. In *Anthropologie et Sociologie*. Paris: Presses Universitaires de France.

Misch, G. (1951 E. W. Dickes trans.) *A History of Autobiography in Antiquity*. Cambridge, Mass.: Harvard University Press.

Nader, L. (1969) Up the Anthropologist – Perspectives gained from studying up. In D. Hymes (ed.) *Reinventing Anthropology*. New York: Random House.

Nicholson, L. (ed.) (1990) *Feminism/Postmodernism*. London: Routledge.

Okely, J. (1975) The Self and Scientism. *Journal of the Social Anthropology Society Oxford* **6** (3): 171–88.

—— (1978) Privileged, Schooled and Finished: Boarding Education for Girls. In S. Ardener (ed.) *Defining Females*. London: Croom Helm.

—— (1983) *The Traveller-Gypsies*. Cambridge: Cambridge University Press.

—— (1984) Fieldwork in the Home Counties. *RAIN* **61**: 4–6.

—— (1986) *Simone de Beauvoir: A Re-reading*. London: Virago; New York: Pantheon.

—— (1987) Fieldwork up the M1: Policy and Political Aspects. In A. Jackson (ed.) *Anthropology at Home*. London: Tavistock.

—— (1991) Defiant Moments: Gender, resistance and individuals. *Man* **26** (1): 3–22.

Olney, J. (ed.) (1980) *Autobiography: Essays Theoretical and Critical*. Princeton: Princeton University Press.

Omvedt, G. (1979) On the Participant Study of Women's Movements: Methodological, Definitional and Action Considerations. In G. Huizer & B. Mannheim (eds) *The Politics of Anthropology*. The Hague: Mouton.

Pocock, D. (1973) The Idea of a Personal Anthropology. Paper presented to the Dicennial Conference of the ASA, Oxford.

—— (1975) *Understanding Social Anthropology*. London: Hodder and Stoughton.

Powdermaker, H. (1967) *Stranger and Friend: The Way of an Anthropologist*. New York: W. W. Norton and Co.

Pratt, M. L. (1986) Fieldwork in Common Places. In J. Clifford and G. Marcus (eds) *Writing Culture*. Berkeley, Calif.: University of California Press.

Rabinow, P. (1977) *Reflections on Fieldwork in Morocco*. London: University of California Press.

Riches, D. (1990) The Force of Tradition in Eskimology. In R. Fardon (ed.) *Localising Strategies*. Edinburgh: Scottish Academic Press; Washington: Smithsonian Institution Press.

Rosaldo, R. (1986) From the Door of His Tent: The Fieldworker and the Inquisitor. In J. Clifford and G. Marcus (eds) *Writing Culture*. Berkeley, Calif.: University of California Press.

Said, E. (1982) Opponents, Audiences, Constituencies and Community. *Critical Inquiry* **9**.

Scholte, B. (1974) Toward a Reflexive and Critical Anthropology. In D. Hymes (ed.) *Reinventing Anthropology*. New York: Vintage Books.

—— (1987) The Literary Turn in Contemporary Anthropology. *Critique of Anthropology* **7** (1), Summer: 33–47.

Silverman, S. (1989) Hortense Powdermaker. In U. Gacs, A. Khan, J. McIntyre and

R. Weinberg (eds) *Women Anthropologists, Selected Biographies*. Urbana and Chicago: University of Illinois Press.

Smith, S. (1987) *A Poetics of Woman's Autobiography*. Bloomington and Indianopolis: Indiana University Press.

Smith Bowen, E. (1954/1964 edn) *Return to Laughter*. New York: Doubleday Anchor.

Stanford Friedman, S. (1988) Women's Autobiographical Selves: Theory and Practice. In S. Benstock (ed.) *The Private Self*. London: Routledge.

Street, B. (1990) Orientalist Discourses in the Anthropology of Iran, Afghanistan and Pakistan. In R. Fardon (ed.) *Localising Strategies*. Edinburgh: Scottish Academic Press; Washington: Smithsonian Institutiion Press.

Turner, V. and Bruner, E. (eds) (1986) *The Anthropology of Experience*. Urbana and Chicago: University of Illinois Press.

Vincent, D. (1981) *Bread, Knowledge and Freedom*. London: Europa Publications.

Wax, R. (1971) *Doing Field Work*. Chicago: University of Chicago Press.

Whitehead, T. and Conaway, M. (eds) (1986) *Self, Sex, and Gender in Cross-Cultural Fieldwork*. Chicago: University of Illinois Press.

Chapter 2

Ethnography and experience
Gender implications in fieldwork and texts

Helen Callaway

> The critical ontology of ourselves has to be considered … as an attitude, an ethos, a philosophical life in which the critique of what we are is at one and the same time the historical analysis of the limits that are imposed on us and an experiment of going beyond them. (Foucault 1984: 50)

The authors in this book examine the self in its many identities and phases, not as a mode of self-absorption or self-voyeurism, but as probings of personal experience in the examination of anthropological practice. Tracing the implications of gender, I look at the ways in which it defines our identities, and helps to shape the gathering of data and interpretations of other societies. Current feminist anthropology gives a central place to the analytical concept of gender as both cultural construct and social relation. Drawing from this scholarship,[1] I turn it back reflexively to raise questions about selves as anthropologists.

While gender is the primary feature of personal identity, for example, gender in professional identity tends to be subsumed in the ideology of the unspecified (or neuter) anthropologist. Male anthropologists usually consider their gender to be consonant with their professional work, while females see the designation of 'woman anthropologist' to be a marked one in the dominant discourse, therefore lesser and demeaning.[2] This feature of the English language differentiating strong/weak or dominant/subordinate forms can be linked to the wider tradition of western discourse structured on binary oppositions (rationality/irrationality, analytical/intuitive and so on) and weighted with greater/lesser values. In this pervading pattern of discourse, men and women are differently constituted as human subjects. A male-oriented default system has been programmed into our language and consciousness, the way in which we view the world, and the discourse we use in analysing our anthropological others. The language we use, then, becomes one of the first areas of critical awareness in seeing the implications of gender for the 'translation' of other cultures.

With gender highlighted, the continuities and disjunctions between field-work and the writing of texts take on greater clarity. As fieldworkers we are necessarily embodied creatures, identified by host societies according to their classificatory systems, gender being a salient feature. Texts, in contrast, are disembodied; the author's gender may be evident only in inflections and nuances. Again, women and men in the field conduct their work in personal, face-to-face encounters through the medium of dialogue. Later, back home, these multiple levels of personal discourse become transmuted into impersonal and distant printed words. These very disjunctions have become issues in current debates.

For Fabian (1983), this break between fieldwork and text allows a cover-up for a fundamental contradiction: ethnographic research involves prolonged interaction with others, yet anthropological discourse conveys the understanding gained in terms of distance, both spatial and temporal. Here I am concerned not so much with the displacement of time but with a related issue, the obscuring of gender through the continuing convention of the transcendent authorial voice separated from the embodied person and from historical time and place.

What are the implications of the anthropologist as a gendered knower? Of field research as a process of personal interaction and flawed understandings, involving what may be vastly different – and not always easily recognised – patterns of gender relations between that of the anthropologist and the society being studied? In what ways does rational inquiry have gendered dimensions? Since there are no ungendered lives, can there be ungendered texts? How does gender relate to the production of knowledge and its power structures (publishers' decisions, professional legitimation and so on)? These questions have been repressed, considered as not worth asking, within the model of objective scientific research carried out and written up by the neutral and neuter knower. Despite the placing of anthropology within the human sciences rather than the more positivist natural sciences and the centrality in the discipline of *participant*-observation, this image of the detached, historically unsituated observer persists.

Often the anthropologist is warned about bringing her own 'cultural baggage' to the field, as if personal and cultural components of one's being could be shed like luggage left in a locker. Presumably gender is part of this baggage. But the opposite case is made here: that a deepening understanding of our own gendered identities and the coded complexities of our being offered the best resources for gaining insights into the lives of others. The project of 'engendering knowledge' (Caplan 1988) requires that the study of other societies, including their gender relations and ideologies, be carried out with scrupulous examination of ourselves as gendered identities. This means continuing scrutiny of the submerged power relations in the discourses and concrete practices of our own society as well.

In fieldwork, gender classifications may be confused and contradictory between the anthropologist's self-perceptions and those of the studied society. Hastrup (1987: 95–9), for example, tells of difficulties during her field research in Iceland because she did not recognise territorial boundaries related to gender. She was exposed to violence, which was fortunately averted and eventually resulted in insights central to her work. Angrosino writes that his training had prepared him to question other presuppositions he would bring to the field, but not his gender identity, 'almost as if we are somehow convinced that such an identity is a universal characteristic that could not possibly cause any misunderstandings' (1986: 64).

Turning to the writing of texts, I would not like to submit to a blind analysis of past ethnographies[3] to determine whether the authors are female or male. It would be unreasonable, I think, to expect any strong gender markers in the majority of texts given the range of factors contributing to their construction. Between the embodied persons interrelating with others in fieldwork and their disembodied texts comes 'genre', the unwritten conventions of ethnography which change through time, depending on shifts in theoretical movements, and demands of universities and publishers. One of the tacit rules of classic ethnography has been the 'neutrality' of the author in the pursuit of a 'value-free science'. Among other exclusions of anthropologists' selves, 'genre' all but eliminated 'gender'.

A strange thing has happened in regard to conventions of ethnography, rather like the dramatic sense of shifts and gulfs discussed by Strathern (1987: 253) in relation to Frazer and Malinowski. Experimental texts, previously recognised as anomalous and outside the great tradition have recently been granted a special place (Marcus and Cushman 1982; Clifford and Marcus 1986). With this new focus, feminist anthropologists have been taking note of women's texts departing from classic ethnography. It is possible now to discern what might be considered a submerged female tradition in 'writing culture'. Numerous examples might be cited, among them Bowen, *Return to Laughter* (1954); Briggs, *Never in Anger* (1970); Suskind, *To Hunt in the Morning* (1973); Myerhoff, *Peyote Hunt* (1974) and *Number Our Days* (1978); Favret-Saada, *Deadly Words: Witchcraft in the Bocage* (1980); Schrijvers, *Mothers for Life* (1985) and Abu-Lughod, *Veiled Sentiments* (1986). Attention has also been directed to texts by 'untrained' wives accompanying male anthropologists in their fieldwork (some of whom later went on to gain academic qualifications): such as, Fernea, *Guests of the Sheik* (1965), and Wolf, *The House of Lim* (1968).

These women wrote against the prevailing ethnographic conventions by drawing more directly on personal experience to show the process of understanding, recording their own puzzlements, sometimes despair, and relating moments of discovery and revelation. By presenting narrative dramas of daily life in foreign settings, they illuminated the general through focus on the particular. Gender difference can be traced here, not to any innate female characteristics, but to learned ways of relating and listening to others, learned modes of representing 'reality' in experiential forms rather than abstractions, the decisions of some to write for a wider readership than is reached by more conventional academic studies, and the marginal authority conferred on their publications by academic departments.

Concerned about the use of the 'personal' and the 'subjective', some of these women anthropologists considered their work to be outside the boundaries of the discipline: Bohannan published her novel under a pseudonym, retaining her own name for her professional work (Preface, Bowen); Myerhoff characterised her ethnographies as influenced by, but not works of, anthropology (Prell 1989: 255). Yet these texts anticipated the oft-cited 'experimental' ethnographies written more recently by Dwyer (1982), Rabinow (1977) and Crapazano (1980).

REFLEXIVITY AND REPRESENTATION

As a mode of anthropological practice, 'reflexivity' entered the conceptual space of anthropology at least twenty years ago. In his programme for an emancipatory anthropology, Scholte set out a critique of the ideology of value-free social science with its widely-held assumption that 'there is, or should be, a discontinuity between experience and reality, between the investigator and the object investigated' (1972: 435). Refuting this position, he proposed the practice of 'reflexivity': in its narrower focus, as the self-reflecting anthro-pologist engaged in the interpersonal relations of fieldwork and, in its broader sense, as a searching probe of the discipline itself, questioning the conditions and modes of producing knowledge about other cultures.

In 1975, Okely published 'Self and Scientism', her themes anticipating this volume:

> In the study of human being by another human being (and what better medium is there?), the specificity and individuality of the observer are ever present and must therefore be acknowledged, explored and put to creative use. (1975: 172)

These implications, in her view, required continuing working through by the individual; the discipline itself needed to develop analytical categories, including gender, to explore various forms of subjectivity.

Lévi-Strauss cited Rousseau's self-division as the origin for a reflexive approach to knowledge:

> To Rousseau we owe the discovery of this principle, the only one on which to base the sciences of man ... in ethnographic experience, the observer apprehends himself as his own instrument of observation. Clearly, he must learn to know himself, to obtain from a *self* who reveals himself as *another* to the *I* who uses him, an evaluation which will become an integral part of the observation of other selves. (1976: 36)

Anthropology offers the possibility of a 'double frame' of reflexivity, as Prell (1989: 241–58) analyses in the work of Myerhoff. In her study of

Huichol religion in Mexico, Myerhoff (1974) includes the reflections of her chief informant, the shaman Ramon, as he introduced her to myths, symbolism and peyote-induced experience, while at the same time she discloses her own revelations and deepening understanding. Her study (1978) of an elderly Jewish group in Venice, California, shows the stages of her own comprehension of how these individuals shaped worlds of meaning out of their experience of two cultures. Her innovative texts reveal the creativity of subjects in thinking about their own cultures as they interact with her and provide data for her layered interpretations.

Often condemned as apolitical, reflexivity, on the contrary, can be seen as opening the way to a more radical consciousness of self in facing the political dimensions of fieldwork and constructing knowledge. Other factors intersecting with gender – such as nationality, race, ethnicity, class and age – also affect the anthropologist's field interactions and textual strategies. Reflexivity becomes a continuing mode of self-analysis and political awareness.

The practice of a reflexive anthropology, as Scholte and others have stated in different ways, properly confronts the politics of representation. Two decades ago from a number of directions (Hymes 1972; Asad 1973; Huizer and Mannheim 1979) came recognition that, as a discipline, anthropology had its roots in the imperialist era and carried with it implicit relations of inequality between an anthropologist from the dominant West and the people of less powerful societies. An epistemological problem was located – summarised in the term 'Orientalism' – used by Said (1978) to expose the problem of how knowledge of other cultures is constituted within unequal relations of political power.

This continuing critique of the discipline links with the widely perceived 'crisis in representation' (Jameson 1984: viii). While associated in anthropology with the literary devices of ethnography, this crisis concerns the deeper movement of 'restructuring' across the range of disciplines in the human sciences (Bernstein 1976, 1983; Giddens 1976, 1979). The critique of an essentially realist epistemology which conceived of representation as a reproduction or mirroring of reality has brought in its wake unsettling propositions of representation as positional, partial and constitutive of reality. The confident truth claims made from the 'objective' perspective of the western élite 'man of reason' have been undermined (Lloyd 1984; Hawkesworth 1989; Hekman 1990). With postmodern ideas of plural voices and provisional truths, narrative came to the fore, first in White's analysis (1973) as governed by tropes and genres, and then 'transformed from a formal pattern or type to an activity in which politics, tradition, history, and interpretation converged' (Said 1989: 221).

GENDER AND AUTOBIOGRAPHY

Coinciding with postmodern ideas – but arising in feminist studies from the practical politics of difference along class, race and ethnic lines – the category of gender has itself become fractured. Grimshaw (1986: 85) argues that while gender inflects much if not all of our daily experience, the relation between masculine and feminine experience is very complex – one is never *just* a man or a woman. In the experience of factory labour, for example, or of poverty and unemployment, working-class women may have more similarities with working-class men; on the other hand, in the experience of domestic labour and childcare, of the constraints and requirements that one be 'attractive' or 'feminine', working-class women may share more with middle-class women. Grimshaw continues, 'Experience does not come neatly in segments, such that it is always possible to abstract what in one's experience is due to 'being a woman' from that which is due to 'being married,' 'being middle class' and so forth' (ibid.). (The same analysis, of course, holds for a man's experience.)

Bordo takes up this 'inflection argument' to contest that while gender can never be said to manifest itself in pure form, this does not mean acceptance of Grimshaw's logical conclusion that 'abstractions or generalisations about gender are methodologically illicit or perniciously homogenising of difference' (Bordo 1990: 150). Bordo points out that in demonstrating the fragmented nature of gender, Grimshaw at the same stroke deconstructs race, class and historical generalities: 'the inflections that modify experience are endless, and *some* item of difference can always be produced which will shatter any proposed generalisations' (ibid.). The 'inflection argument' deflects any analysis of power relations.

Analytical categories, by definition, are abstractions from reality, invented labels for identifying features and placing them in classes of similarity and difference. The choice of analytical categories itself becomes problematic; they are open to instability (Harding 1986). In anthropology, the category of 'gender' has been taken seriously mainly by women informed by feminist perspectives. Yet gender can be seen in many societies as a primary organising principle; in some cases, as Strathern (1988) demonstrates for Melanesian societies, 'gender' reaches far beyond relations of men and women to structure the whole of social relations and events.

Returning to what Said (1989: 212) terms 'the problematic of the observer', which he considers to be 'remarkably underanalyzed' in current anthropology, we confront gender in our own society. Bordo argues that in a culture constructed by gender duality, one *cannot* simply be 'human' any more than in a racist society we can 'just be people':

> Our language, intellectual history, and social forms are 'gendered'; there is no escape from this fact and from its consequences on our lives. . . . our deepest desire may be to 'transcend gender dualities' . . . But, like it or not, in our present culture, our activities *are* coded as 'male' or 'female'

and will function as such within the prevailing system of gender-power relations. (1990: 152)

The autobiography of the anthropologist, the narrative we construct of our lives and work, necessarily unfolds in terms of gendered experience and its inequalities of power and privilege.

THE GENDERED KNOWER

Published in 1970, Golde's collection (1986) was the first to consider the theme 'What it means to be a woman in the field'. Contributors brought out not only gender differences, but also how differences among women were critical – young or middle-aged; black or white; single, married (with or without spouse), divorced, widowed; childless, pregnant, or with accompanying children. Depending on specific societies, they were also given or assumed different identities in the field: an adopted daughter, sister of men, eligible woman for marriage, grandmother and so on.

Reflecting on the book's title, one contributor (Codere 1986: 150) remarked on how foolish 'men in the field' would sound; another (Friedl 1986: 197) considered such a companion volume to be necessary. In different ways, each has a valid argument, one noting the asymmetry of 'women' as a marked category, the other pointing out the danger of setting 'women' off as a separate unit when the issue is that of gender – women *and* men, the experience common to both in fieldwork and the areas where gender makes a difference. Since then, other anthropologists (Ardener 1984; Warren 1988) have explored gender issues in field research; Whitehead and Conaway (1986) raised questions on how a range of differences – sex, gender, age, race, ethnicity and religion – affect anthropologists' interactions in the field.

As these collections have fully examined, women and men meet different practical difficulties. What interests us here are gender differences which set up different patterns of social relations or create differential access to domains of knowledge. Nader suggests a privileged position for female anthropologists:

> Both in Mexico and Lebanon I was respected as a woman somehow different from their women. Consequently I had access to both men's and women's culture. No man, even if he was considered different from the local men, would have had access to women's culture equal to mine to the men's culture. (1986: 114)

This 'privileged position' of women in the field has been questioned, among others, by Gregory, who argues that with persistence male anthropologists should be able to gather the required data, what prevents them is 'the low status of information about the woman's world' (1984: 323). Ardener (1975) traced 'the problem of women' not to lack of empirical data but to the conceptual frameworks of anthropologists.

Continuing the assessment of gender differences in fieldwork, Nader (1986: 114) noted that women and men may take up different topics. Only now, twenty years after her paper was written, are the implications of this observation being examined. Feminist philosophers have claimed that a key origin of androcentric bias in science lies in the selection of problems for inquiry and in the definition of what is problematic (Harding 1986: 652). Are women more likely to study the emotions, for example, as Briggs did among the Inuit Eskimos? In her introduction (Briggs 1970), she tells how she decided at the start that her study of Inuit emotional patterns would require description of her own feelings in particular situations. Well before the current interest in reflexivity, she gave attention to her own interaction as a mode of understanding and placed herself within the frame of her ethnography.

As a topic of special interest, women have chosen to study and write monographs about women from as far back at least as 1915 when D. Amaury Talbot (wife of the anthropologist) published *Woman's Mysteries of a Primitive People* on the Ibibio women of south-eastern Nigeria. Again, in the wake of the 'women's war' in 1929, Leith-Ross (1965, original edition 1939) returned to Nigeria to study women. Kaberry (1939, 1952) published ethnographies of Aboriginal women in Australia and women in the Cameroon grasslands. Landes (1938, 1947) studied Ojibwa women in America and Negro women cult leaders in Brazil. The autobiography of a Papago Indian woman was shaped by Underhill (1936).

One implication of these women writing about women is that – however ethnocentric some of the earlier monographs now sound, however out-moded their conceptual frameworks, whether or not sensitive to the dangers of biological essentialism – they have with greater or less analytical insights created gendered subjects: women within their cultural contexts, women differing from men, women in relation to men of the society. Male anthropologists, however, have seldom created gendered subjects (Clifford and Marcus 1986: 19; Caplan 1988: 14),[4] that is, analysing how their masculinity is socially constructed, perhaps because for the most part they have viewed men as representatives of a society, their masculinity the development of personhood in that social group. As Harding notes: 'The idea of a social construction of masculinity and femininity that is little, if at all, constrained by biology, is very recent' (1987: 8).

The difference that gender makes in how anthropological knowledge is created has still to be explored in terms of choice of area and topic, how field notes and diaries are written, the adoption of analytical categories, selection of 'facts', inferences drawn, unstated premises and patterns of interpretation. In feminist scholarship, the problem of the gendered knower has come to the fore marked by divisions between those who posit a 'women's ways of knowing' (Belenky *et al.* 1986), and those who consider the empirical reach and conceptual scope of the knower to transcend constraints of gender. Postmodern feminists (Hekman 1990: 16) oppose the concept of a 'feminist epistemology' on the grounds that it continues the dichotomies of Enlightenment thought rather than removing the gendered connotations of the process of knowing. To move beyond this apparent opposition, the concept of gendered identity has been redefined from the notion of an essentialist and static subjectivity to one that is fluid and open to change through self-analysing practice (de Lauretis 1984, 1986; Alcoff 1988).

'Experience' is a central concept in de Lauretis's analysis of how subjectivity is not a fixed point from which one interacts with the world:

> On the contrary, it is the effect of that interaction – which I call experience; and thus it is produced not by external ideas, values, or material causes, but by one's personal subjective, engagement in the practices, discourses, and institutions that lend significance (value, meaning, and affect) to the events of the world. (1984: 159)

Pointing to the logical trap set up by positing a genderless subjectivity or one placed within an oppositional dichotomy reverting to biological essentialism, she analyses the 'problem of the subject' in psychoanalysis and semiotic theory. For de Lauretis, subjectivity 'is interpreted or reconstructed by each of us within the horizon of meanings and knowledges available in the culture at given historical moments, a horizon that also includes modes of political commitment and struggle' (1986: 8). Individuals then recognise their own gendered consciousness through self-analysis, act upon the world in terms of their political engagements and become aware of a changing subjectivity.

THE IMPURITIES OF EXPERIENCE

Dumont points out that it was mainly women who wrote autobiographical accounts of fieldwork, at least up to the 1960s. To him, it suggests (with undertones of irony) that women 'were left with the task of conjuring the impurities of experience ... while the men were exclusively doing 'the real thing' (1978: 8). Interestingly, and for whatever reasons – the wider influence of psychoanalysis, less reluctance to reveal intimate personal details, greater acceptance of the relation of personal to professional life, to suggest a few – these autobiographies have been written almost exclusively by Americans: Hortense Powdermaker (1967), who came to London to study under Malinowski, but not her fellow student, Camilla Wedgwood; Margaret Mead (1972), but not her British contemporaries Margaret Read or Audrey Richards; Laura Bohannan (in her fictional account, Bowen 1954), a student of Evans-Pritchard in Oxford, but not Mary Douglas who was also there in the 1950s. In Britain, the autobiographical project by women has been taken up only recently and specifically as a mode of anthropological knowing.

Bohannan's text, *Return to Laughter* (Bowen 1954), has a special place in my library. Finding a secondhand copy in Blackwell's on my way to Nigeria, I read it during my first week there. The book became mouldy and still smells of the rainy season. But only with the 'literary turn' in anthropology have I realised how far ahead of her time she was. The post Second World War emphasis on a rigorous neutral, 'scientific' stance was the obstacle which motivated her to write about her experience among the Tiv of Nigeria under a pseudonym and in a different form. Her book has become a prime example of ethnography as fiction. The moment of Bohannan's rebellion is revealing. This occurs during the prolonged agony of her Tiv friend in childbirth:

> A cool, objective approach to Amara's death? One can, perhaps, be cool when dealing with questionnaires or when interviewing strangers. But what is one to do when one can collect one's data only by forming personal friendships? It is hard enough to think of a friend as a case history. Was I to stand aloof, observing the course of events? There could be no professional hesitation. Otherwise I might never see the ceremonies connected with death in childbirth. (Bowen 1954: 163)

The last sentence rings with irony. Bohannan points up the impossibility of objectivity in such a situation. This was not only a question of research methodology, but also of textual strategy. Her novel, I suggest, was itself a subversive move, particularly during the 1950s when in sociology, but also in anthropology, scientific method with its notion of value-free research was being sharpened and refined. What was pejoratively called 'subjectivity' was disguised and kept out of the text, emotions were discredited, concrete incidents (no matter how illuminating of a general point) were considered anecdotes. Experience, both that of the ethnographer and that of the people, was erased in favour of abstract analysis. The canons of pure science, as set out by positivism, required a literal, unemotional language in representing the world. All the impurities of experience were filtered out. Writing on 'The Novel and Europe', Milan Kundera (1984) questions whether it was an accident that the novel and the hegemony of scientific rationality emerged at the same time. Perhaps, then, it was no accident that Bohannan, in dealing with the harrowing confrontations in her fieldwork, chose the form of a novel.

In the conventional framework of the era, Paul Bohannan wrote up his fieldwork in Tiv country according to various themes – law and warfare, kinship and residence, economics and technology – with both the observer and the colonial presence placed outside the frame of the ethnography. Using the ethnographic present tense, he omitted the history of these people, placing them in a timeless perspective. Morover, he presented his arguments with confidence and closure; in the 1950s ambivalence, ambiguities and open endings were not accepted modes. For that period, he produced approved ethnographies. By the 1970s, fashions were changing. Arguing for the importance of maintaining the liveliness of experience, Dumont writes, 'Nothing seems more fictitious to me now than the classic monograph in which a human group is drawn and quartered along the traditional categories of social, economic, religious, and other so-called organizations and everything holds together' (1978: 12).

Laura Bohannan's novel re-enacts experience – with keenly observed visual details, concrete images of Tiv life, lively dialogue, a polyphony of voices. It is full of incidents and ironic interaction, disclosing misunder-standings and making shrewd guesses at alternative meanings. Postmodern before its time? Yet while ethnographies are now recognised as 'fiction' by such British anthropologists as the late Sir Edmund Leach (ASA meeting, 1987), novels – even realist ones closely based on experience – present an inadequate form of ethnography. Anthropological analysis, beyond a rudimentary approach, is missing, whether at a meta-level in separate sections or as interpretive interplay with experience. The works of the Bohannans stand as 'ideal types' in a study of contrasting modes of ethnographic writing. This example might be cited as a limiting case, extreme rather than representative. Clearly both women and men anthropologists have written a wide range of ethnographies with greater or less emphasis on concrete experience and general analysis.

LIVES OF OTHERS

As a further example from Nigeria, *Baba of Karo* (Smith 1954) shows a similar division between analysis and life experience. In the introduction, the anthropologist M. G. Smith sets out the dimensions of Hausa society along conventional thematic lines. His wife Mary Smith assisted his fieldwork by becoming fluent in Hausa and seeking data in the compounds where women were secluded and inaccessible to stranger men. During their eighteen-month stay, she recorded the memories of a remarkable Hausa woman in her own words. The main part of the book presents this life story of Baba, whose voice, even in English translation, comes through with lively narrative and rhetorical verve.

The rich experience of this ordinary African woman illuminates the wider social world. As Geiger (1986: 341–2) perceptively points out with page references, Baba's narrative frequently contradicts M. G. Smith's generalisa-tions about Hausa society, particularly on such subjects as marriage, divorce, kinship and social relationships among women. As an ethnographic text, this life history is presented entirely through Baba's voice in terms of her memories and reflections. Mary Smith has remained outside the frame. Besides her translation from Hausa into English, Smith acknowledges, without reflecting on the implications, that she re-arranged events into chronological order, eliminated repetitions, and set out chapter titles and sub-titles.

Dwyer (1982: 258–9) has criticised the life histories by Kluckhohn and Radin between the wars for separating the researcher (considered by them to be 'objective') from the informant and his subjectivity, ignoring the specific encounter between the two. The same criticism could be levelled at Mary Smith, since she tells very little about the negotiations that went on between the two women. This silence was the convention of an earlier period, in contrast with Shostak's detailed disclosure of her relations with the !Kung woman, Nisa, in creating her life story (1981, 1989: 228–40). The purposes of these two books were quite different: Nisa's story provides individual experience against a background of anthropological analysis of the lives of !Kung women, while Baba's life stands on its own as 'autobiography'. Would the life story of Baba be more complete, more ethical, if Mary Smith had included the details of her own feelings and thoughts in her relationship with Baba? It would be as dogmatic to insist on this, I suggest, as the previous convention was in excluding the presence of the anthropologist. Yet, in saying this, I would value the autobiography more with an accompanying chapter on the encounter between the writer and the subject and on the problems of shaping the material.

Baba of Karo stands as a magnificent achievement. My regret, again a comment of today, is that the book is not widely available in its original language, Hausa, for the benefit of the generation of Baba's great-granddaughters. But this thought brings new questions. A shift in audience creates new perspectives and meanings for a text. Ironically, against those who argue for detailed disclosure of the anthropologist's relations with the subject, an audience in Northern Nigeria today might well find the presence of Mary Smith, if she had included herself in the story of Baba's life, to be irrelevant and inappropriate.

On the topic of biography and the structure of lives, Langness and Frank (1981: 87–116) discuss the extent to which the anthropologist intervenes to shape the story of a subject's life meant to be called an 'autobiography'. They state that against the assumption of most anthropologists (though one wonders whether this would be held by many who have worked in a non-western society), a life history is not a natural or universal narrative form; placing a microphone in front of a non-literate informant will not necessarily lead to autobiography as we know it. My own efforts at recording the lives of others brought different problems.

In Ibadan, a huge sprawling indigenous city in Western Nigeria, I began work in the late 1960s by undertaking brief life studies of three men (a primary-school teacher, a carpenter and a tailor) and three women (a prayer healer, an *adire* cloth maker and a community nurse). This was a way of gathering data, but, more important, an entry into 'participation' in a vast urban society. I visited their homes and workplaces, met their immediate families and relatives in nearby towns and villages (my offer of transport took me to unexpected places), and attended church services and special events. In retrospect, I realise I was drawn more fully into women's lives not because of the stereotype of a 'natural empathy' nor shared physiological experience, which in any case has different cultural definitions and meanings, but because I was intrigued by what seemed to me then their remarkable independence, and what I would now interpret as their different cultural experience and expressions of gender.

Julianah Olanike (using a pseudonym, a practice in itself problematic) was about twenty when I first ventured into the compound of the Cherubim and Seraphim Society, where she lived and worked. She told me the story of how she had come to be a spiritual healer. Many years before her birth, her father had been told by an *aladura* ('one who prays') that there would be a prophet among his children. Her mother had given birth to eight children, but only two females had survived, and in her childhood Julianah had contracted smallpox and been sent with her mother to the 'bush'. She had stayed alive, miraculously, until the illness passed and her mother could bring her home. Her life, as she told it, was shaped by destiny: a prophet in the family had been foretold and, as a child, she had been brought back from death.

When she reached secondary-school stage, she was sent from the village to Ibadan to stay with her father's brother, a member of the Cherubim and Seraphim Society, and every morning Julianah went with his family to the 5 o'clock service. One morning after she had fasted the previous evening, she came as usual to the service and when she began to pray she felt lifted away from this world, filled with visions of heaven. She remained in the temple unconscious, she said, for an entire week. When she came to, the elders recorded her visions as she related them. For some days after, she 'spoke in many tongues' (translated by a prophet of the Society) and it was recognised that she had unusual insights into people's problems and spiritual conditions. From that day she realised that God had called her to this work and that she must stay at the religious centre. She had been there for three years when I met her.

Several times I went to prayer meetings in the late afternoon, when all those attending were women with babies on their backs, or in various stages of pregnancy, or (she told me) those wanting to get with child. And dressed in the prescribed white, a blouse and cloth wrapped around my waist in Yoruba fashion, I went to the Saturday 'watchnight' services beginning at midnight and lasting for two or three hours. Singing, prayers and hand-clapping in vigorous rhythms; heavy rain slashing against the windows: I hardly needed to suspend disbelief when the 'Holy Spirit descended' to possess several members – swirling, swooning figures in the broad central aisle.

About three years after our first sessions, I searched for Julianah and found her no longer in the Cherubim compound but living nearby and earning a reasonable living, more than many wage-earners, by praying for those who came to her in sickness or in mental distress. She was married now, very proud of her baby son, but living apart from her husband, she said, because of the nature of her work and the need to concentrate on prayer. The story goes on, and I have given only a bare outline. How were the details of others' lives to be transformed into text? Eventually, I used details and themes for papers on Yoruba women (Callaway 1980, 1981), but like the bulk of fieldnotes for most anthropologists, this material became a resource for more abstract analysis and remains unpublished. I have told Julianah's story in the third person because it was pieced together over a number of meetings, not recorded in her own words and not told with the same themes that I think now she would have used to shape the meanings of her life. In effect, I have framed her story within my own perspectives and purposes, suppressing her voice. Although I did not intend this to be the 'autobiography' of an informant with her own reflections on the shaping of her life, yet as I write this I am sharply conscious of a new set of questions about my relationship with her and the alternative texts this might have generated.

These issues have been taken up in the collection, *Interpreting Women's Lives: Feminist Theory and Personal Narratives* (Personal Narratives Group 1989). The authors explore how their subjects structure their life stories according to available cultural trajectories and significant themes. They examine how gender difference shapes the forms of autobiographies in a social group, in one case men structuring their narratives on their work life with women finding different themes and more often using images of rebellion. Assessing personal relations during the construction of the life history of an elderly peasant woman in Tanzania, Mbilinyi (1989) tells how her own strong views on feminism and colonialism were challenged and she was painfully accused of not having listened carefully.

As an example of ethnography placing other women's lives in the same frame as her own, Schrijvers (1985) provides excerpts from novels and life histories of poor rural women in Sri Lanka, showing among other themes their resistance to the domestic violence which pervades this society. She reveals the questionings and disruptions of her research process in 'letters from the field' to her colleagues. Placing motherhood at the centre of these women's lives, she shows this to be a paradox: both the condition of their powerlessness and a source of power. This interpretation, she writes, emerged from her own troubled experience as a mother. As a text, this is experiential, analytical, self-reflexive and open-ended.

LIVES OF SELVES

Can autobiography become anthropology? Several brief experimental texts written in the 1970s place the self at the centre – the anthropologist investigating her own life. This is experience at its most immediate and personal, with the anthropologist as both subject and object. In her paper on boarding education for girls, Okely writes, 'I deliberately confront the notion of objectivity in research by starting with the subjective, working from the self outwards. The self – the past self – becomes a thing, an object' (1978: 110). She probed the memories of her school days to show how the girls' school invisibly provided a preparation for dependence, while the boys' school more visibly educated them for independence and power.

Okely confronts the epistemological status of autobiography: it is retrospective, unlike a diary which records the present; there will be loss of memory and a distortion of the past; this represents a child's perception of events. She notes how a temporal split occurs between the participation of her childhood self and the later observation by her anthropologist self, revealing the fact that she could not articulate her experience in the language of adults at that time. The school world provided the norm, the only rationality, the definitions of reality. She analyses the everyday routines and special ceremonies which imprinted the prescribed class and gender dispositions in girls' minds and bodies. Her study details the all-pervading control of the girls' movements in space and time, in their speech and deportment, with girls internalising the ideals of modesty, humility and the invisibility of self. This brief ethnography is perhaps the more powerful for showing the child's conformity and small acts of rebellion, her bewilderment and embarrassment, through the double lens of refracted memories and the anthropologist's professional analysis. Its importance lies in its rigorous analysis of the social and historical formation of gendered (and class) subjectivity.

Similarly, Callan (1975) found her starting point in her own situation in her study of the wives of diplomats serving abroad. Another example of autobiography, but in this case of the ethnographic present, not of the past. Her own life was her fieldwork. Callan discusses the practical and methodological difficulties in such participant-observation. While she participated both as a member of the group and as an anthropologist, her observation (the outsider stance this implies) violated her status as a diplomat's wife, its definition being commitment not only to official duties but to the implicit meanings of her role and the deeper loyalty this required. Her scrupulous examination of the tacit rules hinted at disloyalty to the diplomatic hierarchy. Wives were not paid and were officially recognised only as spouses; yet they were expected to perform a great variety of duties in the social life of the embassy. Through the insights of her divided self, Callan analysed the gender ideology of 'the premiss of dedication' which hides the ambiguity and stress in the wives' situation. Her counter-narrative, derived from the pain and comic relief of personal experience, undermines the dominant ideology which upholds the wives' subservient position and represses their resistance.[5]

(GENDERED) SELVES, EXPERIENCE, TEXTS

These studies of selves, using gender as the focus of analysis, bring new readings of our own society. They expose a gendered sub-text between the lines of the dominant (no less gendered) version. The close analysis of gendered selves alerts us as well to the submerged operations of gender in other societies and how its rules and negotiations reveal patterns of social organisation. The possibility also arises for dialogues with previously unheard voices and for the discovery of points of difference and resistance to dominant modes.

'Experience', as a term in anthropology refers to the researcher's experience becoming part of the analysis (for feminists, as a basis for claims against misrepresentation by the dominant culture) and also to the 'lived experience' and multiple realities of individuals in the group being studied. As Strathern (1985: 15–16) notes, this term holds weight as a challenge to orthodoxy both within feminist discourse and that of reflexive anthropologists. Yet, in her view, this convergence of interest between the two groups has brought only an 'awkward relationship'. Others from a feminist standpoint (Caplan 1988; Mascia-Lees *et al.* 1989; Morgen 1989: 7–9) have strongly criticised this postmodern movement in anthropology, represented by Clifford and Marcus, *Writing Culture* (1986) and Marcus and Fischer, *Anthropology as Cultural Critique* (1986), for glossing over the contributions made by feminist anthropologists on issues of representation, reflexivity, the politics of dominant positions and constructed notions of otherness, as well as ignoring women's experimental writing.

This 'literary turn', Scholte states (1987: 35), 'consists of a crucial shift from an observational and empirical methodology to a communicative and dialogical epistemology' and 'from the use of visual metaphors ... to a concern with the expressive voice and the constitution of intersubjective understanding'. Some feminist anthropologists, working separately, have already registered this shift by adopting a dialogical methodology which rejects the division between subject and object, places the self within the field of investigation, evaluates positionality and power relations, and creates an intersubjective matrix for knowledge.

Recent attention to the analysis of ethnographic texts has brought criticism from those who consider the 'literary turn' to be a detraction from the central concerns of anthropology: fieldwork and social analysis. Some feminists, arguing this position, ignore the significance of women's experimental ethnographies. But others (Personal Narratives Group 1989) have explored how textual analysis and self-conscious textual creation cannot be separated from research and analysis of society. Whose voices are included in the text, how they are given weight and interpreted, questions of priority and juxtaposition are clearly anthropological and political concerns. They are, at the same time, textual strategies.

Those holding a strong political commitment (including some feminists) criticise versions of postmodernism for eroding the foundations of political analysis. As Fraser and Nicholson point out, 'There is no place in Lyotard's universe for critique of pervasive axes of stratification, for critique of broad-based relations of dominance and subordination along lines like gender, race and class' (1990: 23). But Lyotard's analysis (1984) of the post-modern condition of knowledge cannot be taken as definitive. The loss of 'grand narratives' of legitimation (such as the Enlightenment basis for scientific certainty) does not necessarily mean the loss of political analysis or political projects. Exploring the possibilities for a postmodern feminism, Hekman (1990: 175–90) finds in Foucault's writings the potentiality for a coherent programme of political action based on a local, contextual and historical approach. She calls attention to Foucault's conviction that 'the analysis, elaboration and bringing into question of power relations ... is a permanent political task inherent in all social existence' (Foucault 1982: 223).

Anthropology has shifted from its early concentration on small, isolated groups, preferably on remote islands, through a series of phases to its current concerns with interrelated societies. New issues have come to the fore, such as: populations and environmental degradation, ethnicity and identity in plural societies, the migration of former colonial subjects to the West, colonial and neo-colonial discourses, fundamentalist religions and neo-patriarchy, and the effects of television flashing images of Dallas to Damascus. The discipline now includes the analysis of power relations in an interconnected world with multiple diversities. For our continuing work and experiments in going beyond past limitations, the 'critical ontology of ourselves', as gendered selves, remains central.

NOTES

1 Feminist anthropology began by criticising the conceptual limitations of some classic monographs, then by analysing the changing experience of women in many settings, and, more recently, by theorising gender issues. Moore (1988) analyses the central issues and cross-currents in this field; Morgen (1989) provides an introductory essay on gender and anthropology, critical reviews of topics and areas, and extensive bibliographies. Articles reviewing this scholarship include Lamphere (1977, 1987), Rapp (1979), Rosaldo (1980), Atkinson (1982) and Strathern (1985).
2 Audrey Richards, for example, protested vigorously against being called a 'woman anthropologist' (personal conversation, 1984).
3 The difficulty of recognising authors became clear at a seminar given by Jonathan Benthall at the Institute of Social Anthropology, University of Oxford, 16 May 1986, when he presented unidentified excerpts on the nature of anthropology from the writings of selected well-known anthropologists.
4 See also Callan (1984).
5 A notable exception is Herzfeld (1985).

REFERENCES

Abu-Lughod, L. (1986) *Veiled Sentiments. Honor and Poetry in a Bedouin Society*. Berkeley, Calif.: University of California Press.

Alcoff, L. (1988) Cultural Feminism versus Post-Structuralism: The Identity Crisis in Feminist Theory. *Signs* **13** (3): 405–36.

Angrosino, M. (1986) Son and Lover: The Anthropologist as Non-threatening Male. In T. L. Whitehead and M. E. Conaway (eds) *Self, Sex, and Gender in Cross-Cultural Fieldwork*. Urbana: University of Illinois Press.

Ardener, E. (1975) Belief and the Problem of Women. In S. Ardener (ed.) *Perceiving Women*. London: Malaby Press.

Ardener, S. (1984) Gender Orientations in Fieldwork. In R. Allen (ed.) *Ethnographic Research*. London: Academic Press.

Asad, T. (ed.) (1973) *Anthropology and the Colonial Encounter*. London: Ithaca Press.

Atkinson, J. M. (1982) Review Essay Anthropology. *Signs* **8** (2): 236–58.

Belenky, M. F., Clinchy, B. McV., Goldberger, N. R. and Tarule, J. M. (1986) *Women's Ways of Knowing: The Development of Self, Voice and Mind*. New York: Basic Books.

Bernstein, R. (1976) *The Restructuring of Social and Political Theory*. Oxford: Basil Blackwell.

—— (1983) *Beyond Objectivism and Relativism*. Oxford: Basil Blackwell.

Bordo, S. (1990) Feminism, Postmodernism, and Gender-Scepticism. In L. J. Nicholson (ed.) *Feminism/Postmodernism*. New York and London: Routledge.

Bowen, E. S. (1954) *Return to Laughter*. London: Victor Gollancz.

Briggs, J. L. (1970) *Never in Anger*. Cambridge, Mass: Harvard University Press.

Callan, H. (1975) The Premiss of Dedication: Notes Towards an Ethnography of Diplomats' Wives. In S. Ardener (ed.) *Perceiving Women*. London: Malaby Press.

—— (1984) Introduction. In H. Callan and S. Ardener (eds) *The Incorporated Wife*. London: Croom Helm.

Callaway, H. (1980) Women in Yoruba Tradition and in the Cherubim and Seraphim Society. In O. U. Kalu (ed.) *The History of Christianity in West Africa*. London: Longman.

—— (1981) Spatial Domains and Women's Mobility in Yorubaland, Nigeria. In S. Ardener (ed.) *Women and Space*. London: Croom Helm.

Caplan, P. (1988) Engendering Knowledge. *Anthropology Today* **4** (5): 8–12; **4** (6): 14–17.

Clifford, J. and Marcus, G. (eds) (1986) *Writing Culture*. Berkeley, Calif.: University of California Press.

Codere, H. (1986) Field Work in Rwanda, 1959–1960. In P. Golde (ed.) *Women in the Field*. Berkeley, Calif.: University of California Press.

Crapazano, V. (1980) *Tuhami: Portrait of a Moroccan*. Chicago: University of Chicago Press.

Dumont, J.-P. (1978) *The Headman and I*. Austin, Texas: University of Texas Press.

Dwyer, K. (1982) *Moroccan Dialogues*. Prospect Heights, Ill: Waveland Press.

Fabian, J. (1983) *Time and the Other*. New York: Columbia University Press.

Favret-Saada, J. (1980) *Deadly Words: Witchcraft in the Bocage*. Cambridge: Cambridge University Press. French edn 1977.

Fernea, E. W. (1965) *Guests of the Sheik*. New York: Doubleday and Co.

Foucault, M. (1982) The subject and power. Afterword in H. Dreyfus and P. Rabinow *Michel Foucault: Beyond Structuralism and Hermeneutics*. Chicago: University of Chicago Press.

—— (1984) *The Foucault Reader*, P. Rabinow (ed.). New York: Pantheon.

Fraser, N. and Nicholson, L. J. (1990) Social Criticism without Philosophy: An Encounter between Feminism and Postmodernism. In L. J. Nicholson (ed.) *Feminism/Postmodernism*. New York and London: Routledge.

Friedl, E. (1986) Field Work in a Greek Village. In P. Golde (ed.) *Women in the Field*. Berkeley, Calif.: University of California Press.

Geiger, S. (1986) Women's Life Histories: Method and Content. *Signs* **11** (2): 334–351.

Giddens, A. (1976) *New Rules in Sociological Method*. London: Hutchinson.

—— (1979) *Central Problems in Social Theory*. London: Macmillan.

Golde, P. (ed.) (1986) *Women in the Field*. Berkeley, Calif.: University of California Press. First edn 1970.

Gregory, J. R. (1984) The Myth of the Male Ethnographer and the Women's World. *American Anthropologist* **86**: 316–27.

Grimshaw, J. (1986) *Philosophy and Feminist Thinking*. Minneapolis: University of Minnesota Press.

Harding, S. (1986) The Instability of the Analytical Categories of Feminist Theory. *Signs* **11** (4): 645–64.

—— (ed.) (1987) *Feminism and Methodology*. Milton Keynes: Open University.

Hastrup, K. (1987) Fieldwork among Friends: Ethnographic Exchange Within the Northern Civilization. In A. Jackson (ed.) *Anthropology at Home*. London: Tavistock.

Hawkesworth, M. E. (1989) Knowers, Knowing, Known: Feminist Theory and Claims of Truth. *Signs* **14** (3): 533–57.

Hekman, S. J. (1990) *Gender and Knowledge: Elements of a Postmodern Feminism*. Cambridge: Polity Press.

Herzfeld, M. (1985) *The Poetics of Manhood: Contest and Identity in a Cretan Mountain Village*. Princeton, NJ: Princeton University Press.

Huizer, G. and Mannheim, B. (eds) (1979) *The Politics of Anthropology*. The Hague: Mouton.

Hymes, D. (ed.) (1972) *Reinventing Anthropology*. New York: Pantheon Books.

Jameson, F. (1984) Foreword to J.-F. Lyotard, *The Postmodern Condition: A Report on Knowledge*. Minneapolis: University of Minnesota Press.

Kaberry, P. M. (1939) *Aboriginal Women: Sacred and Profane*. London: George Routledge and Sons.

—— (1952) *Women of the Grasslands*. London: HMSO, Colonial Research Publication No. 4.

Kundera, M. (1984) The Novel and Europe. *The New York Review of Books*, 19 July.

Lamphere, L. (1977) Review Essay Anthropology. *Signs* **2** (3): 612–27.

—— (1987) Feminism and Anthropology: The Struggle to Reshape Our Thinking about Gender. In C. Farnham (ed.) *The Impact of Feminist Research in the Academy*. Bloomington and Indianapolis: Indiana University Press.

Landes, R. (1938) *The Ojibwa Woman, Part I: Youth*. New York: Columbia University, Contributions to Anthropology, vol. 31.

—— (1947) *The City of Women: Negro Women Cult Leaders of Bahia, Brazil*. New York: Macmillan.

Langness, L. L. and Frank, G. (1981) *Lives. An Anthropological Approach to Biography*. Navato, Calif.: Chandler and Sharp.

Lauretis, T. de (1984) *Alice Doesn't*. Bloomington: Indiana University Press.

—— (1986) Feminist Studies/Critical Studies: Issues, Terms, and Contexts. In T. de Lauretis (ed.) *Feminist Studies/Critical Studies*. Bloomington: Indiana University Press.

Leith-Ross, S. (1965) *African Women: A Study of the Ibo of Nigeria*. London: Routledge & Kegan Paul. First edn 1939.

Lévi-Strauss, C. (1976) Jean-Jacques Rousseau, Founder of the Sciences of Man. In *Structural Anthropology*, vol. 2: 33–43. New York: Basic Books.

Lloyd, G. (1984) *The Man of Reason: 'Male' and 'Female' in Western Philosophy*. Minneapolis: University of Minnesota Press.

Lyotard, J.-F. (1984) *The Postmodern Condition: A Report on Knowledge*. Minneapolis: University of Minnesota Press. French edn 1979.

Marcus, G. and Cushman, D. (1982) Ethnographies as Texts. In B. Siegel (ed.) *Annual Review of Anthropology* 11: 25–69.

Marcus, G. and Fischer, M. (1986) *Anthropology as Cultural Critique*. Chicago and London: University of Chicago Press.

Mascia-Lees, F., Sharpe, P. and Cohen, C. (1989) The Postmodernist Turn in Anthropology: Cautions from a Feminist Perspective. *Signs* 15 (1): 7–33.

Mbilinyi, M. (1989) 'I'd Have Been a Man': Politics and the Labor Process in Producing Personal Narratives. In Personal Narratives Group (eds) *Interpreting Women's Lives*. Bloomington: University of Indiana Press.

Mead, M. (1972) *Blackberry Winter*. New York: William Morrow.

Moore, H. L. (1988) *Feminism and Anthropology*. Cambridge: Polity Press.

Morgen, S. (ed.) (1989) *Gender and Anthropology. Critical Reviews for Research and Teaching*. Washington, DC: American Anthropological Association.

Myerhoff, B. G. (1974) *Peyote Hunt: The Sacred Journey of the Huichol Indians*. New York: Cornell University Press.

—— (1978) *Number Our Days*. New York: Dutton.

Nader, L. (1986) From Anguish to Exultation. In P. Golde (ed.) *Women in the Field*. Berkeley, Calif.: University of California Press.

Nicholson, L. J. (ed.) (1990) *Feminism/Postmodernism*. New York and London: Routledge.

Okely, J. (1975) The Self and Scientism. *Journal of the Anthropology Society of Oxford* 6 (3): 171–88.

—— (1978) Privileged, Schooled and Finished: Boarding Education for Girls. In S. Ardener (ed.) *Defining Females*. London: Croom Helm.

Personal Narratives Group (eds) (1989) *Interpreting Women's Lives*. Bloomington: University of Indiana Press.

Powdermaker, H. (1967) *Stranger and Friend*. London: Secker and Warburg.

Prell, R.-E. (1989) The Double Frame of Life History in the Work of Barbara Myerhoff. In Personal Narratives Group (eds) *Interpreting Women's Lives*. Bloomington: University of Indiana Press.

Rabinow, P. (1977) *Reflections on Fieldwork in Morocco*. Berkeley, Calif.: University of California Press.

Rapp, R. (1979) Review Essay Anthropology. *Signs* 4 (3): 497–513.

Rosaldo, M. (1980) The Use and Abuse of Anthropology: Reflections on Feminism and Cross-Cultural Understanding. *Signs* 5 (3): 389–417.

Said, E. (1978) *Orientalism*. New York: Pantheon Books.

—— (1989) Representing the Colonized: Anthropology's Interlocutors. *Critical Inquiry* 15 (Winter): 205–25.

Scholte, B. (1972) Toward a Reflexive and Critical Anthropology. In D. Hymes (ed.) *Reinventing Anthropology*. New York: Pantheon Books.

—— (1987) The Literary Turn in Contemporary Anthropology. *Critique of Anthropology* 7 (10): 33–47.

Schrijvers, J. (1985) *Mothers for Life*. Delft: Eburon.

Shostak, M. (1981) *Nisa. The Life and Words of a !Kung Woman*. London: Allen Lane.

—— (1989) 'What the Wind Won't Take Away': The Genesis of *Nisa – The Life and Words of a !Kung Woman*. In Personal Narratives Group (eds) *Interpreting Women's Lives*. Bloomington: University of Indiana Press.

Smith, M. (1954) *Baba of Karo*. London: Faber and Faber.

Strathern, M. (1985) Dislodging a World View. *Australian Feminist Studies* (1): 1–25.

—— (1987) Out of Context. The Persuasive Fictions of Anthropology. *Current Anthropology* **28** (3): 251–81.

—— (1988) *The Gender of the Gift*. Berkeley, Calif.: University of California Press.

Suskind, J. (1973) *To Hunt in the Morning*. New York: Oxford University Press.

Talbot, D. A. (1968) *Women's Mysteries of a Primitive People. The Ibibios of Southern Nigeria*. London: Frank Cass. First edn 1915.

Underhill, R. (1936) *Autobiography of a Papago Woman*. Memoirs of the American Anthropological Association, No. 46. Washington, DC: American Anthropological Association.

Warren, C. (1988) *Gender Issues in Field Research*. London: Sage Publications.

White, H. (1973) *Metahistory: The Historical Imagination in Nineteenth-Century Europe*. Baltimore and London: Johns Hopkins Press.

Whitehead, T. L. and Conaway, M. E. (1986) *Self, Sex, and Gender in Cross-Cultural Fieldwork*. Urbana: University of Illinois Press.

Wolf, M. (1968) *The House of Lim*. New York: Appleton-Century-Crofts.

Chapter 3

Automythologies and the reconstruction of ageing

Paul Spencer

In this chapter, I wish to consider personal anecdotes, told and elaborated before an audience, as a form of structured autobiography. Erving Goffman (1969: 28–40) has drawn attention to the element of performance in such presentations, with role play and the manipulation of reality to create an effect. In this way a contrived self-image is built up which inadvertently may even captivate the teller, hence my title. The aim here is to discern the relevance of exaggeration in recalling episodes of one's past for an insight into autobiography, and ultimately even the record of history itself. Both history and biography are concerned with processes in time and are bound up with the life courses of individuals. Autobiography gives a uniquely personal insight into the process of history, but may view the memories of earlier times through the distorting lenses of later life, and these in turn are moulded in part by the social construction of ageing.

To illustrate this, I have chosen two autobiographical anecdotes that relate in the first instance to the self-image built up by a colourful Maasai elder. The second is of a misencounter of my own during my first spell of field-work, narrated years later. Each can be viewed in its historical context and both are shown in the concluding section to relate to the interpretation of maturation and ageing in the relevant culture.

THE MAASAI WHO WOULD NOT GROW OLD

Popular accounts of the Maasai give a larger than life portrayal of a proud, tradition-bound people who once dominated a whole region of East Africa. While these accounts are open to question, the larger than life aspect at least is fostered by the Maasai themselves who remain convinced of their stature. This is not only for the benefit of tourists, but is found also in remoter areas where it is the tourists who are the spectacle, and even today when there is a new status quo in Kenya with the Maasai officially relegated to little more than an extension of the game parks.

While working among the Maasai, much of the information I collected, even from the most reliable informants, was dogged by this element of exaggeration. Collecting autobiographical accounts, then, had its dangers, especially when the informant projected his own role prominently. In one respect, however, any autobiography was a valuable resource. The Maasai are a semi-nomadic people, and no one with whom I had close contact early in my stay was still living with the same neighbours a year later, and many were no longer even in the same neighbourhood. Nomadism creates a situation in which a community study extended over time, comparable with Turner's Ndembu (1957) or Middleton's Lugbara (1960), is not feasible for the anthropologist. For the actors, on the other hand, there is a lifetime experience of an extended community. They see themselves over the years as itinerant members of a much larger slice of their society, making visits as well as moving with their herds, and constantly re-establishing social contacts that have lapsed in the course of migration. Autobiographical accounts provide an introduction to this wider community, albeit coloured and distorted by tricks of the memory and trips of the ego.

In Matapato in 1976, this dual aspect of autobiography was vividly illustrated by 'Masiani', an elderly Maasai who as an informant was not particularly interested or well informed. He was deaf, self-centred and impetuous, but also generous and a lively raconteur. His flamboyant narratives of his various encounters with other Maasai could hold an audience, giving the impression of a spirited young man (moran/warrior) who had never quite settled down to the more subtle ways of elderhood. I managed to collect enough of these anecdotes to piece together his life story over a period of historical change. This was complemented by rather different interpretations of some of the same events and of his character by his age mates and members of his family. An intriguing aspect of his self-centred perspective was his inability to fit together the two ends of his experience of the tense father–son relationship, first as a truculent boy and later as an overbearing patriarch. When collecting his fragmented account, the strong element of exaggeration reminded me of *The Life of Benvenuto Cellini* (Cust 1935). As a Renaissance 'lie', Cellini's autobiography gives a vivid picture of the ethos of his times. Similarly, Masiani's colourful account was a Maasai 'lie', and the licence he assumed in his actions and recounting is a feature of Maasai society which increases with age. On his own terms, Masiani's self-portrayal provided an ideal type, riddled with Maasai clichés, and as much a truth of Maasai ideals as a distortion of biographical and historical detail.

Take, for instance, the incident when Masiani was punished by his age-set for being involved in a drunken brawl. He drew blood by retaliating against an age mate who had attacked him. This was a ritually dangerous offence for an established elder, and Masiani had to make reparation even though he claimed to be the innocent victim of the attack.

'The elders of my age-set told me to give the man I had fought a sheep so that he could drink the liquid fat and we could become friends. But I refused: "I wont give anything to that man who throttled me until I wet myself and beat me until he thought I was dead", I said. I had many sheep, but I had none I was prepared to give that man. So they went round calling one another [to mount an age-set posse to punish Masiani's disobedience]. One night I could hear them yelping not far away. I had a quiver with poisoned arrows, so I went out of my village determined to shoot them as they approached. Another young man of our family came with me and told me not to shoot. The posse came and settled down to a discussion. We both lurked in the darkness to overhear what they said. They were as far away from us as that thorn-fence over there. One said: "Oye ... let's not rush in and grab his cattle: let us be careful in punishing this elder". And another said: "No. Let's rush in and beat him". And a third said: "He should not be rushed or beaten. We must get him carefully". My young friend then turned to me and whispered: "You said just now that you would shoot them all; but do you want to shoot men like that who are shooting away from you [and advising restraint]? Wouldn't that be bad?" And I said: "It would be bad. Let's forget about shooting at them". So we got up and walked slowly towards the discussion. And addressing these elders, I said: "Oye ... dont again suggest that you should rush in and grab my cattle". And they replied: "Forget it, for we are not going to rush in". And I went on: "When I overheard that you wanted to rush in and grab my cattle – I didn't beat that man recently nearly as hard as I would have beaten you, the one who made that suggestion. And you are that man's brother, you goodfornothing (*laka iposo*)!" So they came and grabbed two of my cattle: a heifer and an ox ... I did get that ox back again though. It had been placed by the elders in another herd and one day it strayed. So I stole it back and drove it away. I then swapped it for a white heifer elsewhere, and drove that one back to my own herd. The man who was looking after the ox came to search for it, but he never knew that it was me who had taken it, getting my own ox back.'

The incongruity of this account is that Masiani was not just an implacable rebel. He was well connected within his own age-set and popular for his loyalty and the colour he brought to their ageing reputation. The whole episode – taking up his bow against his age mates, haranguing them, and then recovering his ox after it had strayed – overstretches credibility, as do many of his other stories. His excessive rashness at each stage, the coincidence of the stray ox combined with the incompetence of the herder simply does not ring true. Taken as a fantasy surrounding Masiani's punishment, on the other hand, the account seems to portray his feelings quite vividly: the urge to defend his herd; the voice of caution from a younger kinsman whom he was not obliged to obey; the desire to rise above his punishment by first boasting over the heads of his age mates and then staging an audacious counter-theft; and implicitly his ultimate loyalty to his age-set in submitting at least to the minimum fine of just one heifer. These expressions of the ambivalence that surrounds the defence of a man's own domestic interests as against his submission to age-set discipline would be perfectly intelligible to a Maasai audience. The tension between these two types of involvement alters in the course of the life span and is expressed in their ideology and in various Maasai stereotypes (Spencer 1988: 225–6). Masiani's audacity may have been largely that he was prepared to fantasise in public what others would have felt in private. Rising in his own estimation above his adversaries, he also tried to show that he was prepared always to defer to higher Maasai ideals. At worst, he paid for his excesses by having little personal influence in the local political scene, but he still carried weight as a virile member of a dwindling age-set who refused to bow to old age. What he sometimes lacked in personal dignity, his age-set gained in popular acclaim placing them above trivial conformity. Their occasional flamboyant excesses displayed the irrepressible spirit of younger men, and to this extent old age itself had to be respected not only as the ultimate achievement, but also for its own irrepressibility. Historically, it was a period when ultimate power was felt to have slipped into the hands of younger men encouraged for the first time by an alien black administration. Against this trend within the local community, older men could retain their prestige so long as they could hold an audience with stories that glamorised their role and responses within Maasai tradition. Beyond the flamboyance of the performer, the element of exaggeration becomes intelligible in the wider context (q.v. Gulliver 1963: 38–9; Spencer 1988: 216–19).

It is perhaps significant that the setting for this episode was not, for instance, Samburu. The Samburu are up-country cousins of the Maasai and generally less competitive (Spencer 1988: 250). I suspect that a Samburu Masiani would have projected his fantasies and tales on to some peripheral third party, identifying himself as story-teller with the conformist majority. The struggle for power between senior age-sets was altogether weaker among the Samburu and to this extent, older men were in a more secure position than among the Maasai. Such accounts as I collected from older Samburu were essentially oral histories rather than self-centred fantasies.

THE APPARITION IN THE BUSH

Masiani's account opens up the disquieting question of the extent to which all our Goffmanesque presentations of ourselves – even to ourselves – contain an element of autobiographical distortion, giving coherence and meaning to our being. Given that any anthropological account is inevitably reflexive and indirectly autobiographical, this in turn throws doubt on the anthropologist's own judgement. To what extent, in other words, are my own accounts of the peoples of the Maasai region distorted by unresolved dilemmas of my own past and present? To what extent do I too respond to my perceived audience, and possibly in different ways on different occasions? Let me try to unravel this.

Writing about such peoples as the Maasai for an unknown reader, I feel obliged to be largely impersonal and essentially serious. Yarning about field-work with friends on the other hand, I find myself frequently resorting to personal anecdotes, rather like Masiani, and not altogether aware of the extent to which the retelling of these stories takes on new complexions in the effort to gain an effect or to hold an audience. The frequent theme of such stories is the incongruity of the encounter between two cultures wrapped up in a joke.

Take, for instance, my recollection of an episode that I have retold on a number of occasions. This concerns a time when I had just acquired a Land Rover, and I then ended my first long stint of fieldwork among the Samburu with a trip to their close allies, the Rendille. There I was faced once again with a new language and an unfamiliar culture. I simply did not have the energy to start all over again; and this made me realise that I needed a break. A motor road nearby led me to hanker for a dose of English culture, to be able to relax with others in my own language, and to indulge in some privacy. I had been struggling with these feelings for several days, when my lethargic research efforts with some Rendille elders were interrupted by an apparition. A boat had suddenly appeared, perhaps 40 feet long, sailing majestically above the sparse bush cover. I could not have dreamed up a more incongrous diversion. Even the elders seemed disconcerted. Then as we looked, the boat came to an abrupt halt. That day was clearly not destined for untangling Rendille kinship organisation. I ran towards the boat, half expecting to discover some uncharted lake, but at least certain that any vessel that had run aground in the middle of this remote wilderness was in trouble or lost. This was the excuse I needed to get away from the Rendille and even to grapple with a western problem in English. I arrived at the roadside to find not just a stranded boat, but a line of stationary trucks with the boat perched on top of one of them. There was no lake and no sign of trouble, just some heavy vehicles and, beside them on the roadside, a huddle of Europeans looking at a map. This was my cue. Even if I could not help them unground a shipwreck, at least I could make out that I knew the area – and in English. 'Can I help?', I asked. They looked up with mild surprise and then down towards my feet. One of them said 'No thank you', and they turned back to their map. I too looked down and realised that I was wearing a well-seasoned blanket, a pair of sandals made from car tyres, and clutching a stick and a notebook. Had I been a Samburu – or if they had been Samburu – I would simply have stayed where I was and looked on. As it was, they were of my own kind and I wanted to escape. In desperation, I looked at my left wrist, as if wearing a watch that would remind me of an urgent appointment. 'Good heavens!', I said, 'I must be going! Bye bye'.

They looked up again and said 'Goodbye', and then returned to their map. I turned and fled into the cover of the bush. That, then, was my slice of English culture for the present.

Years later, I came across an account by Hilary Ruben portraying an aspect of Africa that was fast disappearing. She and her family were members of this amphibious expedition and she gives a diverging account of the same incident. Possibly for effect, the encounter appears to be cited more than one hundred miles further north in an even more remote part.

> One day ... a fantastic apparition appeared in the midst of all that nothingness: a white man, wearing shorts and shirt [sic] and a pair of thonged sandals [sic] like the nomads. He walked like a nomad too, with the same long [sic], springy gait. He smiled, waved [sic?], enquired whether everything was all right, and before we had time to catch our breaths and ask whence he came and whither he was going, passed on. Mad dogs and Englishmen, I muttered ... Months afterwards, we were to discover that this man was an anthropologist living mostly with the Samburu, and partly with the Rendille. It was in fact Paul Spencer ... (Ruben 1972: 160–1)

The two accounts are sufficiently similar to identify the same event, but they differ enough to raise questions. I am now unconvinced by at least one detail of my own version: it is altogether unlikely that I would have been wearing a blanket in the heat of Rendille country; a cloth just possibly, but even this would have been unlikely at this early stage of my research among them. Somehow over the years, the elaborations of this story seem to have taken over from the reality of the encounter. In my mind's eye, I do not see Hilary Ruben or her two daughters, but only a group of men, studiously trying not to look at me. The story has become part of my self-image. Even in writing about it now, I wanted to substitute a cloth for the (less plausible) blanket, missing and yet effectingly demonstrating the point I wish to make. I am equally unconvinced concerning minor details in the other account. Each version gives a different slant on this fleeting encounter. The normal view of the English meeting in remote Africa is of a spontaneous warmth that would be inconceivable anywhere in England. And yet here, in an unusually remote area, the very unexpectedness of the encounter appears to have led to a very English reserve on both sides. In my own account, they did not respond to my overture, and in Ruben's account I did not even give them a chance. Exaggerations in each of our anecdotes apart, we appear to have revealed – or rather concealed – something of our national character to each other. We had brought the stiff upper lip with us to Africa, barely camouflaged by brief pleasantries.

A feature of this self-portrayal (but not necessarily of the encounter itself) was that I was setting myself apart from the very people whose company I was seeking, as if unable to resolve the gulf between the two cultures. In elaborating the story – inventing the worn blanket for instance – I suspect that I was trying to insinuate how far I had gone to incorporate myself into Samburu/Rendille society, contrasting it with the world of maps, expeditions and affluence. This may well have been a pose, but it was in tune with my feelings of ambivalence towards my Englishness at this time.

The period was in the wake of the Suez crisis, which even today is remembered by many as a watershed between two eras of British policy. It was an episode that had split the nation (and my own family for that matter) between the believers in British imperialism and those embittered by the hypocrisy of an outdated paternalism towards the Third World. Decolonisation was already in progress, but after Suez a veil of disinformation had been swept to one side and the moral issue seemed to resolve from a matter of dignified enlightenment to one of naked self-interest. Having already launched on my own anthropological career in a mood of benign and innocent optimism, I now found myself ashamed of my nationality and irritated that the evidence of Suez had somehow become blurred once the issue ceased to be news. What had been a myth of my own schooling had been exposed and yet remained intact. The believers for the time being – my own kith and kin – could continue to believe. The episode had no direct effect on my approach to research, but it clarified the moral issue. In Kenya, I avoided those who represented in my mind the ultra-believers: the white settlers. In elaborating on my encounter with the convoy in the bush, clothed like a local (according to my story) and unable to make contact with those who spoke my native language, I was implicitly identifying myself with the exploited. Carrying the symbol of my profession – my anthropologist's notebook – I was at the same time legitimising my position there. Wrapping this up as a joke was, of course, a useful way of holding an audience, but it also permitted a certain licence to emphasise the gap between cultures and possibly to exaggerate my own isolation somewhere between them. The breakdown of communication within the society I had left less than a year before was replicated by a comedy of misencounter in the bush.

ADOLESCENCE AND THE BOTTOMLESS PIT

If the elaborations of this incident bore on my response to the Suez crisis, then this in turn evoked memories of my childhood at a deeper level. The Suez crisis can now be seen as a telling episode in the history of changing attitudes towards decolonisation, exposing the ugly side of ideas that so many of us had grown up with. Seen retrospectively, history and growing up were entwined, and the uniqueness of my experience was in part the uniqueness of the time in which I lived. As a child I had unquestioningly accepted the supremacy of British Empire, along with the sanctity of the family and the unambiguous truth of Christianity. My growing up in a time when each of these was put to the test was experienced as a series of painful episodes, each leaving me more uncertain than the last, and each perhaps priming me towards a value-free discipline, such as anthropology. What had once been an ideological commitment, pieced together in the comfortable certainty of my childhood, was exposed step by step as a self-deception, piercing the fragile shell of my innocence. For me personally, the Suez crisis in the mid 1950s was not a major watershed, but it hurt and left me angry precisely because it exposed my own gullibility and replicated the truths behind diplomatic lies that I had faced in the late 1940s, splitting the family in new ways.

The earlier period of disillusionment occurred during the years of adolescence, dulled by the absence of my father at home and the drabness of an undistinguished boarding school in Yorkshire. The transition at the age of thirteen from a southern background to the north was itself unnerving. The revelation of my parents' divorce two years later came as a blow that took years to come to terms with. In the late 1940s, divorce rates were climbing steeply, but within the cocoon of a prudish school that upheld Christian values, divorce was regarded as an outrage. With a sense of utter shame, I kept this family development from my schoolfriends, hiding it like some inner deformity. At home during the holidays, it was a topic that we simply did not discuss or admit to neighbours. We continued to live as we had before as though nothing had happened. If we had only discussed it among ourselves, then we might have come to terms with it and worked the grief out of our systems. As it was, there was an unresolved feeling of unreality about home. I was surprised that I had always accepted my father's absence as quite normal. Why had I never sought an explanation or even toyed with the most obvious one? It was as if my whole childhood had been a facade, undermined by an ugly truth that had been so well concealed that I did not even think of asking the most obvious questions.

My education had encouraged me to ask questions and yet at the same time to accept some basic dogmas. To question these dogmas was to lay bare a bottomless pit. Now, with no certainty to draw round me and a sense of divine injustice, I felt cheated and the questions started to flow. If there was no room for divorce in my religion, then somehow I did not belong. It was in this spirit of niggling doubt that the firmly held beliefs I had grown up with started to crumble. Within a year, what had been an unquestioning faith simply evaporated before my gaze. Belief gave way to immovable disbelief. At first, it was as if I had woken up from the comfort of a dream to find myself involved in a nightmare. My faith – whatever that had been – was destroyed and I was terrified. There was no one up there and nowhere to go after this life had run its course. Why should there be? I had discovered the fragility of my own mortality. The great cosmic mystery now shifted from the uncertainties of death and afterlife to the inscrutable fact of life itself. All I could rely on was the unique sense of my own existence to shield me from oblivion.

Once again, I felt that the facts had always been there, and yet my whole upbringing, as in the case of my family background, had blinded me to them. The facade of family unity seemed replicated at a higher level by an empty facade of religious belief in a society of half-believers. It was my own way of adjusting to a new set of values and to what has, after all, become a commonplace experience in the post-war decades. I was just one of many who encountered and had to accommodate a major historical trend in their own private way. Disenchantment with the assumptions that have surrounded childhood and schooling is perhaps a very general aspect of attaining adulthood, especially in times of change. To become an adult, one has to disengage from childhood. Autobiographical memory is then transformed into a kind of myth, rather like a Kuhnian paradigm. For me, this was the memory of a lifestyle infused with a set of beliefs that served to hold the family together but did not stand up to close scrutiny – or to being displaced by a new set of beliefs and perhaps a new myth. It was not so much the historical trend that was so shattering as the suddenness and stark intimacy of the realisation.

Other aspects of my world-view remained intact and I clung to these. I even assumed the basic integrity of the (southern) English way of life as something to which I could return after leaving school. Academically, my inclination was towards some unambitious scientific career, working among fellow beings, but concerned with inanimate problems associated with progress. However, at heart this vague notion of progress seemed part of the myth of my childhood. It did not answer the desire to recreate some kind of order, some meaning out of life itself, and it was this that gripped my need for understanding and pointed the only way out of my mental confusion. From a wholly uninformed start, the foundations had been laid for a search that was to be realised years later when I first came across social anthropology, which seemed to promise some insight into the fundamentals of human existence, and second the Samburu. These discoveries in themselves entailed a random element of chance. But the way in which I responded to each in turn seems to make sense in terms of my curiosity for understanding things that appeared hidden from me. Changing the course of my career, prior to the vociferous 1960s, was also a silent form of protest against a system that rang hollow and seemed based on half-truths and self-deception, especially after the Suez crisis.

To express this in Bernsteinian terms, it was as if my education encouraged an elaborated mode of thought along channels bounded by restricted dogma that ranged from Christian values to the mindless conformism of my own peer group. Once the dogma had been breached at one point, nowhere was it sacrosanct. An unrestricted elaborated mode of thought spiralled out of control, and life itself lost meaning.

If, as I have suggested, the dilemma of my youth had been the impasse of a search for answers in an endlessly elaborated mode of thought with no fundamentals of faith, then the highly traditionalist Samburu seem an odd object of study and my enchantment with them as a people even odder. Here, I wish to argue that the erratic course that led me eventually to the Samburu somehow offered a way forward; but I was not exactly aware of it at the time and have never quite been able to spell it out clearly. The impasse of one extreme and a sceptical view of progress led me stumbling towards a people who embraced the opposite extreme, whose resilient traditionalism was highly restrictive. From a family background that had seemed to evaporate inexplicably, I was heading towards a kinship system that had a benign halo of certainty and encompassed almost endless ramifications that I could explore at length. Emotionally, as I learned to accommodate this system and taking my adoption into a particular family seriously, it was like re-entering the primitive world of childhood. I had to be eased out of my bewilderment, not by my own ill-formulated questions, but by the questions that Samburu repeatedly asked me and that I in turn had to learn to turn back on them. Reflexivity was a term I had not then heard of, but the principle was inherent in any attempt to enter an exotic culture, to master the language and make conversation – any conversation – on topics that emerged from the context of the moment. The luxury of selecting my own topics had to wait until I could reformulate them.

Like so many others who have had dealings with the Samburu, I was wholly captivated by them. At times, I felt thoroughly drawn towards them and wanted to stay almost indefinitely. At other moments in the still of the night, I would sense the faint and solemn ticking of a clock, reminding me of the one at home during my childhood, and the ticking would then fade as I listened. Why my childhood? Or was this fantasy somehow bound up with the make-believe watch that beamed me away in my joke? Was it reminding me that life's opportunities were ticking away? Whatever my feelings for the Samburu or private misbeliefs, I could not completely rid myself of an inner Protestant ethic that always reminded me to use my time and to work to my open-ended brief. I had to separate my personal involvement from the task of research. Only by completing this research, ultimately as an outsider, could I justify the whole exercise to everyone concerned, including myself and including the Samburu, whose future was by no means certain in an independent Kenya. I had to transform my involvement with them into an involvement with a model about them as an outsider and disbeliever, aware of the contradictions within their system and of wider issues when viewed from outside. Again this was experienced as a very personal problem and yet is common for the anthropologist, whose attempts to empathise in order to analyse entails a moral dilemma. This stems at least in part from the fact that anthropological fieldwork in practice can never be value-free any more than it can be an emotionless experience, for it lies at the interface between two cultures rather like my joke.

In writing up this research as a thesis (1965), some aspects had a certain autobiographical relevance at one stage removed. These included: the angry reaction of youths (*moran*) to the narrow constraints of their upbringing; the ritualised nature of knowledge in manipulating the young; aspects of religious conversion in the course of socialisation; and tensions between the nineteenth-century middle-class family and boarding schools which I compared with the Samburu age system. I do not wish to dwell on these here since there were other equally important themes that were less autobiographical. To the extent that this study might now be seen as functionalist, I would question a widespread view that this approach represented a pre-reflexive phase in anthropology and was unsuspectingly caught up in a colonialist mode of thought (Asad 1973: 18). A more valid criticism of studies such as *The Samburu* is that they reflect too close an identification with a widespread African sense of tradition and too little an awareness of processes of change. In other words, they are *too* reflexive at the expense of the historical context. Certainly, Evans-Pritchard as my supervisor was more concerned that my thesis should reflect my own personal experience of the Samburu than that it should embody a watertight argument. Today, this advice sounds surprisingly modern, reflexive and unfunctionalist (q.v. Pocock 1961: 72).

Yet it remains that the principal thrust of my research was to construct a meaningful whole out of the premises of Samburu society in order to demonstrate to myself that this could be done. Piecing together a self-contained argument out of fragmented field data was like piecing together a fragmented past. If order could be made out of chaos, then as a matter of faith other things could make sense. If this was a functionalist stance, then at least it echoed the self-awareness of such peoples as the Samburu for whom the concept of tradition was strong and implied no change. The warmth that they exuded was one of absolute certainty in their way of life within an unquestioned system of beliefs. There was a sense of wholeness, of wholesome integrity shared by nearly everyone, that I needed to replicate in my writing. It was the anthropology of Durkheim with collective representations, collective sentiments and a collective life in which society itself rode above the fragile dilemmas of the individual.

There was, need I say, a strong element of transference in my attachment to the Samburu, which built up as my relationship to one clan became firmer and more secure. Correspondingly, writing this up entailed an element of counter-transference with all the difficulties of disentangling myself from an emotional experience. Or a better metaphor perhaps would be that I had fallen in love: not with any individual, but with an idea that I associated with a community at large and the way of life of a people who had cast their charm over me. Writing this up was not so much a falling out of love, or grief at the loss of a loved object. It was more a matter of consummation, a necessary fulfilment of the relationship I had formed and of the conditions on which that relationship was based. The whole experience had been contrived, and yet its creative potential had led me towards a sense of completeness. I would suggest that this total experience was not idiosyncratic, but must be very common in the early careers of social anthropologists, and highly pertinent to any volume on their autobiographies.

CONCLUSION: CLINGING TO YOUTH, DISENGAGING FROM CHILDHOOD AND THE AUTOBIOGRAPHICAL RECONSTRUCTION OF HISTORY

Let me conclude by returning to Masiani's autobiographical encounter as compared with my own, each of us concerned with ambivalent views of our own society. Both were narratives in which the author presented himself presenting himself to his own culture, stepping into a realm of partial fantasy. The contrast between Masiani's account and my own stilted attempt here seems to be broadly the contrast between restricted and elaborated modes of thought: an older man conforming to an acceptable stereotype and a younger man out on a limb.

However, the Maasai are restricted only up to a point, since as I have noted, there is a competitive edge to their society that is generally lacking among the Samburu. Masiani's brand of nonconformity set out to stir a receptive audience. He emerges as a Maasai, competitive and thrusting among his peers, but perhaps a little more so than normal, as if to test the system to its limit and reassure himself of his position. The flavour of his account was not just his own irascibility, but also his faith in the certainty and strength of Maasai society. His reminiscences generally, and his boasts, were tinged with Maasai ideals. In the above episode, as elsewhere, he was using the latitude permitted an elder in late middle age to project himself as an undaunted spirit, clinging to youth with all the bravado of a committed *moran*, while maintaining his claim to seniority and respect as the occasion demanded. In a highly age-conscious society and within the restrictions of Maasai convention, he was playing with his age to an extent not permitted to younger men.

In my own joke, I seem to have been projecting myself as a serious-minded research student who had lost contact with his own culture. In emphasising the unbridgable gap, I was implying how far I had gone in identifying myself with the Samburu, and perhaps gave the impression that living among them was an end in itself. But in making this a joke of my past self, I had clearly come back among friends and the end lay in my research. In an odd sort of way, preparing my thesis was a replication of the joke, reliving episodes of my life among the Samburu and Rendille, identifying with them in an attempt to understand; and yet now in the telling, slanting this experience as a bridge across the gap between their cultures and ours for the benefit of my audience: the hypothetical western reader in my mind's eye. The flavour of the joke was only made explicit in a brief preface: 'By adopting me into their numbers. .... accepting me. .... as a *moran* ... Time meant something quite different; and under this spell, three years of my life slipped past unnoticed' (1965: xiv). Note again the element of fantasy in expressing my enchantment: it was after all largely an adoption on terms of my own choosing; and what about the breaks in my fieldwork, what about that inner ticking reminding me of the seconds – and years – slipping away? Wrapped up in a joke or tucked away in a preface, I was projecting this whole episode of my career into a timeless limbo, suspended between a troubled youth and settling down. In a sense, like Masiani, I too was playing with my perception of ageing. Implicitly, I seem to have been viewing my development with its liminal period of separation as a rite of transition that had its counterpart among my Samburu peers: bush-loving *moran* in their twenties, socially suspended between childhood and elderhood (1965: 140, 162, 259–60). Once I had completed my thesis, I could settle down to whatever lay ahead. This left me apprehensive of the future, but with a sense of completion in respect of the past and a renewed confidence. Disengaging successfully from the Samburu had a therapeutic effect. It replicated and in some ways marked the end of disengagement from my childhood. At that point I determined to leave anthropology.

Perhaps it is in the nature of autobiographies to end inconclusively in mid-stream (*vide* Cellini). There is, however, a tail-piece here which bears on a broader issue. If, as I have suggested, my own experience as a novice anthropologist probably parallels that of others, then extrapolating the point, to what extent does fantasy infect the perception of our careers subsequently? How far does the recent popular history of anthropology echo real shifts in approach and genuinely new insights? Or how far is there an element of autobiographical fiction in all this, a self-deluding myth coined by a whole generation of scholars swept along by fashionable claims? This is not to deny the development of the subject with the accumulation of ethnographies and scholarship, and shifts of interest and opportunity. But it is to follow the argument posed by Malcolm Crick in this volume that the outpouring of anthropological concern for the 'self', reflexivity and related concepts are not as new as we often suppose, but have always been a necessary part of anthropology. This is to imply that many of us do not read (or re-read) earlier texts with the same reflexive care that we claim for our field studies. And if we misperceive the recent history of our subject, we are misrepresenting to ourselves our own pasts. A collective myth infiltrates our clouded memories and autobiographical self-regard. We often suggest that as students, we were swept along by prevailing fashions and the misperceptions of our mentors, but who are the mentors now?

The implication is oddly reminiscent of some biographical commentaries on Malinowski and Radcliffe-Brown (to name but two), who are now seen to have cultivated their own images as our hero ancestors, manipulating the historical record in the course of establishing their careers (Kuper 1973: 34–7; Langham 1981: 244–300). From Malinowski especially, we have inherited a discipline with a polemic touch of messianism (or indeed of Masiani); and as Crick notes, the claims and expectations of something new outstrip the record of history and trigger polemic responses. But this is the essence of myth and says something about the subject of anthropology and its excitement, in which our careers too are embroiled. The Malinowskian flame lures us like moths, and in the pursuit of changing fashions and a personal sense of achievement, we are all vulnerable.

This then raises the question, ironically: to the extent that we misconstrue the past – even our own pasts – is it because we too are caught up in the autobiographical restructuring of our ageing? Is this perpetual rearrangement of the anthropological scenario really a development of the discipline or is it in part a false time perspective, a construct of our developing careers as successive generations reach for the fruits of middle age? Who is maturing, the discipline or us? And how will our future biographers view this confusion of history and ageing? And what was I letting myself in for in my second conversion to anthropology after a lapse of nine years? Another worn blanket?

REFERENCES

Asad, T. (ed.) (1973) *Anthropology and the Colonial Encounter*. London: Ithaca Press.
Cust, R. H. H. (1935, trans.) *The Life of Benvenuto Cellini*. London: Navarre.
Goffman, E. (1969) *The Presentation of Self in Everyday Life*. Harmondsworth: Penguin Books.
Gulliver, P. H. (1963) *Social Control in an African Society*. London: Routledge & Kegan Paul.
Kuper, A. (1973) *Anthropologists and Anthropology: The British School 1922–72*. London: Allen Lane.
Langham, I. (1981) *The Building of British Social Anthropology*. Dordrecht: Reidel.
Middleton, J. (1960) *Lugbara Religion*. London: Oxford University Press.
Pocock, D. (1961) *Social Anthropology*. London: Sheed and Ward.
Ruben, H. (1972) *African Harvest*. London: Harvill Press.
Spencer, P. (1965) *The Samburu*. London: Routledge & Kegan Paul.
—— (1988) *The Maasai of Matapato*. Manchester: Manchester University Press.
Turner, V. W. (1957) *Schism and Continuity in an African Society*. Manchester: Manchester University Press.

Chapter 4

Spirits and sex
A Swahili informant and his diary

Pat Caplan

INTRODUCTION

In recent years, as part of an increasingly reflexive trend in anthropology, a number of books have examined the nature of the relationship between anthropologist and informant. Some have presented portraits (e.g. Casagrande 1959; Dumont 1978; Read 1965; Turner 1967), some have reproduced their words as texts (e.g. Griaule 1948) or their dialogues with them (Dwyer 1982), or a combination of these (Crapanzano 1980); some have presented informants through autobiography or life history (e.g. Shostak 1981).

This chapter uses a number of these techniques in its attempt to explore the changing nature of my relationship with two particular informants. On one level it may be seen as a fable – the moral tale of the relationship between a married couple in a village on Mafia Island, Tanzania, and how the adulteries of one of them led to quarrels, fights and ultimately a painful divorce as it unfolds over a twenty-year period, covering three visits by the anthropologist. Events which arouse such painful emotions are worked out by the actors in terms of accusations of witchcraft through control of spirits. Human anger and jealousy are projected on to the spirit world, where they can more easily be dealt with.

Much of the data in the chapter comes less from narrative, than from two kinds of texts. In the first part of the chapter, extensive use is made of the diary kept in 1966–7 by the husband. This gives both his own world-view, and also allows him to present himself as a Don Juan and magician. In the second half of the chapter, the data comes from the dialogues of the anthropologist with both husband and wife in 1976, a time when the marriage was irrevocably breaking up. This time, the voice of the wife is heard more clearly, as she recounts her story and we begin to see the diarist/ informant very differently, as anti-hero, perhaps villain. This time, the anthropologist is drawn into events.

The chapter also considers the nature of the relationship between anthropologist and informants, and the reasons why this changed over time, affected not only by my close friendship with both of them and our mutual interdependence, but also by events in our lives and changes in ourselves.

Their attitudes towards me shifted as I moved from being seen as young, naïve and rather anomalous in terms of gender identity during my first period of fieldwork, to being seen as mature and more clearly gendered at the time of the second and third trips. My feelings about them and their relationship also altered, not only because of the events recounted in this chapter, but also because of my greater knowledge of them. In addition, my premises have also been affected by my changing perceptions of male–female relations, not only in their society but also in my own. Thus my interpretation of the data given to me by these two people has also shifted over time, and continues to do so.

This chapter, then, explores the nature of exchanges between anthropologist and informant, between men and women, including husbands and wives, and between spirits and humans.

Part 1 THE INFORMANT AS DIARIST, THE ANTHROPOLOGIST AS CONFIDANTE, 1965–7

Mohammed and Mwahadia

I met Mohammed (not his real name) on my first day in the village of Kanga, northern Mafia Island, on 11 November 1965. He was introduced to me through my cook, Salum, with whom he had once worked on the same dhow.

Mohammed had been born in Kanga, but he didn't know in what year. I estimated that in 1965, he must have been around thirty years of age, seven years older than myself. He was sent to Koran school at an early age but as an adolescent, he ran away and got jobs as a sailor on the dhows travelling up and down the coast. Later he went to Zanzibar and picked cloves for a couple of months on three occasions. Then he married a classificatory cross-cousin, Mwahadia, by whom he has had a large number of children.

In my notebook for that day I record 'Mohammed refused to budge until Salum more or less threw him out' and the next entry, for the following day, notes that he borrowed one shilling off me, the first of many such 'loans'. After that, Mohammed was a more or less constant visitor to my house and we talked a good deal.

I also became friendly with Mohammed's wife Mwahadia (also a pseudonym), and spent a good deal of time with her.

When I went away from the village for a month in the summer of 1966, I asked Mohammed and one or two other men to keep a diary of the events which I would miss. I did not ask any women to do so, mainly because the ones I knew best, like Mwahadia, were illiterate. Mohammed's was the longest diary, and it proved so rewarding that I asked him to continue to keep it up during the remainder of my stay in the village, and after I left Kanga to work in the south of the island.

Mohammed, who was not literate in Roman script (*Kizungu*) wrote his diary in Arabic script (*Kiarabu*), which I did not read very well. Most of the entries were relatively brief, but in the sessions we had for transliteration, he developed the themes, and I took notes. At the beginning, entries in the diary were records of current daily happenings in Kanga or the surrounding villages, such as births, deaths, rituals, meetings, disputes etc. Later, however, Mohammed also added events or stories from the past. In some of them, he himself was involved at first hand, in others, they were reports from hearsay.

To write such a document indicates, of course, a high degree of self-consciousness on the part of an informant, especially one coming from a culture where few books, other than the Koran, were available to him, and where diary-keeping was unheard of. What I now realise is particularly interesting about this document is that he was the one to choose the topics contained in it, not I. It is thus scarcely surprising that I began to learn about whole areas of Swahili culture which I had missed before. Ostensibly, Mohammed wrote the diary for me, and would not have done so had I not been there. None the less, I suspect that to some extent, he came also to write it for himself; it may also be described as part journal, part autobiography.

Towards the end of this first period of fieldwork, when I had moved to another village, I began to go through my notebooks, checking points which were unclear, and I then spent a good deal of time with informants, often Mohammed, obtaining clarifications. Mohammed would come to stay, sometimes together with Mwahadia, sometimes alone, for a day or more at a time. (I had a large house with a spare room, and was 'chaperoned' by my cook Salum.) In many respects, we became closer during this period as I found this new area of fieldwork very difficult, and welcomed familiar faces. In addition, we could talk even more freely, since I had not yet established close relations in the new village, and received fewer visitors. In addition to the diary itself, more texts were built up in this way.

By this time Mohammed and Mwahadia had become my friends, as well as informants, and this was symbolised by Mohammed's parting gift to me – a coconut tree, for which he solemnly wrote out a deed of gift in *Kiarabu*, and I of acceptance in *Kizungu*. He explained that he was a poor man, and coconut trees were his sole form of wealth. The tree would be mine and, whenever I came to the village, I could use its produce. I was moved that he had given me something valuable and which symbolised on-going rights in the village, but amused too as I thought that he knew full well that he would continue to benefit from it.

One of the questions which occurs to me now is why Mohammed and I developed such a close relationship, given our differences of gender, race and culture. On his side, one factor was undoubtedly the material benefits which he gained from it – Mohammed is a relatively poor man who has sold much of his inheritance, as he himself admits, to give gifts to his lovers, as well as to support his large family. During the first period of fieldwork he 'borrowed' constantly from me, and during the second and third trips, I paid him for sessions during which he helped transcribe tapes, or update old censuses.

A second reason is his own interest in the relationships in the village – Mohammed loves gossip, the stuff of ethnography. Aside from his own numerous relationships, both sexual and otherwise, he seemed to have an unlimited capacity for and interest in ferreting out knowledge of other people's lives. He may have gained some of his information on the verandahs of the village shops, where he, like other village men, spent hours talking during the afternoons and evenings. But he obtained a great deal more from his assiduous attendance at virtually all northern Mafia spirit possession rituals which always include divination sessions at which a wide range of problems are presented to the possessed shamans.

The Spirit World

Mohammed is not a shaman, although he has inherited a relationship with a spirit, which is his guardian. He never gets possessed in rituals but communicates with the spirit regularly in his dreams, often by burning incense (*kutia buhuri*) before he sleeps to achieve such an end. Much of his explanation for events in his own life and that of others is in terms of spirits and their doings.

There are two kinds of spirits in northern Mafia Island (cf. Caplan 1975, 1979). The first is that of land spirits (*mashaitani*) who are appeased by such rituals (*ngoma*) as *kitanga* and *mwingo*, which usually include the slaughter of a cow and the drinking of its blood, a practice which is, of course, forbidden by orthodox Islam. Such spirits are also guardians of the bush fields, and offerings are made to them at regular intervals during the cultivation cycle. *Mashaitani* are almost all possessory spirits, but possession follows descent. Not all descendants of a medium will become possessed, but all are supposed to give offerings to the spirit. Mediums are members of guilds led by shamans, who are believed to have some control over their possessory spirit. This control can be used either for divination to ascertain the causes of a particular misfortune, or the shaman can use the spirit to protect clients or punish their enemies – the latter especially is likely to be termed witchcraft (*uchawi*).

> The spirits are like people. Some are stronger than others. If a spirit tries to get hold of a person already protected by another spirit, the latter will say 'This is my child!' (*kengeja wangu*) and the other will say, 'If I go away, what will I get?' 'Go and follow that person who sent you, they will give you something.'

The second category of spirits are those of the sea (*majini ya bahari*) who are appeased by the rituals of *mkobero* and *tari*; the animals slaughtered in these rituals are goats, not cows. Although there are sea spirit shamans, they do not practise withcraft or divination through their spirits, indeed, most of them do not even get possessed. Rather, it is their knowledge of Islamic charms (*hirizi*) and of the Koran which enables them to deal with such spirits.

Although my fieldwork initially started off concentrating upon kinship and land tenure, I became increasingly fascinated by spirit possession and its dramatic rituals. This was encouraged by my local supervisor at the University of Dar es Salaam. Another factor was that two of my major informants, Mohammed and another man, Athman, were both heavily involved in spirit possession cults, and that in listening to their explanation for events, spirits and their doings frequently entered the picture.

Mohammed's diary – adultery and its consequences

Mohammed's diary covers a multiplicity of topics (my index contains around eighty), but one which occurs very frequently is that of adultery. Sometimes this results in fights between husband and lover, sometimes in a husband divorcing his wife, sometimes in angry wives beating their husbands or husbands' mistresses.

However, often cases of adultery do not lead to violence on the part of husband or wife, but to suspicions of witchcraft. In such cases, the violence is projected on to the world of spirits. Cuckolded husbands and jealous lovers seek the help of shamans and their spirits to punish or even kill rivals. In the case of Mohammed's own life, encounters with spirits, often because of sexual behaviour, are a constantly recurring theme in his conversation or, as below, in his diary:

> There are many men who hate me and are my enemies, because I have broken their houses [i.e. committed adultery with their wives].
>
> She [Mwahadia] was married in Zanzibar, and her husband was a witch [*mchawi*]. My mother didn't want me to marry her because she was afraid I would be killed (by the ex-husband). But I said even if I marry her on Thursday and die on Friday (I don't care) ...
>
> I threatened to change my name, go away and never see them [my family] again [if they wouldn't agree]. My mother was afraid I would commit suicide, and finally I got my own way.
>
> The wedding took place on the 13th day of the month. The next day, I went to build a fence together with my father. But he became ill and died on 15th day, and everyone said 'He has already been eaten' [i.e. by the spirit sent by the ex-husband].

This relationship between adultery and witchcraft in the form of being 'eaten' by a spirit is a dominant one in his diary:

In Bweni and Kanga there are many people who hate me because of their wives. [During one period] They watched me to see which house I go to a lot and decided to put a spirit there to catch me.

On the day after a *kitanga* [a spirit possession ritual] in Bweni, my mother's brother became possessed and said 'My friend, I have something I want to say to you, but I am afraid.'

'Say it.'

'They suspect you [*wana shaka nawe*] but they have not yet seen you [actually committing adultery], so they have put a spirit there [i.e. to catch him].'

So I didn't go to that house again.

But being the victim of vengeance witchcraft is not the only way in which sexual activity leads to the intervention of spirits as Mohammed explained to me:

Committing adultery is called *kuzinga*, *kuzini*, or *kufanya fuska*. If you do this at or near a *panga* [spirit shrine], it is inevitable that you will be harmed, you will be caught. You will have to give a cow as a punishment [to the spirit] for being 'dirty' in its 'town'.

Given that much illicit sex takes place in the bushland which is supposed to be guarded by land spirits, it is not surprising that those conducting such affairs lay themselves open to retribution from the spirit of the area, as Mohammed found to his cost on several occasions. One day he told me:

I met my lover in a neighbouring village and arranged to meet her again somewhere else. But on the way, I encountered a spirit, which caused me to have a high fever and to hallucinate. I was only cured after several weeks and the intervention of my father's brother, a shaman, who invoked our family spirit to protect me and drive away the invading spirit.

Land spirits are said to dislike the 'dirt' of sex, especially that out of marriage, although for an appropriate fee, they can sometimes be persuaded to further amorous affairs by disabling or punishing rivals, as has been shown in some of the above cases.

Sea spirits also dislike sexual activity between humans, although for different reasons. A sea spirit, which usually possesses a woman, is often thought to be a 'love spirit' (*jini ya mahaba*) and so to be jealous of human lovers:

Once I was rendered impotent in this way. I went to an assignation with a woman from a neighbouring village and I couldn't manage anything. I asked her if she had a sea spirit. She said that she had a *tari* spirit and that he took her under the sea, and also penetrated her. So the *jinn* must have been the reason for my failure, and as soon as we both realized this, I became all right. Later, the woman wanted me to marry her.

Given the dangers involved in sexual activity, then, people like Mohammed need to seek protection. On one occasion, he arrived wearing a new charm and told me:

> I have recently been given this charm [*hirizi*] by a ritual expert because I had a dream in which I saw the husband and relatives of my current mistress in the place where I usually meet her.
>
> As it happened, the next day I met you [Pat] near the same spot and you gave me 10/−, so the second half of the dream came true. I was afraid that the first part might do so as well, so I avoided my mistress that day.

Mohammed had something of a reputation in the village for his knowledge of love magic recipes, as well as for methods of rendering rivals impotent and ways of ensuring that cuckolded husbands did not find out about affairs. Some of his knowledge he learned or bought from others, but some he claimed to gain from dreams, which were frequently about spirits:

> On Sunday night, I was asleep and I dreamed that my spirit told me that he wanted his present, and his spirit friend also said that he wanted his money. I woke up right there and then.
>
> *Pat.* What do you see?
>
> *Mohammed.* A man and his friend. It is for their help in guarding me against all harm that they ask for a present.

On another occasion, he dreamed that his spirit came and told him I was ill, and sure enough, when he came to visit the next day, he found that I had been sick the previous night. He said to me very seriously:

> Patrisha, never hate me, never take against me, or it will be dangerous for you on account of the spirit. I am telling you because I am fond of you, and I tell all my mistresses the same thing.

In diary and conversation, then, Mohammed projected a view of himself as an irresistible Casanova:

> If I had married all the women who wanted me, I would have had six or seven wives by now. When I go to Bweni village, the whole place shrinks, I mean they see me as a lion [*nchi yote inakonda – manaanake wananiona kama simba*].

Why did Mohammed confide in me to such an extent? I did not solicit information about adultery, much less about his own – it was offered. At the time, I just assumed that all information which came my way was grist for my mill. I was determined not to be shocked by anything I learned, especially in regard to sex, not only because of my anthropological training in 'objectivity', but also because I saw myself as a product of an enlightened era, the 1960s, which had cast off the repressive puritanism of our parents' generation.

At that time, what struck me most forcibly about gender relations on Mafia Island was their apparent 'liberatedness' in regard to sexuality. Sex was openly celebrated in the marriage ritual, as well as in the boys' circumcision and girls' puberty rituals. Both women and men appeared to have sexual relations outside of marriage. Yet in looking back now, I realise now that such matters were in fact far from being as unproblematic as I thought at the time. Sexual liaisons were dangerous activities, from both a practical and supernatural viewpoint. It was perhaps for this reason that Mohammed chose to make me his confidante – there was, after all, no one else he could have told with such impunity.

During this first period of fieldwork, I tried hard to appear as asexual as possible, seeking to play an ungendered role so that I could move freely between male and female space. To some extent, this tactic must have worked, because people sometimes made remarks such as 'We find it hard to know if you are a man or a woman'. They knew that I had a 'fiancé' (*mchumba*) back in England.

For both of these reasons, it did not really occur to me that other women, such as Mwahadia, might see me as a potential sexual rival, and that this might be a reason why she did not confide in me at that time. She must have been well aware of his adulterous behaviour and yet she never mentioned it to me. Or perhaps it was because she saw me as just a young girl, too immature to be given such information. However, in retrospect, I wonder whether in fact she did tell me, but I failed to understand. On going through my notebooks recently, I found an entry for January 1966 to which I had paid no attention at the time:

In evening, Mohammed and Mwahadia came, latter asked me for money to buy kangas. She claims she wants to divorce Mohammed. He didn't give her any of the money he earned recently by building a hut for someone.

I mentioned this to the cook Salum, Mohammed's great friend, but he said that they were just 'having me on'. However, in October 1966 there is another entry in my notebook concerning their marriage:

Mwahadia is trying to persuade her husband to go to Zanzibar to live and says if he won't, then let him divorce her. She says they have no clothes, no hope of betterment. He should rent out his coconuts and get his older brother (who lives in Zanzibar) to help him get a job and she can plait mats and do other things. But he says she will run away from him once there.

Mwahadia's complaints related largely to their state of poverty and Mohammed's squandering of money. She herself had to earn cash for basic household necessities by making clay pots in addition to all her other work. It can thus scarcely have been coincidental that at the same time as

Mwahadia was trying to persuade him to migrate to Zanzibar, Mohammed was in the throes of another passionate affair. My diary for October 1966 notes that 'Mohammed has a new girlfriend'.

In this society, gift-giving is an integral part of sexual relations. A man 'pays' for sex with his wife by providing her with food and clothes, and a song sung by women frequently is

What are you [husband] waking me up for if you've nothing to give me?

Similarly, in sexual relations outside marriage, a lover 'pays' his mistress for sex by gifts. Mohammed told me once:

I had an affair ... and the woman gave me a bread, and I gave her two cloths [kanga]. Now she runs away from me because our love [mahaba] is finished and there is none left. Once she had got the kangas out of me, she got fed up. That is typical!

In other words, an extra-marital affair by a husband inevitably means that he diverts (usually scarce) resources to his mistress, and it is of this, even more than of sexual jealousy, that wives complain. Somehow, I did not see clearly at the time that while Mohammed discussed adultery in terms of sex, Mwahadia did so in terms of deprivation of her rights to food and clothes.

However, I ask myself now how I was able to put aside conflict of loyalties between the two of them, and pretend to Mwahadia that nothing was amiss when Mohammed was constantly coming to tell me of his liaisons with women in Kanga and the surrounding villages.

Aside from the fact that she herself did not raise it, and I did not wish to break Mohammed's confidence, there are two further reasons for this. I had been taught that an ethnographer did not make 'subjective' judgements about informants, one tried to accept them as they were. Secondly, I did not really see Mwahadia as ill-treated wife, and Mohammed as philandering husband. After all, I reasoned, if Mwahadia had wanted to have affairs in the way that her husband did, she could have done so. Other women must have been having them, if even a fraction of Mohammed's stories were to be believed, and his accounts were confirmed by the instruction given by the ritual expert at the girls' puberty ritual, which included the advice to:

Wash yourself before you go on a journey. You never know whom you might meet on the path and want to go with. (cf. Caplan 1976)

I also thought that they had a good relationship in spite of Mohammed's infidelities. In this, I was perhaps wrong, or was it that things changed so much during the nine years I was away?

Part 2   DIALOGUES: THE INFORMANTS AT WAR: THE ANTHROPOLOGIST AS INTERMEDIARY, 1976

The end of Mohammed and Mwahadia's marriage

Two years after my departure, Mohammed wrote to tell me that Mwahadia had left him:

> She has asked me to divorce her. What do you say? She is at her place. She went there without my permission very suddenly. Quickly, speedily, I want an answer.

This separation, like the previous one, was only temporary for in the following letter he told me that 'Mwahadia and I are together at the moment, and we have had a son.' Four years later, at the beginning of 1972, they had run into problems again, but on this occasion too, they were reconciled, this time by their eldest son, as Mwahadia told me later.

I returned to the village for a brief visit in May 1976 to make arrangements to shoot a film later that year for the BBC. It was nine years since I had left, and in the interim, I had married, finished my Ph.D., done fieldwork in Asia, had two children (then aged five and three) and become involved in feminism. Inevitably, many of my perceptions were somewhat different.

It was the period of harvest, and I had to go out to their bush field to be able to speak to Mwahadia, who was busy guarding the ripening crop. She had had four more children since I left – twin girls, another boy and a girl, and she was pregnant again. So she still had several small children at home, just as I did at the time. We spent the day harvesting and cooking. For the first time, partly because of my changed feminist consciousness, partly because of my own experiences, I noticed how little Mohammed did to help, except to go and fetch a little water. Mwahadia took advantage of his absence to unburden herself and told me that she planned to leave him after the harvest. I recorded her words in my notebook:

> We have quarrelled a lot – he never stays at home. He never ever buys me anything. I have had enough, I am tired. He has accused me of bearing a child by another man. But illegitimacy isn't on the female side. If I get a child it will be *my* child. Only on the father's side can it be illegitimate.

I was impressed at the time with this statement as conveying both the meaning of cognatic descent, and also women's autonomy, but was sceptical that she would actually carry through this idea. I asked her if she intended to remarry, wondering whether she had already got someone in mind, but she retorted bitterly that no one would marry a woman with seven children. She maintained that, anyway, she was fed up with being married and would rather stay with her mother, now widowed.

On my return to the island in July with the film crew to begin the shooting, I was immediately greeted at the airport by Mohammed's elder brother with the news that Mwahadia had indeed left. It was Mohammed whom I met first on arrival in the village and he insisted on telling me his version of the story:

> When the time came to move back to the village [from the fields], she went to her mother's house. She didn't tell me, nor did she tell the elders. She just went and she took everything with her . . .
>
> I went to tell the chairman of the village and said I was to get a report if she went to any rituals or dance. I said I had not taken her back to her parents. She had gone of her own accord.
>
> I won't divorce her even though that is what she wants. I would marry again if I had any money and leave her to it.
>
> It is all her fault – I always gave her clothes, kerosene, food. Now she is sick and claiming that I put a spirit on her.

The next day, Mwahadia came to give her version of events. She was not only pregnant but also quite unwell:

> I've tried all kinds of medicines – charms, hospital etc. I've been to a diviner and been told that he's put a spirit on me. I've done what I told you I'd do – I've gone to my mother's place. He won't divorce me – I don't care, I want a rest, I've been married long enough. He has done such terrible things, he threatens me he'll cut off my ear or my nose. He's become like an enemy, he hates me and I don't want to see him.

Once again, most of Mwahadia's complaints against Mohammed were less about his adulteries, or even his violence, but more about his profligacy, the fact that he would not handle money wisely and did not contribute to the household as he should have done. Mohammed was aware of her feelings, and told me angrily:

> Every time I do anything now [i.e. since their separation], especially if I buy anything, whether it be fish, clothes or whatever, someone goes and tells her.

Only occasionally did I get hints from Mwahadia that his adultery had also hurt her:

> He has insulted me, he says other women are better than me. Am I his wife if he talks like that? And then he threatens me and hits me.
>
> No, I don't want a court case, I don't want for us to go on to the *baraza* and insult each other – you went with so and so, you went with so and so. He has no shame, but I have. I told the chairman [of the village] I just want my divorce certificate [*talaka*] and the chairman went to tell him. I want my divorce not to get married again, but to be alone, I want to be whole again [*uzima*], I want my certificate.

I was very shocked by her allegations of his violence against her, which were later confirmed by their teenage daughter, particularly as I had never encountered violence in any marital relationship in the village. Mwahadia made it plain that she had resisted Mohammed's violence, but that in the end, she had felt compelled to leave him. However, while this may have enabled her to escape physical harm, she was still sure that he was finding other ways of hurting her:

> Now I'm seven months pregnant – he says it isn't his child. But in any case, he is a big shaman. He knows a lot of things, he has put a spirit on to me, and he is trying to kill the foetus and kill me as well. He really hates me now.

The next day, as requested by Mwahadia, I tackled Mohammed when he came to visit:

> *Pat.* She wants a proper divorce.
>
> *Mohammed.* Well, I won't give it to her. She can stay there as long as she likes and I'll get married again. I told her if she wants her certificate she can pay me 3,000/–. Why should I give my property away for nothing?
>
> *Pat.* She says you have threatened her and also bewitched her.
>
> *Mohammed.* If I had wanted to do all the things which she says I have threatened her with, what would stop me? It isn't true. And as for this spirit business, this has been going on for 5 years now. She keeps going [to diviners] and getting told that it is different spirits, four or five, how could I have bewitched her with all of those? I'll tell you what happened – she tried to bewitch me – yes, she has spirits in her family, but my spirit was stronger and got hold of hers, and so she got caught. That's why she is sick ...
>
> *Pat.* She says you agreed to a separation.
>
> *Mohammed.* Well, if I did why didn't she wait for me to take her to her parents? When she was sick I looked after her. I did everything for her – I even cleaned her up after she had defecated. Is that the way I am rewarded?

It was true that Mwahadia was supposed, like Mohammed, to have an ancestral connection with a spirit. It was also true, as Mwahadia confirmed, that the previous year, when she had been so ill, it was Mohammed, rather than her female kin, who had nursed her – a quite unusual situation. Perhaps Mohammed's brother was right when he came to urge me to reconcile them, saying

> That woman, he is her man, and that Mohammed, she is the only one for him. They really want each other. Yes, I know there has been a lot of bitterness and quarrelling, but they should make up. They have borne children together.

A few days later, I received a message in the early morning from Mohammed that Mwahadia had given birth two months prematurely, but the baby had been born dead. I went to her mother's house, where she was staying. Someone came to ask if there was any incense for the funeral, and one of the women present suggested they should go and ask Mohammed for some since he was the father. But her mother rejected the idea bitterly: 'This is his work [i.e. the death of the child]. Don't ask him. Ask someone else.'

Two days later, Mohammed came and asked me to go and see her on his behalf; he was obviously wanting a reconciliation.

> Ask her why she didn't go and see my father's brother if she was dissatisfied. Ask her where I took the money and other things, if I didn't bring them home, as she says. Ask her which women I went with, if I went with women. And tell her that saying such a thing can be a cause of quarrels (*fitina*), serious quarrelling – the husbands of such women would fight with me.

Mohammed was obviously seeking to justify himself not only to me, but to his relatives, and perhaps even to himself. The next day Mwahadia came to my house, and I duly asked her whether she had any intention of returning to him:

> No, I am tired, I have put up with things for many years, but I have had enough, I can't go on ... No I can't go back to him. We got to the point where we were fighting on the path once – we spilled the water, and I can show you the piece of wood he hit me with. And if he hadn't bewitched me, I wouldn't have lost this baby. That is his doing, and even now, I still feel unwell, he wants to kill me ... I can't go back to him now. This has been going on for several years – he has changed towards me, and with the things he has done, he is no longer my partner (*mwenzangu*), so how can I live with him?

In spite of the fact that she had taken unilateral action to end her marriage, the sympathies of most people in the village were with Mwahadia. On one occasion when Mohammed was sitting in my house, one of the most respected men in the village, a Koranic school teacher, came in and began to berate him:

> How is is that you, with grandchildren, can behave in this childish way? You go after other women, you don't stay at home. [To me] Why can't you reconcile them, it is not good that they stay like this.

Mohammed denied this, but reserved his anger until the man had left:

> He has no right to say that, you see he is on her side. But the law is on my side – she had no right to up and leave like that unless I had taken her back to her family, or unless I divorced her. And her mother and brother could be taken to court for harbouring my wife.

Although even Mohammed's own relatives felt that he had behaved badly, they were still anxious for a reconciliation. His elder brother came again to see me:

Brother. Well, did you manage to see Mwahadia? What did she say?

Pat. She might change her mind in time – she is fed up with living at her mother's place. And Mohammed keeps coming and talking about her to me, and has been by to see how she is. But if only half of what she says is true then I feel sorry for her.

Brother. Yes, sympathy is all very well, but that isn't going to feed the children. These days it is hard enough for two people together to manage, how is one person alone going to do it?

Shortly afterwards, Mohammed was in the mood for compromise:

> Now I want you to tell her this. There will be no peace in the house if one of the parties does as he or she likes. If I the husband am going away, I should tell her [*kuagananaye*], and she should not go out anywhere, to fetch water, or to a ritual without my permission. Because once one does that, then the other one does the same, and so it will go on like that. I think that is how our quarrel started. If she comes back, then it must be resolved that each tell the other what is happening. Don't you think so? Doesn't your husband know where you are? Didn't you discuss it before you came? Yes, well, it is the same here as in Europe.

Interestingly, Mohammed addresses me as a married woman here in seeking to reiterate the norms of reasonable behaviour in marriage.

Just before I left I asked Mwahadia what her intentions were:

> *Me*. Will you return to Mohammed?
>
> *Mwahadia*. My heart hasn't yet agreed. Maybe I will go but not yet. Someone has already been sent [by Mohammed] to ask me to return. But it's all very well for you and him. You don't have to live with it – the quarrelling and the insults. I know I am having difficulties since I separated, but that man is too much for me.

Discussion

In 1976, I became much closer to Mwahadia, and during my visits in 1976, she talked particularly freely to me. On one occasion she said 'I've no one to tell my troubles to, no one asks me how I am.' She felt herself unsupported even by her natal family who all had their own problems. However, there was no doubt that she saw me differently, now that I had finally 'grown up' in her eyes by marrying and bearing children. For the first time, she even discussed Mohammed's infidelities.

For my part, I was particularly shocked at what she and and her daughter told me of Mohammed's violent behaviour towards her. In some ways I was the more shocked because I had been so sure for so many years that they had a good relationship. I was not perhaps as angry as I might have been because Mwahadia made it plain that she had not passively accepted violence from

Mohammed, any more than she had from her first husband – she had, literally, hit back. I admired her ability to cope with the situation, her resolution to live on her own and run her own life, even if it would be difficult. Around that time, we filmed a number of divorced or widowed women living on their own by cultivating and selling their mats, and this added to my perception of women's relative autonomy in this society. This was reinforced by the degree of support which Mwahdia enjoyed from other villagers, including Mohammed's own relatives.

Now that I try to analyse my attitudes towards the break-up of their marriage in 1976, I can see that in many ways, once again, my implicit point of comparison was my own society. A question which ran through my research was how did the position of women in this society compare with that in my own? At this time, one of the major questions being posed by the women's movement in the West concerned the battering of women, and there had been a good deal of publicity about the reasons why women put up with being battered, how few alternatives there were for them, and the necessity of creating places of safety for women subjected to domestic violence. Here in Mafia, it seemed that if a man was violent to his wife, other people intervened and that, furthermore, women themselves would not passively submit.

I did not see it as my job to persuade Mwahadia to return to Mohammed against her better judgement. But I did not feel able to break my relationship with Mohammed, perhaps because their marriage had already finished when I knew about its worst details, perhaps because I still needed him as an informant. Perhaps also because in the end, I saw him as increasingly pathetic. He seemed to be losing not only Mwahadia, but all the arguments and the support of other villagers, ranging from the chairman and council, to his own relatives. In conversations with the two of them, then, I saw myself as intermediary, not mediator.

Part 3   EPILOGUE – RECONSIDERATIONS 1985

On my return visit in 1985, my point of comparison had shifted: this time I was not only studying women and implicitly comparing them to women in my own society, but also gender relations, comparing males and females with each other on Mafia in terms of health, food and fertility. My findings forced me to rethink to some extent my previous view of gender relations, as my work revealed just how disadvantaged women are in terms of work-load, morbidity, more pregnancies than they want, and a less adequate diet than men receive (Caplan 1988, 1989).

This does not mean that I now consider that my previous work was 'wrong' in its depiction of women's relative autonomy, both in sexual and economic terms (Caplan 1978, 1982, 1983). While continuing to maintain that women do have some room for manoeuvre in this society, I would add that the costs of autonomy are often high. Women on their own have a lower standard of living than those supported, even not entirely adequately, by husband.

Similarly, I now realise that in spite of an unofficial ideology condoning sexual freedom, it would in fact have been very difficult for a woman like Mwahadia to have had lovers in the way that Mohammed did. Aside from the risk of divorce if her husband found out, she was pregnant no fewer than twelve times by Mohammed, and many of her pregnancies were difficult with frequent bouts of ill-health. Furthermore, because of his lack of support, she had to work even harder than most women in order to get some cash.

When I returned in 1985, Mohammed and Mwahadia were still living apart. Mohammed had acquired a fine house, built by his eldest son who worked in Dar es Salaam, and had living with him his second daughter, currently divorced, and two of her children, as well as his youngest son and daughter, both still at school. He was in his usual poverty-stricken state, and was trying to get together a consignment of raffia-grass to sell in Dar es Salaam. He complained that he did not have any female help in drying the grass, and I asked him why he didn't get married again. He said he wanted to – he had a lot of difficulty living without a wife to help to cultivate. On another occasion he said plaintively 'I feel so cold these nights on my own' and when I asked him again why he didn't re-marry, he replied 'Yes, I want to, if I can sell my cow'.

Mwahadia had refused to live in the house built by her son, even in a separate section. She had moved away from her natal family's cluster, and was building a small hut to live in with her youngest daughter, next to that of her third daughter, currently divorced, and her children.

I put the same question to her – why didn't she re-marry? She replied that she had been betrothed to a man in a village in the south, but that he was killed by a spirit. She did not seem keen to embark upon another marriage:

I won't be deceived by a husband with other women or over money – claiming he has none every evening when you know he's been working or felling coconuts. I won't put up with *that* again.

Yet paradoxically, in 1985, I felt that Mohammed was the worse off of the two in spite of his fine house. He was lonely, 'cold at nights', no longer a 'lion', while Mwahadia was managing on her own, refusing another marriage, busy with building a new hut, enjoying visiting her married children and their families, now scattered from Mafia to Dar es Salaam to Zanzibar. In short, she appeared in control of her own life.

At this period, when neither of them was engaging in sexual activity, they appeared untroubled by spirits.

Conclusion

A relationship with an informant is crucial for an anthropologist – sooner or later it becomes vital, and more and more time is spent with one for s/he has the kind of knowledge the anthropologist needs (Dwyer 1982: 265). However, as Crapanzano has pointed out, 'The anthropologist's presence is of paramount importance to the informant and governs his tale' (1984: 954). Plainly, Mohammed would not have written his diary and confessed his adultery had I not been there and I suspect that he might not have done so had I been male.

In one sense, the anthropologist chooses the informant, but in another, the reverse is equally true. Why did Mohammed choose me? While he gave gifts to his lovers in return for their sexual favours, I gave him gifts for his time and information, including, of course, the diary. This meant that our relationship was the reverse of that which usually obtained between males and females. When I left, he obviously felt it important to give me a parting gift of some value, thus restoring the balance of reciprocity to some extent.

Rabinow has suggested that the most important part of such intervention lies in the way in which anthropologists inevitably train people to objectify their life-world for them, thereby creating a 'doubling of consciousness': 'consequently, the data we collect is doubly mediated, first by our own presence and then by the second-order self-reflection we demand from our informants' (1977: 119). Informants must interpret both their own culture and that of the anthropologist, which they do by first becoming self-conscious about it and objectifying their own life-world, and then by presenting it to the anthropologist. As a result of this, Rabinow suggests that the anthropologist and the informant create a liminal world remaining external to both of them (ibid.: 153). But does this mean that other cultures do not 'objectify' their own life-worlds? This would be a somewhat surprising suggestion, thirty years after the publication of *Ogotemmeli* (Griaule 1970).

Another question is whether, by demanding such information from our informants, we, from a 'confessing' society, actually 'torture' them (Crapanzano 1984: 956). Plainly, circumstances differ. In this particular instance, I certainly did not feel that I was torturing my informants, indeed, I felt rather that I was being used as confidante, as intermediary, perhaps even 'confessor' or therapist.

Thus, it is not necessarily the case that informant and ethnographer create a liminal world, external to both of them. In this particular case, what happened was rather that I was drawn to some extent into the informant's world – like Favret-Saada's involvement in witchcraft in the Bocage (1980) – and became caught up in the doings not only of humans, but even of spirits, at least in the eyes of my informants, and sometimes, in my own.

REFERENCES

Caplan, A. P. (1975) *Choice and Constraint in a Swahili Community*. Oxford: IAI/ Oxford University Press.

—— (1976) Boys' circumcision and girls' puberty rituals among the Swahili of Mafia island, Tanzania. *Africa* 46(1).

—— (1978) The Swahili of Chole Island, Tanzania. In A. Sutherland (ed.) *Face Values*. London: BBC/RAI Publications.

—— (1979) Spirit possession on Mafia Island, Tanzania. In *Kenya Past and Present*. Kenya Museum Society.

—— (1982) Gender, Ideology and Modes of Production on the East African Coast. In J. de Vere Allen (ed.) *From Zinj to Zanzibar*. Wiesbaden: Franz Steiner Verlag.

—— (1983) Women's Property, Islamic Law and Cognatic Descent. In R. Hirschon (ed.) *Women and Property, Women as Property*. London: Croom Helm.

—— (1988) Engendering Knowledge: The Politics of Ethnography. *Anthropology Today* 4(5): 8–12, 4(6): 14–17.

—— (1989) Perceptions of Gender Stratification. *Africa*.

Casagrande, J. B. (ed.) (1960) *In the Company of Man*. London: Harper and Row.

Crapanzano, V. (1980) *Tuhami – Portrait of a Moroccan*. Chicago: Chicago University Press.

—— (1984) On the Life History (review article). *American Anthropologist* 86.

Dumont, J.-P. (1978) *The Headman and I*. Austin, Texas: University of Texas Press.

Dwyer, K. (1982) *Moroccan Dialogues*. Baltimore: Johns Hopkins University Press.

Ellen, R. F. (ed.) *Ethnographic Research: A Guide to General Conduct*, ASA Research Methods in Social Anthropology 1. London: Academic Press.

Favret-Saada, J. (1980) *Deadly Words: Witchcraft in the Bocage*. Cambridge: Cambridge University Press.

Griaule, M. (1970/1948). *Conversations with Ogotemmeli*. Oxford: Oxford University Press.

Rabinow, P. (1977) *Reflections on Fieldwork in Morocco*. Berkeley, Calif.: University of California Press.

Read, K. E. (1965) *The High Valley*. London: Allen and Unwin.

Shostak, M. (1983/1981) *Nisa: the Life and Words of a !Kung Woman*. Harmondsworth: Penguin.

Turner, V. (1967/1970) Muchona the Hornet, Interpreter of Religion. In *The Forest of Symbols*. Cornell: Cornell Paperbacks.

Chapter 5

Putting out the life
From biography to ideology among the Earth People

Roland Littlewood

> I know Science has to search me out
> to fight me, to check me out. I have
> to love them. You got to put it down
> as it come to you' own senses.
> Mother Earth

The Pinnacle villagers had warned me about the Earth People. Dangerous and unpredictable strangers to the coast, they were no friends to a White. Immediately I arrived in this fishing village to look at local understandings of health and sickness, I had been told about the community established nine miles away, which its members knew as the Valley of Decision or Hell Valley. A few weeks afterwards I happened to see three of them exchanging sacks of coconuts for a cutlass in one of the village stores; they looked at me with surprised disdain (I was the only White along the coast except for the two Irish Dominicans at Toco), but otherwise ignored me. A few months later I took the opportunity to join some of the villagers on a Government forestry expedition into the bush near the Earth People, both to see the forest and mountains but also, it was evident, to visit the Valley.

One of the foresters had met Mother Earth on her march to town in a previous year and offered to take me. Leaving the abandoned *ajoupa* (forest hut) which had served now as our base camp for two days, we passed along a disused track, waded through a turbid stream, occasionally recognising among the scrub and forest debris the relics of the wooden houses which, twenty years before, had comprised small hamlets along the shore, to climb to a small plateau facing the sea, backed by the mountains which descended to behind the settlement and then on either side dropped down to a rocky bay some thirty feet below. The Valley of Decision is hardly a physical valley, a declivity really.

The most outstanding characteristic of the settlement is surely its neatness and precision. The lower slopes of the mountains are cleanly cut into well-tended terraces, planted with banana, plantain, tobacco and *ground provision* – yam, tannia, dasheen, cassava. Between piles of slowly burning scrub remain breadfruit and papaya, orange and avocado trees, coffee and cocoa. Nearer the house, pumpkins and coconut palms frame the first lawn I have seen since leaving Port of Spain, the grass cropped short by a couple of goats.

The lawn stretches down from the house to the track along the edge of the cliff, down which a slippery path twists along the rock face, down to an elaborately carved canoe and two rafts resting up on the shingle. A shallow ravine can be seen passing along the side of the house and then across the lawn while the area near the house is neatly paved with rocky stones. The house itself is the only building remaining of a once thriving village: a large wooden hut with an attic, boards unpainted apart from the words 'HELL VALLEY, THE DEVIL LIVE HERE' facing the sea; window and door spaces open, fronted on one side by a small silk-cotton tree and on the other joined to an open-sided and rudely fashioned extension, the bottom of which comprises basket-work receptacles woven into the supporting posts and containing extraordinary quantities of harvested fruit and provision. Unlike other isolated country huts, there was no rubbish, no rusting tins or discarded tools lying about, no fragments of clothing, old papers or fading copies of the farmers' almanacs. Everything here was wooden, simply carved, polished through use, giving a strong sense of permanence, of place. Tall, aged, dignified, the house existed for itself, not as the outpost of some society located elsewhere, in town, in Britain or in the United States.

The sound of axes could be heard from behind the house. Chickens picked underneath: like all those in rural Trinidad, it is raised up on short stilts. In the space where a door had once hung stood a middle-aged woman of African ancestry, medium stature, naked, her hair in short dreadlocks. Two small children played around her on the threshold. She greeted us with polite reserve, discreetly avoided shaking hands and acerbically admonished my companion who had, as usual, thrust our cutlasses into the earth when we neared the hut: 'The Earth is the Mother'. He seemed ill at ease, refused an invitation to stay and wandered off, saying he would return to pick me up later. I entered, accepted some coconut water in a calabash together with a Valley-rolled cigar, and was told that my visit had been anticipated in a dream the previous night. Indeed I was late. I stayed in the Valley of Decision on and off for over a year.

THE BEGINNING OF THE END

Few people in the West Indian island of Trinidad have not heard of the Earth People, a small community established on the north-east coast above the rough seas where the Atlantic meets the Caribbean, not far from where Columbus obtained his landing in the New World on his voyage of 1498, and whose local Caribs he identified as living in the Earthly Paradise; not far, either, from the rocky point where, within a hundred years, the remnant of one Carib group were to leap to their deaths rather than face slavery, and where, another three hundred years later, Melville and Frances Herskovits conducted among their African successors fieldwork for the first ethnography of the English-speaking Caribbean.

In a country long familiar with the millennial religious response of the Shouter Baptists, frequently gathered by the roadside in their coloured robes, intoning lugubrious 'Sankey and Moody' hymns and ringing their handbells, and also with the newer Rastafari movement, taciturn and reserved, recently introduced from Jamaica, the Earth People remain an enigma. Their appearance in the villages or in the capital, Port of Spain, causes public outrage, for their most obvious characteristic is that they are naked. Public opinion favours the view that these young men, carrying cutlasses and with the long matted dreadlocks of the Rastas, are probably crazy: if not the whole group then certainly their leader Mother Earth whose visions gave birth to the movement and who leads their annual marches to town. Every year they come from the coast to Port of Spain to pass on their message and gather new recruits from the poorer working-class areas around the capital, Belmont and Laventille, Pitch Road; areas which appear to have missed out on Trinidad's new-found oil wealth. Communication is hampered by the Earth People's characteristic language, their studied and frequent use of obscenities, and Mother Earth's striking teachings. She informs Trinidadians, a largely devout if not exactly church-going population, that she is the Biblical Devil, the Mother of Africa and India, Nature herself.

The community of the Earth People, Hell Valley, straddles a coastal track, some nine miles from the nearest village. The local smallholdings of coffee and cocoa have long since returned to forest; their owners either left the area for good or moved back to the village. The mountains behind the Valley, never settled and seldom crossed, remain part of the island's extensive forest reserves, exploited for wood only on their southern side where they meet the central plateau. The track follows the coast, occasionally passing over headlands and allowing a glimpse of the sea, but usually winding along the mountains through the dense bush of secondary forest, hidden from the sun, occasionally dipping down to ford small rivers and mangrove swamps. Through the tangled foliage of overgrown coffee and cocoa and the tall, spreading *immortelle* trees planted eighty years ago to give them shade, the occasional traveller can glimpse the remains of abandoned *cocoa boxes*[1] and rotten wooden huts. This coast is regarded by Trinidadians as the most desolate part of the island, 'behind God's back', a fitting retreat for the handful of Black Power activists who established themselves there briefly in 1972 after blowing up the village police station. They were tracked down and shot by the Regiment, Trinidad's modest armed forces.

A year after the 'guerillas' were killed, Jeanette Baptiste, a thirty-nine year old woman from Port of Spain came to the coast, together with six of her twelve children and her partner. The family settled in the remains of one of the deserted hamlets midway along the track, where it overlooks on one side a small rocky bay, and on the other a long, curving beach bisected by a river which, laden with mangroves, slowly enters the sea as a gentle delta. Initially, they were paid by an overseer to collect copra but after an argument they continued to squat on the land by tacit agreement, growing their own food.

Two years after they arrived, when Jeanette was eight months pregnant, she had a dream in which the moon told her she should have her child on top of a hill. Not understanding why, she followed the dream nevertheless and gave birth to twins under the roof of the broken-down house. When they were five months old, Jeanette, in a period of inspiration, sang a song to Yemanja, the Yoruba mother deity of the *shango* cult, and started burning all her possessions: neither she nor her family understood at this time what was happening, but her husband, a Shouter Baptist, presumed some hidden meaning in it and did not interfere. When questioned by her family, Jeanette gave answers that flashed into her head: her actions were those of a Natural Spirit in her. The burned objects she now relates to her life back in town, to religion (the Bible), science (her spectacles) and to her domestic tasks (bedding, kitchen utensils and the sewing machine with which she made the children's shirts). Together with the destruction of all their clothes, the Burning resulted in the family remaining naked, cooking in the embers of an open fire, sheltering together at night against the cold Atlantic winds.

Pondering over these extraordinary actions, Jeanette realised that the Christian doctrine of God the Father as creator was false and that the world was really the work of a primordial Mother, to be identified as Nature, as the Earth. Nature had originally created a race of Black people, but her rebellious Son/Sun re-entered his Mother's womb/moon to gain her power of generation and had succeeded by producing White people. The Whites, the Race of the Son, enslaved the Blacks and have continued to exploit them. The Way of the Son is that of Science, of Society, of cities, clothes, schools, factories and wage labour. The Way of the Mother is that of Nature: a return to the simplicity of the Beginning, a simplicity of nakedness, cultivation of the land by hand and with respect, and of gentle and non-exploiting human relationships.

The Son, Science, in his continued quest for the power of generation has now succeeded in establishing himself in *Africans* and *Indians*[2] and is also on the point of creating mechanical non-human beings. The Mother, who has borne all his behaviour out of her love for him, has finally lost patience. The current order of Science will end in nuclear war or in a catastrophic drought and famine, a destruction wrought through the Son's own power, after which the original state of Nature will once again prevail.

Jeanette herself is a partial aspect of the Mother who will only enter into her fully at the End. Her task now is to facilitate the return to Nature by organising a community on the coast, Hell Valley, the Valley of Decision, to prepare for the return to the Beginning and to Put Out The Life, her life, to her people, the Black Nation, the Mother's Children. She has to combat the false doctrine of *religion* which places the Son over the Mother, and to correct the distorted teaching of the Bible in which she is represented as the Devil. She stands for Nature and Life, in opposition to the Christian God who is only her Son, the principle of Science and Death. As the Devil she is opposed to churches and prisons, education and money, contemporary morals and fashionable opinions.

As God is 'right' Mother Earth teaches the Left, and the Earth People interchange various common oppositions: 'left' for 'right'; 'evil' or 'bad' for 'good'. Conventional obscenities are Natural words and should be used for She Herself is the Cunt, the source of all Life. The exact timing of the End is uncertain but it will come in Jeanette's physical lifetime. Then Time will cease, disease will be healed and the Nation will speak one language. The Son will return to his Planet, the Planet Sun, the Planet of Ice, which is currently hidden by Fire placed there by the Mother–Fire which will eventually return where it belongs, back to the heart of a nurturant Earth.

Since her visions in 1975 which marked the Beginning of the End, Jeanette's immediate family have been joined by numbers of Black Trinidadians, usually young men, sometimes with their partners and children. The community has a high turnover and, while over fifty people have been associated with the Earth People, when I stayed with them in 1981–2[3] there were twenty-three living in the Valley of Decision, with perhaps twenty close sympathisers in town. About once a year the group march into town to Free Up The Nation and present their message in the central streets and parks, in particular Woodford Square, the popular site for political demonstrations next to the Parliament building. After a few weeks of Putting Out The Life, and visits to friends and relatives, they return to the Valley to continue to Plant For The Nation. In Putting Out The Life Jeanette harangues the crowd; she poignantly retells her personal struggles, identifying them with those of Nature. The men of the group chorus agreement, and explain and argue with the bystanders.

PUTTING OUT THE LIFE: THE MOTHER

The idiom of childbirth is fundamental both to Mother Earth's formal cosmogony and to her understanding of current relations between women and men. The experience of motherhood has played the single most salient role in her life, as it does for the women in the nearby villages who recounted their lives to me. It is through her own motherhood that Mother Earth represents herself as all Black women.

She was the eldest of ten children born to the domestic servant of a White family in Port of Spain. She only met her father 'once or twice' as she recalls; he died when she was about thirty: 'He call me then. I was not very interested but I go'. At sixteen she left home to live with a boy. This relationship broke up and she returned to stay with her grandmother, a follower of the *orishas* of *shango*, and then lived with one of her mother's previous *friends* by whom she herself had three children. As for most working-class Trinidadian women, emancipation from parents and emergence into adulthood came, not with chronological age, education, employment away from the household or even sexual relations, but with childbearing. She *scuffled* – borrowing, bartering and getting by through help from relatives, and boyfriends: 'a little job here, a next one there. I often plan to get marry but something happen, I ai' fuss.' Her life was similar to that of many poorer women in the town and she recalls she was not aware at the time of any particular anger, any wish for change, just facing the endless round of bearing children and caring for them. Only one aspect of her life in town produced any immediate resentment:

> Something happen to me in hospital once which I didn't like at all. Was with one of my babies, I don't really like the labour room because I find the bed is too high, it is too cold, the plastic they put on it is too cold. You have to lie down on this wet cold plastic and in my pain I like to be walking.
>
> Whenever a pain take me I jump off the bed and I gone, up and down, up and down, until it ease again, I go back and lie. But in the labour room you cannot do that: you have to bear the pain on the bed there. To me, I get more pain by being lying down there twist up. So I never like the labour room. So what I do is ease my pain on the outside, in the yard, and I remain there whenever it take me and walk: walk until it get very hot and I know when it is time to deliver, I just jump up on the bed and my baby will come. When the baby come I call the nurse. The nurse did just pass and see me comfortable so, when she come back now, she say 'What happen?' I say 'the baby, the baby' ... When she look she say 'Look what you making a mess, you making a mess in the place, look what you doing on the bed! You making a mess! Get up and go in the labour room! I bet you I push it back'. And she hold it, [part] of the baby, and push it. I fire a kick because I feel a pain! An' when I fire the kick my foot pass near her face. When I start to cry one time I say 'Sorry, I didn't really mean to do that but you push it and you hurt me' ... You know and I cry and thing and I make it look [right].

Not until the Burning did Jeanette realise this was a prefiguring, a purely individual representation of the universal striving by which the Mother's Son, indeed all men, tried to return to the mother's womb, to destroy this root of natural fertility and to gain its power, later to attempt to transcend it altogether through science in a purely mechanical creation.

PUTTING OUT THE LIFE: HER CHILDREN

The Earth People as a community may be seen as a generalisation and a reinterpretation of personal experiences, Mother Earth's certainly, but also those of their own which resonate with hers. They are not a passive mimesis but a transformation, commentaries, 'experiences put into circulation' (Turner 1986). As Shirokogoroff (1915) noted, 'imitative mania' alone cannot become social rebellion. Nor a community. The Earth People do not take Mother Earth's experiences and interpretations as 'metaphor', as merely emblematic. They are Life for them as for her, to be realised through action in the everyday world.

Do the lives and experiences of each member of the Earth People replicate those of Mother Earth's life – generating a *homologous* structure of social organisation and values – or does each member *reciprocally* relate to Mother Earth in the community (cf. Jakobson 1960)? We find both: homology in those aspects which relate to the historical and political situation shared by Black people in relation to Whites (for all the members are Black); and reciprocity in those aspects which concern the relations between Black mothers and their children, and between women and men (for the majority of the permanent members are young men).

The Earth People consider themselves a family arranged around Mother Earth, a family that corresponds to the original Mother Nature with her Black Children. Indeed the Mother is somehow the same person in both. The primordial family of Black Children is already recreated in the typical Afro-Caribbean family, and parallels between it and the group in the Valley are continually stressed. In theory there are no other distinctions beyond that of Mother herself and that of Earth Person (or *fruits*, for each new member takes a fruit or vegetable name); there are no recognised sub-groups, no hierarchy. Mother Earth is regarded with warm, affectionate feelings by everybody as their Mother. Nor is there a sacred text for the Valley of Decision: its origin and continuation lie solely in her past life and in her personality. It is Mother who relates everyday incidents to their central purpose. It is in her that the awesome powers of Mother Nature will finally be manifest. Her mood both follows the events of the day and is itself quickly reflected in the feeling of the others. If she feels unwell, the Earth People are subdued; if lively, they are filled with new energy and confidence. Her usual station is by the central cooking area: shouts of 'Mother want you' are quickly relayed to those working away from the house, and as immediately obeyed. Her critical comments on the progress of the cooking, the tidiness of the men's house or on general morale are listened to with quiet attention and her wishes anticipated. At the same time this is done with much playful abuse. On one occasion, soon after my arrival, she helped herself to Coconut's calabash of *fig* (plantain). He protested 'That my own fig'. Breadfruit immediately reproved him: 'That Mother Earth own. All

food come from Mother Earth', but added, to general laughter, 'And she ai'
got no fucking manners!'

Until the End comes she does not see herself as having ultrahuman powers
in any physical sense; this would anyway be unnecessary for all is Nature:

> I is the Mother, the Beginning. But I ai' play chief. You think I want to sit
> on high throne? ... Imagine you self Ruler of the Earth! It real dread you
> know ... Not to take it as a kingship. I don't want a crown. The Children
> are my crown.

How did the Earth People come to join Mother Earth? They themselves told
me of their poverty compared with other, particularly White Creole,
Trinidadians. Like all working-class men in the shanty areas of Port of
Spain, they accept that *tibourg* (middle-class) *society* is not interested in
them. They maintain that they had never really dedicated themselves to the
material pursuits of the *respectable*[4] classes: by contrast they had experienced a
need they described as 'spiritual'. Some of them joined the Shouter Baptists
until they realised that these were only 'partial' and had not come to terms
with the historical and political relationship with Whites. They had then
grown their *natty* (dreadlocks) and adopted Rasta idiom and some Rasta
ideas but, again, felt that this was not enough, that Rastas were not living the
natural life they proclaimed.

Breadfruit had grown up near Mother Earth who had been a neighbour of
his mother and tried to combine Shouter Baptism with the *natural* parts of
Rastafari:

> And then I let natty grow again and one day minister take me in church
> and he say 'Why do you don't go and comb it?' I say 'Why?' He say 'For
> society'. So I think I don't want it; I for meself. So I didn't go to church
> again ... And at night I go out naked and lie on the ground and say 'Why
> not pray to a Mother for a few days?' So I do! [Soon he saw Mother Earth
> again on a visit to town] Me mother always go by she. I see her a next
> time in '79 when she go up to Laventille. I use to talk about Selassie and
> thing but she show me my senses. The next day I had a vision and see me
> self natural, run about with little children. Next day I just put on bag
> [sack] and start go about with she. What made me see me self was that I
> see self and see this Black woman naked and walk about with school girls
> in uniform and I fly by her side. And I move and kiss earth and I burn
> Bible. And when Mother come up I free to talk it again.

Potato was seventeen when he came to the Valley:

> What Mother Earth say it all 'bout, my mother did and so [preparing
> local food] but Rastas didn't like it. I hardly go off on it [Rastafari], hat
> and so, and I start going 'bout with bare foot. I didn't like the city,
> fighting with pollution. This world too crucial to the flesh. Old time

people more natural: my old grandmother used to tell us to gather round when she cock up her leg an' pee. Now you run home hold your legs together! ... We live here natural. When we go to town I ai' shit for a week. We come back in bush and take deer bush and pow! Free up yourself! When we little they talk of God the Father. And me say 'Who he?' And they talk of Mary, Mother of God and me say 'What!' and I get brain tie up. And now Mother gives me senses. Like we all come from down here [the Earth].

To what extent can we argue that the members who joined the group were in some sense consciously 'looking for a mother', attempting themselves to return to an earlier and harmonious life as a child, some frozen replication of one phase in the family cycle? They themselves argue the reverse – that the human family provides a replication of the original family of the Mother and Her Black children. As a community they feel that they are part of this family, and the Valley as a whole appears to reflect the working-class Afro-Caribbean family. The two possible 'structural imbalances' of the group, which I thought threatened its continued existence, derive from its rooting in the original Mother–Child cosmogony and from the rarity of women members.

Mother Earth is the Mother of every member and yet she has a consort, her partner Jakatan, but the only person resembling a consort of the parthenogenic Mother is her incestuous Son, the God of the Whites: in the group there can be no ultimately grounded status for Jakatan, except as one of the Mother's Children. Although he is much younger than Mother, it was he who had first suggested that the couple and their children should move to the bush and, although he loyally supports her in public, on occasions he leaves the community to visit his family. At other times he takes a select group of Earth People to the *high woods* where he has built a small hut. In his absence Mother Earth decries this 'high woods group' and complains that 'he plays at boss man there'. At times of bitter argument she harangues the group about the role of fathers in general, how they desert women and leave them to look after the children. She retells the story of her life. She is the West Indian mother complaining to her children about the vagaries of their father. While there is much genuine affection between Mother Earth and Jakatan there are times when I thought he resents the role he has in the group as a sort of elder son, particularly when he is berated by Mother for not taking a more active role in encouraging the less experienced members, a role which is in any case restricted in that there is no position for a 'father' in the group. Again the situation recalls the self-perception of the Black Creole family in Trinidad, constantly measured against their idea of the *respectable* White family.

The other 'unbalanced' feature, the absence of *mothers* (women), recalls the problems of sexuality between the siblings of any family. While Mother

Earth is certainly correct in saying that it is Black women who have particular difficulties in abandoning town to come to the Valley because of their more *respectable* aspirations, she herself finds it difficult to accept women members, particularly if they are likely to form liaisons with her male Children. Whilst celibacy is no explicit part of her teaching, Mother Earth strongly hints that the time is not yet ready for sex:

> Roland, they could go off for a woman but it ai' in them. They work to preparation for having children. I show them how to live to love the mothers. Their outside life ai' no preparation.

PUTTING OUT THE LIFE: THE WHITES

> The attentive reader will have grasped no doubt from what has been said so far that in what I am about to relate I was a witness and not an actor. I am not the hero of my tale. Nor am I exactly its bard. Though the events I saw convulsed my previously insignificant existence, though their full weight still bears upon my conduct, upon my way of seeing, in recounting them I wish to adopt the cold impassive tone of the ethnologist: I visited this sunken world and this is what I saw there. (Perec, *W or The Memory of Childhood*, p. 4)

I realised that my own stay with the Earth People would involve two particular difficulties, for them and for myself. Fieldwork with new religious groups is rare because uncommitted outsiders are not easily welcome, particularly when initial enthusiasm is palling and conflicts develop about the extent of accommodation with the outside world, and splits in the group are common. The Valley awaited recruits not students. Conversely, departure can only be a betrayal.

The very specific beliefs of the Earth People were the other problem. Whites are the Children of Science, the historical oppressors of Black people. Given its history of genocide, slavery and colonialism, no White in the Caribbean can anyway conceive of themselves as any sort of 'neutral' observer. The European is already an integral part of the local classification (see note 4); the White ethnographer is already an element in the society (s)he comes to observe. My invitation to stay in the Valley, the sheer improbability of the situation – the arrival of a White male psychiatrist – was an inversion of the earlier situation when, after Putting Out The Life, Mother Earth had been sent by a magistrate to the Port of Spain psychiatric hospital (until rescued by the group in a night raid). The parodic absurdity of my arrival confirmed some sort of implicit Natural meaning. For a world already upside-down, reconciliation could only be absurd.

It was after a few daytime visits, for which I was dropped off by boat from the village or stayed nearby in an abandoned cocoa box, that I was told to remain for a night and then for longer stays. At about this time, after going swimming in the river with Pumpkin and Cocorite, I emerged from the water and walked back to the house naked, to general derision, acclaim and amusement. From then onwards I lived in the Valley for a few weeks at a time over a period of a year. I did not sleep in the men's hut but occupied a space near the central fire, in between Mother Earth and her family, together with the new members. The possibility of my joining fully, cutting my ties with the outside world, was raised occasionally but discreetly. There seemed no great pressure on me to do this and I assumed it was generally recognised that I would eventually return to Britain. Towards the end of my stay, the group persuaded me, over my objections, to bring a camera and tape recorder. I photographed them. They photographed me. My wife and our daughter came to stay also on a few occasions. My daughter's name is Letice and this resulted in our all being given *fruit names*; we were jokingly known as the *short-crops*, the Trinidadian term for 'European' crops newly introduced. At this point, at the suggestion of Mother Earth, I gave an interview in Port of Spain to a magazine (*The People* 1981) and a lecture about them at St Ann's Hospital, and wrote with the group an article for publication in the *Trinidad Guardian*. I recognised I was an immediate bulwark against any action by the police or the hospital, someone who could help gain public support when the Valley faced any concerted campaign in the press for government action against it, as it frequently did (*Trinidad Guardian* 1982).

My stay inevitably led to changing notions of Black and White, leading to a general transformation that Whites could be Black 'inside', and Blacks White, an idea that Mother Earth herself already held in parallel with the more dichotomised schema favoured by the Rastas. I resisted this but settled into working together with Mother Earth on such diversions as determining which culture heroes were already representations of the Son. Prometheus and Jesus? Of course. Odysseus? Probably. I offered suggestions derived from structural group therapy on resolving communal 'tensions', but I became confused as to what was a structural model of what. Could I have a model of a tranformation of which my model was itself an element? I still sought distance, innocence, Perec's 'cold impassive tone'. 'How very White you are', sighed Mother Earth, 'still Science'.

For the more Rasta-orientated members my stay was difficult (see *The Bomb* 1982). Their problem was the same as mine: a need for an unadulterated community, a synthesis shorn of its dialectical power. We had frequent discussions as to my implications for the immediate practical concerns of the group, let alone its eschatological aspect: would I too live at the End? Would the police come and rescue me? On many occasions I told everybody that I felt I was making needless difficulties for them but was always told to be quiet and to stay. 'Don't get you' mind tie up now.' In spite of these public demands to stop worrying I remained uneasy about 'universalising' the teaching and my effect on the existing daily conflicts. While I am not now, ten years later, convinced that I 'should' have stayed, at the time I allowed myself to be persuaded by Mother Earth, who as the founder and leader of the group instructed me firmly to remain, saying that my arrival was both predicted and a necessary development of the End. An all too easy persuasion? Perhaps, but for the anthropologist to claim total responsibility is to deny power to the people whose lives we reconstruct for our own purposes, and who at times reconstruct ours. On my final visit to the Valley I recorded her Message to the World, a message of communal singing and Mother retelling once again the story of her Life and her people, and of the coming End.

MYSELF?

A biography is the intersection of two lives. Myself? (as the personal ads at the back of *The New York Review of Books* put it). A White male. Middle-class British childhood, father of Yorkshire radical Nonconformist stock, a Swiss mother whose uncle was associated with the Zimmerwald movement. Provincial ennui and the worthy *Manchester Guardian*, then, but also Bunyan, Robin Hood, *The Wind in the Willows*, Richmal Crompton's *William*, *Captain Blood* and *Westward Ho!* Grammar school, Rider Haggard, 'backwoods cooking' in the Scouts, Conrad, *The Golden Bough*, Kropotkin's *Conquest of Bread*, Meister Eckhart, Schrödinger's *What is Life?*, *Là Bas*, *The Divided Self*. On leaving school, six months at Shivanandra's ashram in Rishikesh, then St Bartholomew's Hospital Medical School, the Dialectics of Liberation at the Roundhouse, casual work on the periodical *Black Dwarf*, medical support to the LSE occupation, the Revolutionary Socialist Students' Federation, failed and retook surgery finals, the quasi-hippie Electric Garden and Indica, art school in Whitechapel, house jobs at Barts, psychiatry in Hackney, Jaspers and Dubuffet, psychotherapy training, Rastafarian patients, research on statistical phenomenology, lectureship, first book on racism and psychiatry, anthropology at Oxford (my Jude's Syndrome resolved[5]), last paintings, parenthood, Trinidad.

Plotting some points for my biographical trajectory like that (and we have a variety of selectable trajectories with or without the psychological realism which constructs them as plausible narratives for others) to the moment at which it intersected with that of Mother Earth, the question is hardly 'Why did I choose the Earth People?', rather 'How might I have failed to choose them?'. After some months in the village I was getting a little complacent. Everything was reasonably easy, too easy as I was later to understand. I'd finally finished reading Proust and was on course for yet another routine ethnomedical monograph on a small village community (but one totally bereft of any apparent theory, the astounding pragmatism of the villagers' bush medicine seemed to put paid to any neat structural Marxism), when an argument with a *long eyed* fisherman who wanted thirty dollars to disclose the prayers for curing *maljo* (evil eye: they wouldn't work after they'd been sold, I knew that much, and he knew more about fieldwork than I did), turned my thoughts again to the Earth People. A long-standing interest in radical Puritanism, some sort of Romantic yearning for a primitive *Zwischenmenschliche*, the rumours that Mother Earth had been in the psychiatric hospital in Port of Spain? Of course. 'The Pinnacle villagers had warned me ...,' 'the most desolate part of the island ...' indeed: classic appeals to the reader to consider the intrepid ethnographer's narrative as colonial adventure, the Victorian valley utopia which both presents and opposes the Other as 'other'.

Of course. But not just that. I'd often wondered how religions got themselves started: not the routinisation and elaborations, the consolidation of dogmas and hierarchies, but the earlier bit, where the mundane and the fortuitous somehow became central, where personal contingencies and experiences become universal truths, where the nocturnal traveller on his way to Emmaus is recognised as the recently executed prophet, where Mother Ann Lee's endless pregnancies transform the Christian God into the Shakers' bisexual divinity, where transient dysphorias become the very foundations of Hell. (As the Digger Gerrard Winstanley put it, offending against seventeenth-century Calvinism, 'if the passion of sorrow predominate, then he is heavy and mad, crying out he is damned'.[6])

The passage of personal lives, with all their routine accidents, into the stuff of established culture and hagiography had always seemed a little mysterious. Does Christianity demonstrate the personal experiences of Jesus, or of St Paul? Who knows? The biographical fallacy, arbitrary and unprofitable speculation. And yet.

If the random sources of my own religious systems continued to fascinate me, I was contemptuous of the half-baked psychoanalytical speculations of Devereux and La Barre, even Erikson, and bored with the typologies of the sociologists of religion who, too, used the idiom of 'pathology' to qualify any millennial movement of which they disapproved (most of them, it seemed). The Earth People offered me a return to the problem of the interactions between individual experience and social representation, between a psychopathology closer to biology (my first degree had been in biochemistry, and I knew that Mother Earth had thyrotoxicosis) and the procedures of social anthropology: questions that remained vital to me, not to be dispersed in some Foucauldian elision. I still found biological knowledge interesting – biological potentialism, the constraints on our social choice of natural symbols.

If I had chosen the Earth People, they had chosen me. As I learned, Mother Earth herself was concerned with revising the opposition between Nature and Science. More than that, it was perhaps an opposition that could only be resolved through my arrival as their 'Other': male, White and a scientist, my periphery to their centre. A re-enactment by us both. She stipulated that I would live with her community only on the condition that I wrote my D.Phil. thesis about them, as some sort of near final squaring off (or reconciliation?) with Science, the procedure left up to me.

I had been twenty-four when my country relinquished its colonial power over Trinidad. And yet its measure of values remained inescapably European. The models for education, economy, political process and the texture of everyday life are those of Britain and the United States. The marginality which this engenders has been said to present the West Indian with 'no target to aim at, no ideal vision, that is not ultimately self-defeating' (Lowenthal 1972). In the European perception of the West Indies the countries have never been identified with any civil society but rather with nature, raw material awaiting exploitation through heavy capital investment and cheap labour. Disappearing from the European gaze when sugar ceased to contribute significantly to the metropolitan economy, the West Indies have recently re-emerged, but now as a tourist paradise of unsullied nature whose inhabitants exist to provide refreshment and entertainment, and to seduce visitors into discarding temporarily their metropolitan responsibilities – 'Islands in the Sun'. Such a prelapsarian state of nature, what Aimé Césaire has called a mock paradise, compromises:

> environmental delectability, effortless subsistence, carefree disposition, devotion to sensual pleasures (music, dance, sex) and easy racial intermingling ... When nature is so agreeable, houses are seen more as luxuries than necessities. (Lowenthal 1972: 16)

If the Valley of Decision was an appropriation (yet an affirmation) of such a vision, it was also one which contained an explanation of our fall from grace. If in its apparent autonomy, Mother Earth and I collaborated in a renactment of what Pratt (1986) has called 'the first contact scene', we nevertheless fought for an unattainable reconciliation, a starting over again. And one which was not just personal but a reconciliation whose success or failure carried a heavy burden. My transcribed tapes and photographs are less indexical fragments, snapshots *en route*, than set pieces, posed, self-presentations by Mother Earth and myself, not bits of 'as it was' but declarations of 'how it should be', 'how it couldn't be'.

'My' chapter then is less 'about' Mother Earth than it is part of Mother Earth, not in some modish deconstruction but as an explicit element of her cosmogony, explicitly predicted, demanded by her, an intersubjectivity. As is your reading of it. A conventional 'Russian Doll' display of the structures of her biographies (see Figure 5.1) fails to show my, your, interaction with her, our engagement, our role in the historical oppression of Black people and our potential liberation from history. If the Son, the parodic God of White Science, has produced us through our commodification of Black people, through male domination of women, through our rape of Nature,[7]

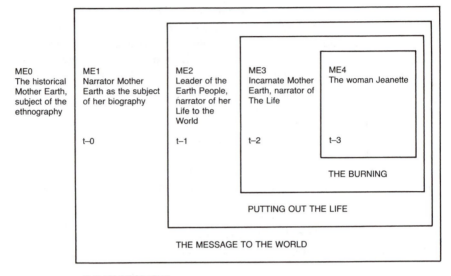

THE ETHNOGRAPHY

N.B. I have adapted the schema of Umberto Eco in *The Role of the Reader* (1979) and *A Portrait of the Elder as a Young Pliny* (1985). It is a considerable over-simplification which ignores the effects of my presence in t–0 on the recitation of the events of t–1 . . . t–3.

Figure 5.1 Putting out the life: the structures of the narratives

then the Beginning of the End entails a transformation of us all, subject and object, personal experience and academic discourse alike.

THE MEANING OF A LIFE

I do not claim to have achieved that, but I would not have wished to live with the Earth People had I not resonated with much of their world. (And still do:[8] it was only on my return to Britain that I realised the parallels with what was to become ecofeminism.) I'm not sure that they solved any particular personal dilemmas for me (the reverse), merely that they offered a reassertion of the sort of values in which I was brought up (which raises its own questions as to how reciprocal or homologous my values are to those of my parents), values which I still respect and whose absence in contemporary Britain I profoundly regret: some notion of Dissent, a sense that any authority is inevitably compromised, that the moral life is an individual one to be defined against all institutional power. Adolescent if you will. If the millennium is about anything it is about the suspension of time. Primitivist? An assumption that institutions can be most truly understood through a reconstruction of their origins? It would be naïve to imagine that, at one level, enthnography is not motivated by some personal quest for the fundamental, for ourselves (else we would be as tiresome as sociology). So yes, but at an explicit intellectual level I do not think so.

For what questions, then, may I claim Mother Earth as our answer? Her cosmogony condenses down into a single coherent schema a whole series of fragmented or sub-dominant identities which are refracted through her life – those of Black people, of women, the mad, the dispossessed – through an appropriation and reassertion of the existing local 'strategies of everyday resistance'[9] *bad talking*, *obeah*, *picong* (satire), Calypso, Carnival, *masquerade*, word play, *worthlessness*. But she is not merely seeking the heart of a heartless world, a lost pastoral innocence. More radically, she engages with their White ascription, with complementary parent–child relations, our differentiation from nature, the challenge to traditional ideas of personhood posed by biomedical technologies[10] and by nuclear war, the loss of personal relations in an increasingly commodified world: in short, a multitude of contradictions between experience and meaning.

And yet. Her valuing of Nature over human society and its scientific procedures approaches a hylotheism in which the Creatrix is identified with Her creation. Nature is an active force, form as well as content, and Her representation, Woman is both organising principle and material. Ultimately Mother Earth's eschatology is quietist for it seems that All may well return to the One, recalling perhaps Buddhism rather than the Judaeo-Christian moral and biological dynamic which continues in Rastafari and in psychiatry. The return of the Son to his Mother, of Science to Nature, although implicit, is never clearly enunciated. Perhaps it could never have been, given my own departure. An ultimate *coincidentia oppositorum* between us remained elusive. As she put it, eloquently if eliptically:

If all trees are one tree, that is the Mother.
If all men are one man, that is the Son saying he is the Father.

NOTES

1 Sheds with sliding roofs for drying cocoa.
2 Approximately half of Trinidad's population trace their descent to Indians recruited as indentured labourers in the later nineteenth and early twentieth centuries. The remainder, the Creoles, are *Africans* or *Negroes* (the sociologists' 'Afro-Caribbeans') together with some *French Creoles* ('Whites'). *Society* already refers in Trinidad English to urban life, while *Science* is the term for European (Hermetic) sorcery (Littlewood 1988).
3 On a Social Science Research Council Post-Doctoral Fellowship 1979–81. I returned again in 1988 for three months, and again in 1991.
4 On the dualism of Afro-Caribbean society and values in Trinidad, see Littlewood (1988). Briefly, an egalitarian working-class and male-orientated notion of *worthlessness* (or *nigger ways*) is contrasted with *respectability* which is associated

with church marriage, middle-class and White values, formal education, social hierarchy and chastity, and which is represented typically in women (cf. Wilson 1973).

5 Hardy (1896/1974).

6 Winstanley (1973) p. 351.

7 Science led Man to 'Nature with all her children to bind her to your service and make her your slave', to a 'truly masculine birth of time (in which Man) would conquer and subdue Nature, to shake her to her foundations.' Mother Nature was to be penetrated by Man after he had 'broken her Seale and exposed her naked to the World' (Francis Bacon and Thomas Vaughan, cited by Easlea 1980, pp. 129, 133, 247–8).

8 Our trajectories continue. For the Earth People: the death of Mother Earth in 1983, mutual recriminations and splits, a visit by me in 1988. For myself: an uneasy accommodation with academic status, clinical power and responsibility, phone calls from the Earth People, rejection by a Port of Spain publisher of our joint pamphlet *The Teachings of Mother Earth* (a transcription of the Message to the World).

9 What Schwimmer (1972) terms an 'oppositional ideology': 'inversions or reversals of putative scale values on which the members of the disadvantaged group suppose themselves to be consigned to the pole of marginality or peripherality by those in the 'centre' ... One of the potent ways in which they appear to give meaning symbolically to their communality is by reversing the polarities of the scale to make their values central' (cf. Taussig 1987). Gates (1988) takes Bakhtin's term 'double-voiced' to characterise such ludic tropes as irony, parody and antanaclasis in Afro-American English, Abrahams' (1970) 'direction by indirection' (as Hamlet put it).

10 If Mother Earth's apocalypse seems to reinvent science fiction, read the forty-year programme for transfer of human personality on to computers and our final dissolution as biological organisms as urged by Hans Moravec (1989), director of the Carnegie Mellon University's robotics centre.

REFERENCES

Abrahams, R. D. (1970) *Deep Down in the Jungle: Negro Narrative Folklore from the Streets of Philadelphia*. Chicago: Aldine.

Bakhtin, M. (1971) Discourse Typology in Prose. In L. Matejka and K. Pomorska (eds) *Readings in Russian Poetics: Formalist and Structuralist Views*. Cambridge, Mass.: MIT Press.

Easlea, B. (1980) *Witch-Hunting, Magic and the New Philosophy: An Introduction to Debates of the Scientific Revolution 1450–1750*. Sussex: Harvester.

Eco, U. (1979) *The Role of the Reader*. Bloomington, Indiana: Indiana University Press.

—— (1985) A Portrait of the Elder as a Young Pliny: How to Build Fame. In M. Blonsky (ed.) *On Signs*. Oxford: Blackwell.

Gates, H. L. (1988) *The Signifying Monkey: A Theory of Afro-American Literary Criticism*. New York: Oxford University Press.

Hardy, T. (1896) *Jude the Obscure*. London: Macmillan, 1974 edn.

Jakobson, R. (1960) Linguistics and Poetics. In T. Sebeok (ed.) *Style in Language*. New York: Wiley.

Littlewood, R. (1988) From Vice to Madness: The Semantics of Naturalistic and Personalistic Understandings in Trinidadian Local Medicine. *Social Science and Medicine*, 27: 129–48.

Lowenthal, D. (1972) *West Indian Societies*. Oxford: Oxford University Press.

Moravec, H. (1989) *Mind Children: The Future of Robot and Human Intelligence*. Cambridge, Mass.: Harvard University Press.

Perec, G. (1989) *W or The Memory of Childhood*. London: Collins Harvill.

Pratt, M. L. (1986) Fieldwork in Common Places. In J. Clifford and G. E. Marcus (eds) *Writing Culture: The Poetics and Politics of Ethnography*. Berkeley, Calif.: California University Press.

Schwimmer, E. (1972) Symbolic Competition. *Anthropologica*, **14**, 117–25.

Shirokogoroff, S. M. (1915) *Psychometric Complex of the Tungus*. London: Kegan Paul, Trench and Trubner.

Taussig, M. (1987) *Shamanism, Colonialism and the Wild Man: A Study in Terror and Healing*. Chicago: University of Chicago Press.

The Bomb (1982) Naked British Professor Lived in Trinidad Bush, Port of Spain, 15 January.

The People (1981) Earth People Play Host to English Psychiatrist, Port of Spain, December.

Trinidad Guardian (1982) Nuisance From the Earth People, leading article, Port of Spain, 9 January.

Turner, V. W. (1986) Dewey, Dilthey and Drama: An Essay in the Anthropology of Experience. In V. W. Turner and E. M. Bruner (eds) *The Anthropology of Experience*. Urbana, Illinois: University of Illinois Press.

Wilson, P. J. (1973) *Crab Antics: The Social Anthropology of English-Speaking Negro Societies of the Caribbean*. New Haven, Conn.: Yale University Press.

Winstanley, G. (1973) *The Law of Freedom and Other Writings*, (ed. C. Hill). Harmondsworth: Penguin.

Chapter 6

Racism, terror and the production of Australian auto/biographies

Julie Marcus

In this chapter I argue that the state exercises power to produce both Aboriginal and anthropological selves and the texts through which each shall be known. Bringing this power and violence into view indicates its scale and intent. Moreover, I believe that the failure to explore the racist nature of the Australian state in most Aboriginal ethnography derives from that state power.

The forces through which Aboriginal selves are produced in Australia are such that the writing of ethnography, whether traditional or experimental, becomes problematic. The gaze of the state (Foucault 1977) continues its surveillance, and violence on the 'frontier' remains pervasive. The absence of any discussion of power from Australian ethnographies is central to its continued deployment. The politics of ethnographic texts need not be significantly altered by explorations of the interaction of the anthropological self with the production of that text, that is, by focusing on auto/biographies alone. An examination of the factors controlling the production of ethnographic texts is also required.

The advantages of internal textual analysis and the insights of literary criticism can only be retained by a critical analysis of the ways in which the state produces the chaos, disorganisation and disordered sexuality of the dominated, racialised others who are scrutinised through ethnography. Indeed, the politics of a text can only be determined by taking the conditions of production into account, whether in producing a text or in reading and deconstructing it. The distinction I draw here – that between the internal and external politics of a text – is one that, in other contexts, would be denied. Textual politics themselves are the product of both sets of factors and are often read in this way. The absence, however, of an account of the forces governing the production of texts from some aspects of postmodern anthropology, provides for a de-politicised ethnography rather than one which is politically aware and critical (Marcus 1990).

BIOGRAPHY AND POLITICS

The narrative knowledges of biography and autobiography are held to belong not with science and its 'truths', but with non-science and its 'fictions'. In the case of biography-writing, a conflict arises because the biographer must blur the distinction between the cold, scientific realism of 'facts' and the warm, evocative reason demanded by a literary genre and its market. This perceived clash of genres is found also in anthropological autobiography – between the scientific texts of ethnography and the often charming autobiographical accounts which form their 'other halves' (Caplan 1988). The breakdown of the distinction between the two genres, profoundly unsettling for some anthropologists and a relief to others, has again focused anthropological attention on to the place of the writer within the text, and on to both the biographical and autobiographical elements of the ethnographic text. This section of my chapter addresses the relation of the structures of auto/biographical texts, and the selves constituted through them, to the racist conditions of the productions of these texts.

Let me begin with an outline of the life of a white woman who once aimed to become an anthropologist. Olive Muriel Pink (1884–1975) was born in Hobart, Tasmania. Her imperial values, her concepts of moral correctness and her personal dignity carried her through many tribulations. Those values rendered her increasingly eccentric in the eyes of a newer world. When she died in Alice Springs in 1975, local journalists recorded the apocryphal tales of her eccentricity – of her long, white Edwardian dresses, worn, regardless of the heat, with high collar, hat and white gloves; of her love long-lost on the slopes of Gallipoli; of her clashes with the officers of the government of the day, clashes which led to tales of men crawling along the floors of their offices rather than admit that they were 'in' when she called; and of her long treks through the desert, reputedly on foot and carrying only a large watermelon under one arm. She died in near poverty, having lived over twenty years in a tin 'hut' on the outskirts of the town with little in the way of material comforts.[1]

Unlike many of her contemporaries, Olive Pink had never been afraid of the desert, nor did she fear Aboriginal Australians. All her life she sought to alleviate the conditions of poverty and hardship under which they lived. Her desire to gather authentic information led her to leave the safety of the city and a secure job to travel alone through Australia's arid and remote regions. What she saw there led her to the study of anthropology, resignation from her government job and steady income, and research among the Warlpri and Arrernte people who live to the north-west of Alice Springs. In her forties, she studied anthropology at the University of Sydney and found it both exciting and depressing. Her aim was to get into the field before the 'traditional Aboriginal' finally disappeared, and to collect the scientific information she thought would assist in promoting the well-being of Aboriginal Australians. Her major fieldwork was carried out during the 1930s. At the age of forty-nine, with no previous experience, she climbed on to a camel and set out on a tour of ritual sites. Despite her success in fieldwork, she never completed her thesis and was forgotten as an anthropologist. On her 1988 Australian bicentennial plaque in Darwin's city park, she is memorialised as 'Olive Pink – eccentric'.

How has an anthropologist who carried out substantial research in central Australia, with publications in an academic journal (Pink 1933, 1936), been lost from history? Was Olive Pink simply too eccentric to succeed, even within a profession which has always extended a warm welcome to eccentrics? Or was it, rather, that her 'eccentricity' derived from her vigourous and unrelenting politics against racism? Her politics created problems, both in central Australia and in the universities, which caused her to be labelled as eccentric in order that she could be legitimately excluded. Her anti-racist activities were perceived by anthropologists as destroying the amicable relations with locals on which field research in central Australia depended, and as bringing a 'scientific', hence 'non-political', anthropology into disrepute.[2] Her eccentricity derived also from her more personal, narrative style of writing, one less recognisably scientific. The intersection of her politics with the non-conforming style of her scientific ethnography produced texts on Aboriginal religion that lay outside the framework then acceptable.

To expose the relations of power between settler[3] and Aboriginal Australians in central Australia was in itself a radical and unwelcome act. Conservative in her morality, committed to a view of social justice, an Edwardian to the end in a world that had moved on, she was an ambiguous and restless figure. Her experience with settlers and Aboriginals in central Australia was transformative. Far from being feminist in her original ideals and opinions, her encounters with the realities of racism and with the gendered nature of university life convinced her that Aboriginal well-being was being actively sacrificed to the needs of the male-controlled pastoral and mining industries of central Australia.

In wanting to preserve Aboriginal culture and its supporting economy from destruction, in seeing settler society as polluting to the primordial purity of Aboriginal life and mores, and in her attitudes to the children of settler men and Aboriginal women, Olive Pink was very much of her time and far from revolutionary. Her views, however, contrasted with those of many of her colleagues on critical points. Partly as a result of her attempts to secure a large area of land for the Warlpri, she sought to have administrators of all kinds – missionaries, police and government officials – entirely excluded from the reserves. Missionaries she considered to be great destroyers of Aboriginal culture. She fought to remove Aboriginal Australians from the official supervision under which they were held, to give them spaces of their own. In order to protect Aboriginal women from sexual exploitation and to prevent the reduction of the Aboriginal population through the introduction of sexually transmitted and contagious diseases, she sought the exclusion of all settler males from the reserves.

After several years of struggle with academics and politicians, Olive Pink addressed the Science Congress in Melbourne. While the text of her speech has never been published, an abstract appeared in *Oceania* (1936, **2**(1): 20). Entitled 'Camouflage', her paper reflects despair and frustration in her diagnosis of where the real difficulties for Aborigines lay. She laid the blame on male settlers and male anthropologists. She would have nothing to do with causal psychological explanations. She spoke of a 'clash' of cultures, not just of the neutralised 'culture contact' used by her peers; of a male 'regime' as a structured system of power from which women and Aborigines were excluded; of the way the language of experts 'camouflages' the causes of the rapid decline in Aboriginal numbers. She rejected the contemporary eugenics notion of 'race suicide'.

Olive Pink argued that the constant supervision of every facet of everyday Aboriginal life created the chaos which was central to the representation of dominated populations as primordial problem-children, moral failures in need of even more 'help'. Few colleagues understood her. The difference in perception arose from the impact of personal politics in the creation of anthropological knowledge. Olive Pink saw the results of racial domination and she sought to place her professional work as an anthropologist at the service of the Aboriginal Australians. Holding views incompatible with the anthropology of her time and place, she eventually put aside the scientific study of Aboriginal society in which she had placed such hope and went to live alone in Alice Springs.

AUTO/BIOGRAPHIES

Working in central Australia,[4] I too became increasingly concerned with the ways in which anthropological texts and knowledge reproduce, rather than undermine, structures and practices of racism and sexism (Marcus 1988). Like Olive Pink, I came to see the need to remove Aboriginal Australians from the continuing glare of the settler eye, and to see this as a prerequisite for reducing the atrocities committed against them. But unlike her, I have a newer language in which to describe the conditions which she could only refer to as 'culture clash' and 'camouflage'. I have available the concept of a 'culture of terror' (Taussig 1984) through which relations of domination are deployed into the culture and daily life of the other, dominated, group. And unlike her, I have the recent literary and feminist critiques of ethnographic writing which have drawn attention to the place of selves in the construction of texts about dominated 'others'. I have a language of criticism which speaks of voices, positions, silencing and erasure in ways which are very different from the meanings of those terms in the past.

This new language allows me to suggest a new 'reading' of Olive Pink. Her voice was erased because she produced her scientific anthropology out of a personal politics of active anti-racism. Her eccentricity was manu-factured from the surveillance to which she was subjected; it was legitimated through the charge that her anthropology was not anthropology, but welfare work or politics. In the end, she lived out their fantasies of her self.

The ways in which the anthropologists of the 1930s constructed Olive Pink as eccentric can now be exposed. Her voice can be written back into history, her eccentricity deconstructed. More importantly, recent theoretical developments give her the audience previously denied her. Her voice can now be heard. The obliteration of voice, however, is only one aspect of the problem; the other is with *listening*. The question is how anthropologists deal with the problems of voicing and of listening when the gaze of the state is so pervasive.

Recently these problems have been taken up within anthropology by the critical stances proposed by versions of postmodernism. But they do not address the scale of the problem of racism for Australian anthropology, and the radicalising and silencing possibilities within the encounter. Nor do they examine the specific ways in which a state produces both the texts of a dominated other and the listening positions from which they can be heard or read. These points can be illuminated by asking what so shocked Olive Pink that it determined the direction of the rest of her life. The answer is that she went to court in Darwin, where Aborigines were being prosecuted by settlers. She was horrified at what she saw. Later, carrying out her anthropological research in central Australia, she again saw the problems created for Aborigines by settler 'justice'. She tried to get several cases investigated more fully, and to have the increasing number of charges of 'resisting arrest' examined.

Fifty years later, the operation of the judicial system against Aboriginal Australians still raises serious concern and is again being investigated. Although the actual scale of violence against Aboriginal Australians is probably not known to the general public and is constantly denied, it has never really been hidden. Violence is very much a feature of everyday life for Aborigines, as are the attitudes that sustain it. Violence against Aboriginal individuals is still rarely punished; this, too, is well documented and well known.

The long history of numerous deaths of Aboriginals while in custody indicates the scale involved. Some Aborigines appear to have been murdered; some seem to have been mistreated and denied suitable medical, pharmaceutical or nursing care. Others undoubtedly commit suicide, even though a number of murders are also represented this way. In Marcus (1989) I gave an example of such an allegation, one in which the ramifications of the judicial system for the production of texts and selves became evident.

The embeddedness of Australian Aborigines in a culture of racist terror differs from that described by Taussig (1984) of Indians in Colombia in degree rather than in kind. The 'compliance' of victim and violator in the production of public truths, texts and selves, is also evident. This is a harsh diagnosis, one that many would at once reject as exaggeration. I argue, however, that the terror of direct physical violence produces the chaos that justifies the need for constant supervision and the withholding of basic rights from which Aboriginal Australians are excluded. Aboriginals seen as exemplars of chaos provide the disorderly 'other' against which settler Australians define themselves as civilised, rational, orderly and white. It is as if the limits of the gaze of the state are marked out in physical violence; as if the gaze itself can be extended through violence into the crevices of society that would otherwise be closed to it. This process needs to be recognised and labelled more accurately within anthropological discourse. There is a need to get away from language which sanitises the horror of the practices of racism.

The numerous deaths of Aboriginals in custody[5] can only be explained by taking into account the surveillance of Aboriginal people and the violence against them. They are only too aware of what faces them inside and outside the prisons. They are aware of the fantasies in which they are obliged to participate, of the destruction and reconstituting of the self which those processes imply. Some can no longer face the cyclical violence. The impossibility of seeing a way out of it leads to suicide for those who survive the beatings, whether they are inside the prisons or out.

The surveillance, however, is forever incomplete. No matter how much detail is provided, no matter how strictly interpretations are created through the media, judicial and ethnographic texts, the Aboriginal selves produced within these texts are essentially false. The reality of the other culture constantly slips away, precisely because it is defined as other. The powerful forces of the state do not only produce Aboriginal Australians, they produce anthropologists and their scientific anthropological texts as well. The reality of racism is almost entirely obliterated from the traditional ethnography of Aboriginal Australians,[6] and the anthropological silence on this matter is disturbing.

WRITING ABOUT AN OTHER

In Australia, the production of Aboriginal culture and selves, questions of auto/biographies, and questions concerning the role of anthropologists in the processes by which those texts are produced, are quite literally matters of life and death. Autobiographies are beginning to appear, works by Aboriginal Australians who are literate in English. Sally Morgan's *My Place* (1987) and Ruby Langford's *Don't Take Your Love to Town* (1988) were immediate best-sellers and this genre, which has much in common with recent Black writing in America, will continue to grow. Some Aboriginal Australians have now found their own voice, their own texts and their audience.

Other Aboriginal Australians, however, remain without writing in a textual world and rely for a voice, therefore, on mediation. In central Australia the possibility of an unmediated representation of Aboriginal culture seems rarely to exist, and the racist politics of the centre ensure that information about Aboriginal Australian individuals is limited. The ethnographer feels the need to represent those lives which would otherwise have no voice at all. The apparent need for mediation is itself a product of the complex relations of power between anthropologists and Aboriginal Australians. While some anthropologists have used their knowledge and efforts to assist Aborigines in their claims for land rights, nothing suggests that more information about Aboriginal society collected by anthropologists will advance the Aboriginal cause.[7] On the contrary, the ever-growing mountain of ethnographic 'facts' is often utilised against the interests of Aborigines.

The problem is not one of writing Aboriginals into ethnographic texts in some more cooperative way, nor is it one of writing for an other, even though both these matters are relevant. Rather, it is a matter of writing power back into our texts, of placing ourselves within those relations of power, and exposing the ways in which Aboriginal lives and culture are being violated. Aboriginal Australians, like Morgan (1987) and Langford (1988), who have gained a voice and a place in mainstream literary production, are very clear on the activity of the state in their lives, and it is their accounts of their struggles against it which make such poignant reading.

My choice has been to write about racism rather than about Aboriginal society and culture. Because the interpretation of the detail cannot be controlled by the writer, the anthropologist retains the position of intermediary and structurer, and also of racial dominance. The question is how that position is to be used. It is not only the ethnographer *in* the text that is of political importance, but the ethnographer as *producer* of text and as *analyst* of the conditions of textual production that requires exposition. This aim, derived from my 'reading' of the lives of both Olive Pink and (below) Louisa Montgomery, an Aboriginal woman of Alice Springs, and my framing of those lives within a gendered and racist cultural context, led to my use of the notion of a 'culture of terror'.

THE IMPOSSIBLE TEXT

The sketch that follows is not a biography, for the politics of knowledge in central Australia precludes its possibility. Pieced together from fragmentary notes, diaries and remembrances, the information I give here came from Louisa personally. Because some of it was given to me bit by bit, as part of the traffic in information which circulates within the town, it is what she wanted me to know and think. Some information was given in exchange for services, and to the extent that differing power relations structured feelings and actions between us, accuracy cannot be guaranteed. Other information comes from incidents in which I was both observer and participant. Some of these incidents were too painful to write down at the time and could only be dealt with later. The effects of framing and selection are necessarily severe.

Louisa Montgomery was born in about 1947. Her conception site is north of Alice Springs. Both her conception story and her place of birth are important in determining her status as an owner of town land. Her family moved into the Aboriginal camp near what is now called the Old Telegraph Station, then known as 'Bungalow'. Her first education came under the notoriously strict regime maintained at the Bungalow school. She was a bright and intelligent child, and speaks of her early desire to learn to read, a desire that saw her collecting old labels and pieces of newspaper blowing about the creek bed in order to have something to read.

While still young, she and her family were loaded on to trucks and forcibly transferred from Bungalow to the new Santa Theresa mission located about eighty miles south of Alice Springs. Her family also spent some time at the Aboriginal Mission at Arltunga, set up during the Second World War at an old gold-mining settlement (where the water supply came to have a reputation for carrying with it the seeds of death).

Louisa did well at school; a docile student, during adolescence she thought of becoming a nun. Perhaps because of these personal qualities, Louisa and other young women were sent to Darwin for training as teaching assistants. There were occasional visits from the young men of Santa Theresa; on her return Louisa married, and shortly afterwards her first child was born. The children then arrived regularly until there were seven in all. Louisa and her extended family lived mainly in one or other of the town camps, a peripatetic life based for a while in a tent erected just outside the town on the land that several families were trying to lease. By 1982, Louisa's marriage had disintegrated in a cloud of physical violence and drinking. The batterings of those years have left their scars. Her sister has suffered similarly, and their invisible wounds produce continuing misfortune.

In the 1970s, many of Louisa's family became involved in the politics of land claims. During those years Aborigines set up self-help organisations to challenge settler rights and usages of town land. There was a series of political engagements with the Alice Springs Town Council, strong and bitter campaigns for residential land and sacred sites that could last as long as eight or ten years. Louisa was on several committees set up by the Aboriginal organisations, work which was not paid. In local politics she was constantly called upon, by settler bureaucrats and Aboriginals alike, for information and advice. In 1980, Louisa and many of her family were active in the campaign to prevent important sacred sites in the creek bed from being submerged under a recreational lake. When work started on compiling an Arrernte dictionary, because of her intelligence and fluency in English and Arrernte, Louisa was brought in as a translator. She did well and was asked to undertake specialised training in interpreting. As well as working on the dictionary project, she worked at the Aboriginal primary school, and gave occasional Arrernte lessons to settler Australians in the town. But paid work formed only a part of her daily activities. She, and other members of her family, were called upon to be present at grand events organised by the town that required an Aboriginal presence – like the visit of the Pope, for example.

Her life still strikes me as unbearably responsible, despite the presence of the markers of irresponsibility which settlers place upon it by pointing to her homelessness, drinking and untrammelled behaviour. The political struggles took a severe toll. The consensus sought by Aboriginal organisa-tions required regular meetings and consultations – meetings about school-ing, educational policies and health, sacred sites, the media, recreation facilities and racism. The work of most of the non-Aboriginal organisations also proceeded through consultation – there were therefore meetings about roads, gas pipelines, parks, the trees in the creek bed and telephone lines. The degree of participation in the processes of daily living and daily politics that was required of Louisa and others like her, far exceeds anything known by settler inhabitants in Alice Springs or elsewhere. These demands added substantially to the level of stress with which she and her family lived. If they refused to attend meetings, they risked being labelled as irresponsible; if they did participate, the time, tensions and problems intensified frustra-tion and stress. Political participation is important, too, because of the way in which it constitutes an enmeshment of individual and family with the state.

All this carries a price. In a campaign to save a sacred site from development, for example, Louisa lost her brother and baby son in an accident related to her participation. In addition, disagreements within the Aboriginal community (and naturally, in a situation of oppression and struggle there are many) can lead to protracted personal and political difficulties. During claims to unused land within the town boundaries, Louisa and her family were under constant threat of dispossession and arrest for trespass. Disagreements over the use of a sacred site as the location for an Aboriginal social club, for example, led to some of the younger women being threatened by equally frustrated and desperate men.

In 1984, Louisa managed to rent a house in the town, and her family and relatives moved out of the tent. With her moved her own children, her mother's brother, three children of a divorced sister, and two or three teenaged boys. Sometimes two or more of her brothers also camped there, sometimes a lover. From the tent, she took some bedding and some cooking utensils. A fridge and a washing machine were provided on credit. Various organisations and friends contributed either sheets or cloth to cover the 'picture' windows, a table and chairs, a sofa, and assorted bits and pieces. The lack of furniture and basic household equipment, the stress on the meagre facilities available, and the attractions of the house for homeless friends and relatives led to the rapid collapse of the household. A visit from the Housing Commission resulted in a seven-day ultimatum – clean up or clear out. Various friends moved in to help, but rent could not be paid, repairs could not take place, and in a short time, all Louisa's dependents were homeless again. The anxiety created by such situations is, again, beyond the comprehension as well as the experience of most settler families.

The campaign for living space for her family and relatives focused on obtaining a formal lease on the land just beyond the town boundaries on which they were squatting. The claim was under way for over ten years; each time Louisa and the other families satisfied the official criteria for a lease, those criteria were changed. The Town Council sought to allocate the land to a caravan/camping park for tourists, rather than to homeless Aboriginal people. Whereas water, electricity and telephone could be taken to the site if it were to be 'developed' as a tourist area, the cost of taking those facilities to an Aboriginal settlement was held to be prohibitive, despite the fact that town residents living beyond this site were already serviced.

These are the summary public details of Louisa's life. My reading of central Australian politics has already revealed huge gaps in her history and biography. Certainly there is nothing here to indicate the humour, defiance, affection, manipulativeness and resilience with which she teeters along a narrow path, one from which she could at any moment topple either into self-destruction or revolt. Let me now turn to the way in which Louisa and I worked together in a constrained, racialised and politicised environment which made a relation of close friendship almost impossible.

AUTO/BIOGRAPHY AND ANTHROPOLOGIST

I was fortunate, I think, in meeting Louisa early in my work, and in establishing an immediate personal rapport with her. That rapport was based on mutual recognition of shared interests which meant that the informant-researcher relation was going to be one of constant re-negotiation, anger, suspicion and deep distrust. It also meant that that the researcher was to become, like the informant, a resource-person to be manipulated, a sign of value and a source of *manna* in which every fragment of information was going to cost dearly in both money and personal terms. If I wanted to have a well-placed, canny, politicised, knowledgeable Aboriginal 'friend', I was going to have to pay for it. Liking one another was perhaps a prerequisite, but it had nothing to do with our 'relationship', it was simply the condition which made us ripe for mutual exploitation. I had to try to relinquish the weaponry of cultural and race capital, to leave myself unarmed, naked and exposed.

In no other relationship is it thought wise to leave one's self, one's pocket and one's race, so unprotected, and it is no more wise to do so in Alice Springs than it is anywhere else. In its distance from the relations of anthropologist and informant found within the literature, my relationship with Louisa was profoundly and constantly worrying, especially as, unlike Marjorie Shostak (1981: 30–42) I quickly gave up all hope of ever being able to negotiate what I regarded as a genuine 'friendship' of any kind. Any understanding was going to be entirely one-sided, and it was not going to be done by her. Her understanding was already complete. She had had years of experience in dealing with anthropologists, as she had also dealt successfully with nuns, priests, doctors, bureaucrats, white advisers of all varieties and the police. She knew not only what I wanted (and said so), but what elements of it I absolutely had to get; she understood about guilt and she understood about racism. What I think she knew, and what I at first rejected, was that the structures of racism were all-encompassing, all-determining, and in the end, all-ruining. What I had to learn was that there was no outside position from which to observe, and that giving up my personal power was an exercise of self-delusion that was of no use to anybody.

When we were both drunk, she would sit down and talk to me 'from the heart'. Her confidences were matched by mine, and in this, I felt the poverty of the exchange badly. My lacklustre emotional and political life was, I think, as amazing to her as her active and varied sexual and personal life was to me. 'There must be something more', she used to say, 'tell me some more', until in desperation I told stories of a middle-class suburban childhood and its delinquencies, stories sufficiently exotic to be unexpected enough, thanks to a very unruly childhood, to hold her interest. In retrospect, it was the absence of my punishment by the police that struck her as fantastic.

In these discussions, her affirmations of the value of her Aboriginal life and her rejection of material comforts were heart-wrenching. 'They say', she said on several occasions, 'that they don't know how we can bear it. But we *like* it like this. This is *our* way, our Aboriginal way, and we're alright, we like it. I don't like those women coming up here, those social workers, and saying, "I don't know how you can bear it". They don't know anything about us.' From time to time, snippets of information were passed around in my presence, bits and pieces which I probably failed to integrate in the way that was intended. And on drinking days, in our sessions in the creek bed or our tours around the town, I was shown sacred trees, phallic symbols, told tales of magic and sorcery, and all the time I wondered whether these were Louisa's inventions, dreamt up on the spur of the moment in order to have something to give. Was this the stuff of ethnography?

Then I witnessed an important event in Louisa's life. It was a hot day and several of us had been drinking behind the public toilets near a supermarket. Louisa and her friend, the new 'bush wife' of Louisa's nephew, sat quietly, reading popular romances, and chatting idly. I sat and fiddled disconsolately, wondering what on earth I was doing there, consoling myself with can after can of warmish beer that tasted worse as the day progressed. The police had cruised by, looking; I had lost my nerve, and so we had moved on. At the end of the day, I took the new 'bride' back to her lover who was camped eighty miles out of town, some hour up the track. Rather than stay in camp with her family, Louisa decided to return to town with me.

Next day, Louisa and I set off in high spirits to collect her mother from the camp. As we drove along the familiar road to the north, she sang one of the songs of her country. At the turn-off to the camp, unexpectedly, she told me to stop. Her eldest son came over and whispered to her. In the night, the young bride had been killed; stabbed deep in the upper thigh by her new 'husband', her life had poured away from her. A trivial domestic altercation had erupted into fury. Years of frustration poured out into violence and death.

As we drove sadly towards the camp, Louisa wailed, lamented and hurled abuse at her nephew's name. The scene at the camp was desolate. Everyone was subdued, weeping, and several were covered in ashes. Recriminations, hurled more or less at random, were half-heartedly refuted. Louisa furiously demanded to know why they had not stopped him. There was no answer. She stormed through the camp, hurling abuse in Arrernte and English, collecting her few things, wailing loudly. Her parents sat on the ground and pleaded with her. Louisa's children gathered up their belongings, threw them into the back of the truck, and sat glumly inside. A young cousin who wanted to come with us was refused permission. The killing had divided the family severely, and although the breach would heal, the immediate impact was saddening. The adults waited for the police. The murderer had taken to the bush, but would be picked up easily enough later – he had no bush skills and would be starved out.

The miserable journey back to town was punctuated by Louisa's laments and curses. In her distress, and knowing well what was still to come, she tore up her books, threw a good deal of money out the window of the car, and gave some to me, until her purse was empty. I promised to burn all photographs of the dead woman. In the town, the relatives of the dead girl were already threatening to retaliate. Supernatural sanctions were in the air. There was a good deal of fear, a good deal of bravado, and a good deal of desperation on both sides. No one wants a feud, but the parents of a girl not yet twenty years old were deeply distressed.

Before the funeral at the Catholic church, Louisa and her brothers went up to the camp of the dead girl's family, there to take their punishment. Louisa arrived at the church badly beaten and bruised; her brothers, also beaten, were too frightened to attend. The priest's sermon, aimed at heading off further trouble and at reasserting the supremacy of Christ over 'evil spirits', seemed shockingly irrelevant to the emotions fluttering through the congregation. As he spoke, a low moan wafted through the church, bearing on it the grief and despair of all concerned. At the graveside, the priest spoke again of forgiveness and the love of Christ; the older women wailed and gashed their heads with stones and wooden clubs. The men stood by, muttering sullenly. With the coffin in the grave, we all filed past, throwing a handful of dust on to the coffin, and left. As we reached the cars, fighting broke out among the women. Louisa was abused and called to account, and several large women closed in on her. Cooler heads restrained those not directly involved and tried to get everyone into the cars. I shepherded the children toward our minibus, and helped Louisa's old parents inside, well out of the way. As I turned back to the fighting, I saw a woman run up behind Louisa, club held high, ready to strike. Despite myself, I screamed a warning. Fortunately it was lost in the tumult, and Louisa received only a blow on the back of the skull. Had she turned around to answer my call, the club would have hit her squarely between the eyes. My lesson was severe.

Had this been the end of the matter, things would not have been so bad. But the recriminations and hostility remained, and the mood in the town was uncertain for many months. The campsite was pulled down – no one can live on the site of a death and certainly not such a violent one – and the family was lodged in several of the town hostels. At the hostels alcohol is forbidden, and people sleep one family to each room. Meals are provided, there are washing and shower facilities, but they are crowded and of course, one is again under supervision, even if it is Aboriginal supervision.

The constant supervision of Aboriginal Australians and their desperate attempts to get out of the glare of the official spotlight struck me as one of the most significant factors in Louisa's life. It was this experience with state surveillance that first alerted me to the politics of Olive Pink and her irascible letters. That, and the intensive engagement with the tentacles of a state which was constantly urging self-help and welfare policies which required ever more Aboriginal participation. Louisa, like many Aboriginals, was trapped in a fruitless struggle for what was given to settler Australians by birthright. Efforts to 'improve' Aboriginal welfare all seemed to turn into new sites of struggle. Yet Aboriginal people cannot refuse to play their parts, for to do so would remove the last vestige of hope. The shocking thing is that they have not given up hope and that from somewhere comes the strength to fight again.

In Louisa's case, her claim for living space within the town had to be set out in terms of both Council regulations and Aboriginal, but unrecognised, rights. These claims rendered her ever more visible, more likely to end up back under supervision. The frustrations that result from these structural dilemmas and impossibilities, from enforced choices, direct interference and loss of privacy, produce the symptoms of chaos which justify further state supervision.

The impoverished and dominated groups of any society are constantly portrayed as being in disarray and disorderly. In the Australian case, as in comparable nations, the major indices of disarray and moral turpitude are drunkenness and sexual disorderliness, the combination leading to the 'promiscuity' and 'laziness' that characterise their kind. The factors I saw worked out through Louisa's life were the structural factors of domination being refracted through an individual in such a way that they were sometimes experienced as personal characteristics. But more importantly, her life showed the ways in which the structures of racism and sexism worked through an individual to mystify for settler Australians the sources of Aboriginal oppression and to create the cultural characteristics that could be used in the reproduction of the texts, images and structures of race which lie at the heart of Australian culture. Louisa often drank; she gambled with her pension and her wages, and her engaging personality ensured a constant stream of male admirers. These indices of moral fallibility are used by the state to condemn a life which would, on any other measure, be one of consistent public responsibility. Louisa was not, of course, mystified by the refraction of racism through her being, a refraction which bent her social responsibility into moral degeneracy and criminality, she was simply the more conscious of its terror.

This account of Louisa, written to show the ways in which anthropologists produce even the most intimate of texts about Aboriginal Australians, was, I thought unpublishable. After she and her children read it and corrected some of the details, however, they decided to take *another* risk and to hope that the political benefits of publication overseas would outweigh the disadvantages likely to accrue at home.

RACISM, TERROR AND AUTO/BIOGRAPHIES

It was for women like Louisa Montgomery that Olive Pink fought, and for the sake of Aboriginal Australians that she gave up the science of anthropology that she loved. Just as my understanding of Olive Pink's life depends on that of Louisa Montgomery, so it depends on my own. In my analysis of Olive Pink's life and politics, there is much that draws upon my own experience of race and gender, both in central Australia and in the universities. The similarities bridge the fifty years that separated our ventures into anthropology. My time in Alice Springs showed me the dimensions of that same system, its continuing repressive surveillance and harsh violence. Almost all the members of Louisa's family had had brushes with the law. I came to know many people with family members imprisoned and many women, men and children who had been beaten, harassed, pushed and shoved, and punched or raped[8] by police and by other men in the town. Those assaults were never punished. The police presence, although it is only one aspect of the supervision they lived under, had a constancy that is unknown in those safer havens of middle-class settler Australia.

My aim is not only to write-in Louisa Montgomery and Olive Pink to the narratives from which they have been excluded, but to show the conditions of power within which their texts are produced and to make their voices comprehensible in a way in which they were not before. It is essential to look behind Louisa's 'laziness' and 'drunkenness', to look behind Olive Pink's 'eccentricities' and 'madness' to see what these labels referred to. In Australia, as in other colonising states, those who challenge the interpretations of those fundamental racist narratives of the chaotic 'other' will be targetted, erased, obliterated.

Aboriginal voices speak, but they too, are rarely heard. There are still many who must speak through ethnography and must therefore exist only as representations of themselves over which they have no control. It is therefore important not to abdicate the anthropological task of analysis. The only possible justification for the production of images and representations of other cultures and peoples lies in the attempt to produce some form of cultural critique. I have tried here to expose the ways in which narratives, texts, selves and others are produced and reproduced through the politics of domination, one to which race and gender remain central.

NOTES

1 See Marcus (1987).
2 The Australian National Research Council (ANRC) Papers, National Library of Australia, are relevant.
3 In order to avoid the categories of skin colour, I use the terms 'settler' and 'Aboriginal' as adjectives wherever possible.
4 For background, see Gorey (1952), and Blackwell and Lockwood (1965).
5 In 1988 a Royal Commission headed by Muirhead, who resigned after nineteen months, was set up to investigate Aboriginal deaths in custody. Although its hearings have finished, its report had not been issued before this book went to press.
6 McKnight (1990: 50) relates, for example, how Radcliffe-Brown apparently stayed longer than any other place at Dorre and Bernier, two islands on the north-west coast of Western Australia, but never described the nightmarish scene where Aborigines suffering from a variety of contagious diseases had been chained together and forcibly sent, the women to one island and the men to the other. A recent attempt to deal with this absence in anthropological studies is Cowlishaw's (1988) account of racism in a rural town.
7 In his survey of the place of Aborigines in anthropological literature, McKnight (1990: 43) writes, 'Our knowledge about these subjects has not, unfortunately, been particularly beneficial to the Aborigines.' He concludes that anthropologists have concentrated their research on the traditional patterns of Aboriginal life, leaving it to a political scientist to write about the destruction of Aboriginal society.
8 The Alice Springs businessman who had recently chained an Aboriginal woman so tightly that her genital area was badly crushed was charged by police but defended on the basis of his previous good behaviour. This incident was widely reported in the newspapers.

REFERENCES

Blackwell, D. and Lockwood, D. (1965) *Alice on the Line*. Adelaide: Rigby.

Caplan, P. (1988) Engendering Knowledge: The Politics of Ethnography. *Anthropology Today* **4**(5): 8–12; **4**(6): 14–17.

Cowlishaw, G. (1987) Colour, Culture and the Aboriginalists. *Man* **22**: 221–37.

—— (1988) *Black, White or Brindle*. Melbourne: Cambridge University Press.

Foucault, M. (1977) *Discipline and Punish*. Harmondsworth: Penguin Books.

Gorey, N. (1952) *The Alice*. Adelaide: Country Women's Association of South Australia.

Langford, R. (1988) *Don't Take Your Love to Town*. Melbourne: Penguin.

McKnight, D. (1990) The Australian Aborigines in Anthropology. In R. Fardon (ed.) *Localising Strategies: Regional Traditions of Ethnographic Writing*. Edinburgh: Scottish Academic Press; Washington: Smithsonian Institution Press.

Marcus, J. (1987) Olive Pink and the Encounter with the Academy. *Mankind* **17**(3): 185–98.

—— (1988) The Journey Out to the Centre. The Cultural Appropriation of Aboriginal Identity. In A. Rutherford (ed.) *Aborigines Today*. Copenhagen: Dangaru Press.

—— (1989) Gender, Politics and the Production of Text in Central Australia. Paper presented at ASA Conference, York.

—— (1990) Post-modernism, Anthropology and Australian Culture. In J. Marcus (ed.) *Writing Australian Culture*. Special edition of *Social Analysis*, Adelaide.

Morgan, S. (1987) *My Place*. Perth: Fremantle Arts Centre Press.

Pink, O. (1933) Spirit Ancestors in a Northern Aranda Horde Country. *Oceania* **4**(2): 176–86. Reprinted in *Bulletin of the Olive Pink Society* (1989) **1**(1): 5–10.

—— (1936) The Landowners in Northern Division of the Aranda Tribe, Central Australia. *Oceania* **2**(2): 10–24.

Shostak, M. (1981) *Nisa: The Life and Words of a !Kung Woman*. London: Allen Lane.

Taussig, M. (1984) Culture of Terror – Space of Death. Roger Casement's Putumayo Report and the Explanation of Torture. *Comparative Studies in Society and History* **26**(3): 467–97.

Chapter 7

Writing ethnography
State of the art

Kirsten Hastrup

The conjuncture between anthropology and autobiography is manifest in ethnographic texts. Ethnography itself implies writing and the authorial status of the ethnographer has been brought into focus (e.g. Clifford and Marcus 1986; Geertz 1988).

In this paper my aim is to address the problem of how to write ethnography – and why.[1] Ultimately these two questions must be answered simultaneously. As Barthes has it about the author:

> the author is a man who radically absorbs the world's *why* in a *how to write*. And the miracle, so to speak, is that this narcissistic activity has always provoked an interrogation of the world: by enclosing himself in the *how to write*, the author ultimately discovers the open question par excellence: why the world? (Barthes 1982: 187)

Addressing the question of how to write ethnography is not solely a matter of experimentation with style, it is also a rediscovery of the world. A truly postmodern anthropology denies the presupposition of the independence of form and content (Tyler 1987: 198).

There are dangers, therefore, in discussing the writing of ethnography. Seeing anthropology as essentially a literary vocation implies a risk of aestheticism (Geertz 1988: 142). In turn, this involves a distortion of the criteria by which ethnography must be evaluated. It has to be worth reading for more than literary pleasure. The invention of culture in writing must reflect the way in which cultures invent themselves (Wagner 1975: 30). Above all, ethnography must be 'a rendering of the actual, a vitality phrased' (Geertz 1988: 143). This is not a simple return to empiricism, or to methodology as an anxiety-reducing device (Crapanzano 1977: 69). It is a reframing of the empirical, or a redefinition of the real (Hastrup 1987b). Writing is part of it; but the dilemma is not 'literary'.

Writing ethnography is not reducible to method (Clifford 1986a: 2). The anthropologist is not merely *writer*, but also *author* (cf. Barthes 1982). The authorial craft must be applied with care for the narrative to be convincing as ethnography, that is. Among the narrative constructs used are particular pronouns and particular tenses. Regarding the latter, the traditional use of the ethnographic present has been widely criticised as a means of temporal distancing of the 'other' and of false objectivism (Fabian 1983). I contend the opposite: the ethnographic present is the sole narrative construct of time which can preserve the reality of the ethnographic encounter (Hastrup 1990). In conjunction with other tenses, and with a proper play on pronouns, we may now reinvent ethnographic writings as truly convincing narratives without subverting our message to rhetoric or 'style' (cf. Crapanzano 1986). There need be no 'loss' from fieldwork to writing (*pace* Sperber 1985: 6).

In the following, the basic assumptions behind my conviction about the necessity and creativity of ethnographic writing will be displayed and the argument substantiated. Through discussions of the current status of fieldwork, the ethnographer, the informant, the violence, the text, and the use of pronouns and tenses, we arrive at some conclusions about the meaning of ethnography.

FIELDWORK

Fieldwork is situated between autobiography and anthropology. It connects an important personal experience with a general field of knowledge. The connection itself is of generative impact upon the reality of anthropology (Hastrup 1987b). Like other individuals, anthropologists are also continuous with the space they constitute (cf. Ardener 1987: 39–40).

Due to the fundamental simultaneity between discovery and definition in anthropology, the reality experienced in the field is of a peculiar nature (Hastrup 1987b, 1990). It is not the unmediated world of the 'others', but the world *between* ourselves and the others (cf. Tedlock 1983: 323). Our results are deeply marked by this betweenness and there is no way, epistemologically, to overcome its implications. The ethnographer in the field is the locus of a drama which is the source of her anthropological reflection (J.-P. Dumont 1978: 12). To eliminate the experiential nature of fieldwork is to stick to a radically inappropriate view of the anthropological practice – with which we have been all too familiar in the modernist era (Rabinow 1977: 5).

The condition of fieldwork is fundamentally confrontational and only superficially observational; self and other are inextricably involved in a dialectical process (Fabian 1985: 20). In fact, and quite contrary to positivist wisdom, the main lesson of anthropology in general is that the absolute distinction between subject and object is a modernist artefact, generally belied by social exchange in the non-modern societies traditionally studied by anthropologists (L. Dumont 1986: 257–8, 261). Self and other, subject and object are categories of thought, not discrete entities.

From that perspective, fieldwork for the ethnographer is not unlike a 'possession' in which the subject–object relation also collapses (cf. Fernandez 1986: 247). Fieldwork, we realise, has an ecstatic quality both in its inherent transcendence of the subject-boundaries, and in its performative aspects (Fabian 1985: 22, n. 7). It is a social drama confronting the performers with their unbounded selves.

Fieldwork is also *work*, of course. It is a systematic attempt to acquire knowledge about a different world. The point is that 'systematics' are defined and redefined by the ethnographer's involvement in a particular social drama, for which she could only in part prepare herself. In short, we must admit that the 'ethnographer's magic', in the format of common-sense rules and scientific principles (Malinowski 1922: 6), cannot be applied at a safe distance. The magician is part of the plot; her achievement is not 'pure production' *ex nihilo* (cf. Mauss 1972: 141). It is production from a particular position; gender studies have taught us that the general pretence of neutrality must be abandoned (Conaway 1986: 61). There is no way of eliminating our consciousness from our activities in the field; it is part of reality (cf. Hastrup 1987b).

Association with the 'other' was always a precondition for the acquiring of knowledge. Margaret Mead wrote: 'As the inclusion of the observer within the observed scene becomes more intense, the observation becomes unique' (Mead 1977: 6). And Rosalie Wax stressed that it is in the 'areas of mutual trust and, sometimes, affection that the finest fieldwork can be done' (Wax 1971: 373). The examples are legion; some degree of immersion into the alien space was always recognised. Only, until recently, it was seen as a means to an end: observation at the closest possible distance. Neither Mead nor Wax, writing in the 1970s, appear to have any clue to the extent to which fieldwork participation itself generates the events that are then portrayed as 'facts'. Fieldwork in the postmodern condition is not carried out 'from the door of one's tent'; it is confrontation and dialogue between two parties involved in a joint creation of otherness and selfness (Dwyer 1977: 147). It is this interpersonal, cross-cultural encounter that produces ethnography (Clifford 1982: 144).

Not even the concept of dialogue is new, however. In his fine discussion of primitive philosophy, Radin contrasts outsiders' formulations with a 'true philosophical dialogue' (Radin 1957: xxx–xxxi). Another classic is Griaule's 'Conversation with Ogotemmêlli', which shows the fieldwork dialogue in practice (Griaule 1965). The present use of the term, however, carries more profound epistemological connotations. In the anthropological dialogue, we talk *across* established difference and create a world of betweenness (Tedlock 1983: 323–4). This world is both an intersubjective creation and the object of our analysis. In other words it is the source of our knowledge, and it remains so long after fieldwork itself.

The implications of this concept of dialogue is a fundamental continuity between definer and defined (cf. Ardener 1987: 39). Subject and object merge; 'each one is both subjective namer and objectively named at alternating points in the discourse' (Parkin 1982: xxxiv). In the intersubjective world of fieldwork, both the ethnographer and the informants are caught up in webs of signification they themselves have spun (Rabinow 1977: 151). A reality begins to emerge in the process.

In order to sort out the inextricable links between the interlocutors in the fieldwork dialogue, I shall deal with the generalised subjects of ethnographer and informant.

THE ETHNOGRAPHER

If fieldwork is a personal adventure and belongs between autobiography and anthropology, it implies that the ethnographer is a person with a distinct biography. It is striking how this simple fact has been ignored by the anthropological profession. Owing to feminist anthropology in particular, we have now come to realise that autobiography in general is actually very significant (Okely 1975, 1978). Until this occurred, the ethnographer was portrayed as a generalised male subject. In the modernist stance the masculine pronoun represented the phallic aggression by the West against other cultures 'pregnant' with meaning (Crapanzano 1986: 52).

Thanks to Malinowski it has been convincingly demonstrated how autobiography has informed ethnography (Okely 1975; Stocking 1983) and, conversely, how fieldwork has revealed to the ethnographer parts of his own hidden nature (Stocking 1986). Even Malinowski himself recognised that the essence of ethnographic work is to discover what are the native's main passions and so to confront what is essential in ourselves (Malinowski 1967: 119). Even the all-male modernist subject could not fail to register that his person was the ethnographer's bedfellow in the field. But he never realised that this bedfellow was part of the ethnographic reality. The western male was a positioned subject. Even Margaret Mead thought of the ethnographer as a generalised male (e.g. Mead 1977: 13).

All ethnographers are positioned subjects and grasp certain phenomena better than others (Rosaldo 1984: 192). The position is defined by age, gender and outsider's status, but it also refers to the ethnographer's lived experience which enables or inhibits particular kinds of insight (ibid.: 193). This is another way of stating that the ethnographer cannot remain external to her object of study. If she transmutes the virtues of distance into an epistemological choice, the ethnographer is condemned to see all practice as spectacle (Bourdieu 1977: 1). Ultimately this would lead her back to the false equity between observation and 'scientificness', or between visibility and veracity (Hastrup 1986). Taking participation seriously, and exploiting the paradox of fieldwork as an intersubjective mode of objectivisation, transform the ethnographer from spectator to seer (cf. Stoller 1984: 94), and her knowledge from observation to insight – which is much more than an iconic expression of visibility.

Visualism is on the wane in anthropology or at least under forceful attack (Clifford 1986a: 11–12; Fabian 1983: 106 *et passim*). The ideology of vision as the source of ethnographic authority is on the retreat (Tyler 1986: 130–1). In the postmodernist condition the exotic tableaux have been replaced by 'worlds' that become familiar to the ethnographers during their stay in the field. Familiarity is owed to the ethnographer's being part of the plot. Elsewhere I have described how she finds herself transformed from a first-person 'I' to a third-person 'she' in the 'other' world (Hastrup 1987a). The objectification of the ethnographer, or the particular position she is allotted in the local plot-space, is of primary significance for her coming to terms with life. She is not only a *labelled* ethnographer but also a *named* person to the people involved.

As a subject, she is repositioned in the field. Her 'self' is blurred, not because she has a weak personality and simply 'goes native'. After all, even to go native is to enter a world of one's own creation (Wagner 1975: 9). Her 'self' is blurred because identities are always relational and inventive (Clifford 1988: 10). The ethnographer is reinvented by her position in the field-world, and by her relations to the informants. The experience is one of self-dissolution and it is inherently anxiety provoking. In this case 'method-ology may often be a locus of displacement for the anxiety provoked not just by the data but by the investigator's confrontation with the subjects of research' (Crapanzano 1977: 69).

A further complication is the general feeling that there is something altogether corrupting about being 'there' (Geertz 1988: 97). The ethnographer is suspect because she postpones global reconciliation by creating otherness and objectifying it (cf. Dwyer 1977: 147). Although she may reconstitute herself through the act of writing ethnography (Crapanzano 1977: 72), it must be of a particular nature if the charge of corruption should be avoided. Before I proceed to this discussion, we must consider the other role in the drama.

THE INFORMANT

The objectification of the informant has recently been criticised. In the modernist era the informant became an instrument in the pursuit of a scientific object; in the text the objectification of the informant has been disguised as her disappearance (Dwyer 1977: 144). The absence of the native as a speaking subject in anthropology has (rightly or wrongly) been read as a continuation of the colonial situation in which the 'other' was gradually destroyed.

The theme of destruction is not new. Already Bastian (1826–1905), one of the founding fathers of German ethnology, noted about the *Naturvölker* that 'at the very instance they become known to us they are doomed' (quoted by Fabian 1985: 9–10). At his time this seemed already to be a historical fact.

Today we recognise the epistemological range of this: 'The others' were understood in our own terms. In the modern society 'the savage became the signifier in an anthropological discourse whose signified remained Western society in transition' (Fabian 1985: 12).

As 'other', the informant was seen as a transparent medium of the other culture, hardly acknowledged as of self-reflective capacity. Says Degénerando in 1800, when speaking of civilised man's faculty of *reflection*: 'It would be interesting to know whether the Savage does not possess at least some beginning of so noble a power, or whether he remains always a stranger to himself' (Degénerando 1800; Moore (ed.) 1969: 86). The implicit evolutionary viewpoint shaped the anthropological object almost until this day; difference was cast as temporal distance (Fabian 1983).

Once we realise that 'othering' is part of the anthropological practice (Fabian 1986), and that the identity of the others, *as such*, is relational, we are ready to acknowledge that they have their own self-referential discourse. They have their own project of self-realisation alongside our project of self-transcendence (Dwyer 1977: 148). As 'informants' they may actually be in search of an outside observer to whom they can recount their troubles and reflections (Rabinow 1977: 19). This is epitomised by Barbara Myerhoff's study of an elderly Jewish population in the United States: 'they were the teachers and I, surrogate grandchild, was the student. I was deeply moved and saddened when people blessed me for merely listening' (Myerhoff 1978: 36).

What we listen to are the informants' own voices, but what they speak are not 'cultural truths'; they are circumstantial responses to the ethnographer's presnce and questioning (Clifford 1986b: 107). Once 'informants', the constructed 'others' already spend more time in the liminal, self-conscious world between cultures than in their 'own' world (cf. Rabinow 1977: 39). At that point, the informants may actually become 'strangers to themselves' – not due to their lack of reflective capacity but because of it.

What the informants tell us (their 'others') in the ethnographic dialogue is spoken not from the centre of their world but from the liminal space of the cultural encounter. Self-reflection in this space is based on a 'doubling of consciousness' (Rabinow 1977: 119). The informant's response to the ethnographer's questioning is an externalisation of inner (cultural) experience.

So far, the informants' voices have been concealed in anthropology. The native and the ethnographer have rarely been articulate within the same monograph (Tedlock 1983: 324). Interpretations have been offered in terms of 'indirect speech' – generalising the informants' informations (Sperber 1985: 16–20). It has been criticised as another instance of the anthropological distancing by means of a 'style that suppresses direct quotation in favour of a controlling discourse' (Clifford 1983a: 137, 1988: 47). I contend that however many the direct quotations, the informants' voices cannot penetrate the discursive speech of the ethnographer. We can cite them verbatim and record their speeches as acts made by people who are subjects in their own plot-space. Ethnography is so much more than recording, however. It is writing a culture, which is not an empirical entity but an analytical implication (cf. Hastrup 1990). Going for the implicational order means that all informants become figures within imposed allegories that in a very real sense bypass them (Crapanzano 1980: xi). The utopia of plural authorship which grants the informants the status of writers (Clifford 1983a: 140), posits the anthropologist in an authenticity trap no different from the one inherent in the visualist rhetoric of realism. The displacement from 'I saw it myself' to 'this is what I actually heard' reframes the problem of authenticity, but does not solve it.[2]

However much we replace the monologue with dialogue the discourse remains asymmetrical, like the languages involved (Asad 1986). The purpose of ethnography is to speak *about* something for somebody; it implies contextualisation and reframing. At the autobiographical level ethnographers and informants are equals; but at the level of the anthropological discourse their relationship is hierarchical. It is *our* choice to encompass their stories in a narrative of a different order. *We* select the quotations and edit the statements. We must not blur this major responsibility of ours by rhetorics of 'many voices' and 'multiple authorship' in ethnographic writing. 'The responsibility for ethnography, or the credit, can be placed at no other door than that of the romancers who have dreamt it up' (Geertz 1988: 140).

The acknowledgement of the informant's contribution and of the fundamental equity between individual selves and others is not solely a matter of letting them speak within the covers of our monographs, but of the much more fundamental problem of finally leaving 'representationism' behind. Once that is done, the very concept of informant dissolves (Hastrup 1990). It is less certain, however, if we shall ever overcome the violence inherent in the encounter.

THE VIOLENCE

The drama of fieldwork, as played out on the stage established between ethnographer and informant, implies a degree of violence on the ethnographer's part. Because any scientific discourse must make claims to speak over and above the acts observed or heard (Tedlock 1983: 323), there is an inherent hierarchy in the relationship between the interlocutors. To deny that is also to remain insensitive to the violence inherent in fieldwork. Both parties are engaged in a joint creation of selfness and otherness, but the apparent symmetry at the level of dialogue is subsumed by a complicated asymmetry: the ethnographic project systematically violates the other's project (Dwyer 1977: 147–9). While perhaps enshrined in mutual friendship and even affection, the ethnographic dialogue is twisted by the fact that the ethnographer's questions are unsolicited, and that they will of necessity shape the answers. The ethnographic material is doubly mediated by our own presence and the informant's response to that.

Another point is that one cannot learn what is systematically hidden in any culture simply by entering it (Clifford 1983b: 132, 1988: 67). Revealing the cultural implications requires a degree of systematic violence; the ethnographer must keep up a certain pressure to elicit the information necessary for drawing some general conclusions (Griaule 1957: 14). We hardly respect our informants' right to fall silent. Probing into cultural silences may be merely a symbolic act of violence, but it is violence none the less (Rabinow 1977: 129). For all our rhetoric about dialogue, ethnographic practice implies intrusion and, possibly, pain.[3]

I myself have become acutely aware of the informants' pain from a recent personal experience. The famous Danish experimental theatre, Odin Teatret, staged a play based on my autobiography, including my fieldwork in Iceland.[4] The performance was magnificent and widely acclaimed as outstanding. My life history has been restored in an intense drama, whose main character bore my name. 'I' was performed by another and my story had been reframed. This was what happened to other people, who were 'fieldworked upon' and put into an alien discursive context. When the theatre left to go on a world tour with their play on me, I was left completely naked. With the theatre-group running away with my story and my passions, and presenting them to unknown and distant audiences, I temporarily lost my concept of 'self'. The pain I felt made me understand any other informant's latent sense of loss at the departure of the ethnographer. The moment of self-objectification is suddenly over.

The range of the implied violence is testified to by the touching account of Shmuel, who told his history to Barbara Myerhoff. Towards the end of their last session, Shmuel said:

> 'we finish now. You have all I can give you. Take it and do something with it. What it is I don't know. You have to take it in your own way. How you will do this with all your ignorance, I cannot think, but maybe something comes together and makes sense for you. We'll see. Now, *maidele*, go home with all this package of stories. I'm tired.' Shmuel died the following night. (Myerhoff 1978: 74–5)

Shmuel was old, and his death 'natural', but we must be careful not to miss the point that making other people tell their story may be extremely wearing to them, and symbolically imply their death. Thus, we also know how Crapanzano's informant Tuhami died when he had been written into an allegory that bypassed him (Crapanzano 1980). Even Dwyer's informant, or rather his partner in the transcribed dialogue 'somewhat irreverently ... ended the final dialogue by falling asleep' (Dwyer 1982: 288). It is part of the (western) narrative structure that it must terminate. Unlike the informants mentioned, I can write back and reassert my 'self' within an equal discursive space – thus bypassing the allegory on 'me'. Yet, I shall never forget the pain resulting from having been fieldworked upon.

This pain is related to the fact that meaning is always connected with the consummation of process, with termination and, ultimately, with death (Turner 1986: 97). Only retrospectively may we grasp the meaning of our life histories. That is why my own history being recast as myth implicated my (symbolic) death. It is also why the ethnographer cannot avoid leaving her informants at a loss.[5]

Acknowledging the inherent violence in fieldwork actually rephrases the problem of authenticity. The material elicited through the ethnographer's symbolic violence must be in some sense inauthentic. The ethnographer's presence in the other world already violates it. The identities of the interlocutors in the (asymmetrical) dialogue are mutually implicated (cf. Clifford 1988: 11). The material is no less 'real' for that, only it is the result of intervention and the outcome of violence – even when fieldwork is carried out under a banner of friendship. That would be my explanation for the perpetual portrayal of ethnographic facts as 'brute'.

In *Argonauts* Malinowski says: 'In Ethnography, the distance is often enormous between the brute material of information … and the final authoritative presentation of the results' (Malinowski 1922: 3–4). This is echoed and even doubly stressed by Rosaldo in 1980: 'even the most brute of brute facts I found to be culturally mediated' (Rosaldo 1980: 17).[6] In this case the image of brutality is partly owed to the ethnographer's concern with head-hunting, but even this confirms my point about the ethnographer's eliciting of material being the locus of factual brutality.

If the facts are not seen as brute, they may be portrayed as humble: 'It is a venerable custom among anthropologists to present the *humble* facts of ethnography in *sublime* style' (Boon 1986: 225, emphasis original). I fail to understand how this can be so; 'facts' have no independent existence. Whether brute or humble, whether produced through violence, empathy or both, the ethnographic material is always *written*. The number of voices recorded by the ethnographer is immaterial; writing ethnography is an act which subsumes them all. The empirical is already implicational once it has become ethnography. Even fieldnotes are not external sources to culture (*pace* Barth 1987: 2). Anthropological knowledge is based on empirical difference *and* on discursive hierarchy. Symbolic violence is inevitable, but writing ethnography is not, therefore, an act of oppression. The ethnographic text is of a peculiar and paradoxical nature which defies the simple logic of the western power game.

THE TEXT

If reality *begins* to emerge during fieldwork, it takes shape in writing. Writing may be an act of self-constitution and exorcism on the ethnographer's part; but it is also an act of ethnographic comprehension. In the 1980s this has become a commonplace to the extent that the very right to write ethnography seems at risk (Geertz 1988: 133). 'What once seemed only technically difficult, getting "their" lives into "our" works, has turned morally, politically, even epistemologically, delicate' (ibid.: 130). Why continue, then?

Quite apart from personal career-making, the inducement to produce ethnographic texts actually stems from the fact that they are not mere records of experience, they are means to it. 'Experience became experience only in the writing of ethnography' (Tyler 1986: 138). Even autobiography has to be written to make sense. 'Writing up' is 'making out' – which is different from 'making up' (cf. Geertz 1988: 140). The literary concerns of postmodern anthropology displace literalism and realism as a *genre* – but not realism as *epistemology*. In the anthropological discourse, real differences are posited – and transcended.

Fieldwork experience has become memory before it becomes text; the relics are embellished to pass for ethnography (cf. Boon 1986). The source is inexhaustible. The actual dialogues feed the discourse infinitely. Although fieldwork took place some time in an autobiographic past, the confrontation continues. The past is not past in anthropology; it is ethnographic present. The referential discourse of realism gradually fades when we realise that it was built upon a confusion between genre and epistemology, a confusion which also implied that representation was taken for reality.

Another no less important rejoinder to realism is that fieldwork itself distorts and contradicts the representational discourse (Fabian 1985: 14, 20). It is impossible to *know* fellow humans 'as if' they were truly objects of sort. *Genres* cannot, therefore, exhaust reality. Texts are contextualised truths, under risk from the empirical.

They are written from a particular author's point of view. The monograph presents the confrontational knowledge of a particular ethnographer. At the confrontational level acting and speaking are made by subjects, ethnographers and informants, acting as simple pronouns in the shared space: I, you, she and he, we and they. The multiplicity of pronouns is part of the dialogue – and consequently part of the 'material' in the text. The anthropological text itself, however, is a discourse about something. It refers to a world which it claims to express (Ricoeur 1979: 75). Ethnographic writing requires that the author of this claim stands up and identifies herself. What we write is the meaning of action and speech, not the actions and speeches themselves as events. And meaning is positioned, just as discourse is addressed.

'Authority', then, may be polyphonic or multivocal at the immediate level of ethnographic experience, but textualisation implies an interpretative authority which excludes dialogue (Clifford 1983a, 1988: 43). The peculiar nature of ethnographic writing consists in the concurrent rendering of exchange and dialogue at one level, and discourse at another. The world is an ensemble of references opened up by texts (Ricoeur 1979: 79). In ethnography an infinite number of equal worlds is seen through the framework of a global discourse.

PRONOUNS AND TENSES

We are now in a position to return to the question of how to write ethnography. The position of fieldwork between autobiography and anthropology, and the simultaneous realisations of dialogical exchange and monological discourse, have some important implications which may now be spelled out.

First of all we note that the classical methodological dilemma of participant-observation is now posited as a literary dilemma of 'participant description' (Geertz 1988: 83). Earlier, the anthropologist stated her presence in the field and then disappeared from the text. Today we require that she remains there because her presence in the field was the locus of the field-world. Besides, only by admitting that the anthropologist is part of the plot, can we maintain our authority as based in a truly colloquial situation (Fernandez 1985: 16).

The colloquial situation, however, must be transcended in discourse. The ethnographer *authors* a truth about her people. Before, we could criticise the notion of 'my people' as an instance of possessiveness; it was an impediment to the replication of fieldwork in one's territory (Freilich 1970: 13). Later it was read as a metaphor for 'my experience' (Clifford 1983b: 130, 1988: 37). I would go further and announce the use of the possessive pronoun as a corollary to the author-status. The people are 'mine' not as individuals, of course, but as inhabitants of the world my writing creates. The author's 'I' must be seen, and her imagination acknowledged. There is no way to evade the burden of authorship, however heavy it has become (Geertz 1988: 140).

In the colloquial/dialogical situation there are speakers and listeners, I's and you's. Identities are constructed reciprocally; selves and others are invented and mutually objectified. Given the interlocative nature of fieldwork, the reciprocal identities of speakers and listeners embody the essence of subjectivity.

As anthropologists, we still have a problem of objectification, though, and of transcending the dialogical situation in our discourse. To me the recent attempt by Dwyer (1982) to make a monograph out of transcripts of dialogue completely misses the point, therefore. Although surrounded by 'annotative soul-searching' (Geertz 1988: 97), the dialogues do not question anthropology as such. Although our fieldwork is interlocution between first and second persons, anthropologists still have to write about the third persons, the absent or objectified ones (Fernandez 1985: 19). At this level, there is an author's 'I' which must be identified. She is a discursive subject, a scholar, who writes others into objective existence. The subject–subject relationship between individual equals turns into a discursive hierarchy between the author and 'her people'.

The importance of pronouns, and the use of first, second and third person is paralleled by an equally important use of tense in ethnography. Again we return to the fact that fieldwork is situated between autobiography and anthropology. This implies a particular construction of time in ethnographic writing. In the field we experience a shared time, 'coevalness', with the other, but when texts are eventually produced this shared time is part of an autobiographic past. The result has been an 'allochronic' discourse apparently implying a temporal distancing (Fabian 1983).

This evolutionary viewpoint upon the 'other' also implied a distinct view upon western history as well: it is an invention placed 'out of awareness' and portrayed as nature (Wagner 1975: 158). As a symptom of the West, anthropology too, has obviated its own theories as 'history' (ibid.). The representations and the realities of the others have been confounded. Thus, the essentially stylistic feature of the 'ethnographic present', has been read as a truth about timeless societies (Hastrup 1990).

The use of the ethnographic present, so characteristic of 'realism' has been a prime target in our 'historical' revision. It has been labelled 'a vague and essentially atemporal moment' (Stocking 1983: 107) or exorcised as 'synchronic pretense' (Crapanzano 1986: 51). Following Fabian, Pratt contends that 'the famous "ethnographic present" locates the other in a time order different from that of the speaking subject' (Pratt 1986: 33). She is right, but her criticism is wrong because she confuses the categories of 'the other' and 'the speaking subject'; they do not belong to the same level of the discourse.

Others have taken a different standpoint; writing on the present-oriented style Marcus and Fischer suggest that the challenge 'is not to do away with the synchronic ethnographic frame, but to exploit fully the historical within it' (Marcus and Fisher 1986: 96). I would make an even stronger claim: the ethnographic present is the only narrative construction of time which gives meaning to the anthropological discourse. Fieldwork defies our ordinary historical categories, and the field-world has neither a firm past nor a distinct future because its reality is intersubjectively constructed and depends on the ethnographer's presence in the field. Truly, fieldwork takes place in an autobiographic past – but we are *not* writing autobiography. We are writing ethnography, and the discourse presents an implicational order which must have a general validity beyond the moment of the recorded events. We know that the confrontation and the dialogue continue long after our return to the academic home world. The relics of fieldwork can be embellished in infinite ways, the source is virtually inexhaustible. Therefore, the (autobiographic) past is not really past in anthropology. The dialogue was 'then', but the discourse is 'now'. There is no choice of tense at this level: the ethnographic present is the only construction of time which renders the truth about the 'absent' reality. There would be no point in doing anthropology, if it was reduced to stories of no veracity beyond the fieldwork episode itself. The authority of the text and the author's 'I' are correlated with an ethnographic present.

Any ethnographic reality must be located in time as well as space and at the level of the dialogue we should acknowledge both the autobiographic past and the shared time. But as discourse it transcends both. The use of the author's 'I' and the ethnographic present are narrative constructions that meet this demand. Since we are now in a position to overcome the confusion between representation and reality, the ethnographic present must be redeemed as the discursive instance of anthropology. In using it, we have *not* claimed timelessness to be a feature of other societies, but we do stress that ethnographic knowledge transcends the empirical. Taking the point of departure in fieldwork we present a knowledge which is *out of time*.

To my mind that is one of the most important reasons to practise anthropology: to remind the world – perpetually – that history is no necessity, and that there are powerful cultures out of time. Above all, we should not pre-empt the creativity of the 'others' within our own invention (Wagner 1975: 159). By a narrow historicising approach *we* claim to have exhausted a moment. We have not; meaning is infinite, and the 'other' may have her own project which we should not violate. The discourse must be conducted in the present tense, and by an identified author.

THE MASTER NARRATIVE

Having dealt with the 'how to write' ethnography I should like to terminate this chapter by addressing the 'why'. Ethnographic texts are allegories; and the 'ethnography' itself is a metaphor for a world-out-of-time. As with all metaphors, this may produce action (Fernandez 1986). At one level the action may be a pursuit of 'criticism of the barbarism of civilisation, an openness to otherness, and a commitment to and great suspicion of Reason' (Rabinow 1985: 12).

There is more to ethnography, however, than this double pursuit of critique of selves and recognition of others. We may in fact reintegrate the 'modern' world-view within a more general non-modern one (L. Dumont 1986: 247). That is the main point of present-day anthropology to reclaim a *non*-modern reality which dissolves the history of modernism and the transition to postmodernism.

For ethnography to be able to pull the rugs from under modernism and the alienation of other histories, an acknowledgement of the hierarchical nature of the anthropological discourse is required. If we, as advocates of difference, claim for both recognition and equality, we claim the impossible (L. Dumont 1986: 266). 'There are two ways of recognizing *alter*: hierarchy and conflict' (ibid.). Conflict is in keeping with the modern trend, and the scientific presupposition that wholes have to be put into pieces. We experience conflicts all the time between peoples who have been declared equal but separate. Modernist rationality introduced an absolute distinction between subject and object, as if they were symmetrical parts of a rigidly bounded totality. Oppression followed.

The anthropological recognition of *alter* must be different from this. It is essentially hierarchical. At the level of dialogue, the individual interlocutors are equals. 'You' and 'I' are engaged in a joint creation. But we are both subjects engaged in a process of objectifying our reciprocal identities. There are selves and others, but no absolute and exclusive categories of *ego* and *alter*. Difference is continually transcended. However, at the level of discourse the 'others' are textually fixed; the absent people are recognised as embodying an alternative culture.

When this is realised, we also know that writing ethnography is not inherently oppressive. On the contrary: by describing the non-modern worlds, we may be able to reintegrate our decomposing modern world within a more common human universe. Not-writing would imply a failure to recognise the human values inherent in the modernist's *alter*.

In ethnography we atone for the sin of language: to separate words and things (cf. Tyler 1987: 172). Ethnographies are realities, and their very incongruity reminds us about the plurality and generosity of the world. The fanning out of the modern universe into a collection of flat ideologies and scattered sciences may be reversed on account of this. While the grand Master Narratives lose their authority because of their single-mindedness, anthropology flourishes as the postmodern narrative par excellence: multi-vocal, heteroglot and essentially inexhaustive.

Because the writing of ethnography was always essentially *non*-modern, anthropology now has both the opportunity and the duty to provide the world with a global discourse about itself. That is why the writing of ethnography is not solely a literary problem.

NOTES

1 Allegedly, this marks the end of modernism, if anthropology was ever modern (Ardener 1985; Strathern 1987; Rabinow 1986: 252; cf. also Lyotard 1984; Clifford 1986a: 13).
2 I am thinking of the works by Paul Rabinow (1975, 1977) and Jean-Paul Dumont (1976, 1978) in particular. My purpose is not to belittle the significance of the personal reflections that were published subsequently to their 'proper' mono-graphs. On the contrary, they have been important steps in the direction towards an integration of the field-account and the monograph. However, by now we must take the next step, and integrate the 'I' with the ethnography produced.
3 The theme of anthropology as practice has been further explored in Hastrup (1990). An important inspiration is Fabian (1986).
4 A full account of my encounter with Odin Teatret is given in (Hastrup, in press).
5 I am not denying that there can also be gains. Thus, Myerhoff reports how some of

her elderly informants actually found her quest for their stories invigorating (Myerhoff 1978: 38–9). But I do think that in order to take our informants seriously as persons and not just as 'voices', we must start by acknowledging the potential violence of the entire anthropological practice.

6 Rosaldo's work on Ilongot head-hunting is actually one of the finest examples so far of a postmodernist ethnography. The author is present, the informants are there, history is there, as well as a general anthropological insight. That is why his notion of brute facts is so telling.

REFERENCES

Ardener, E. (1985) Anthropology and the Decline of Modernism. In J. Overing (ed.) *Reason and Morality*. London: Tavistock (ASA Monograph 24).
—— (1987) Remote Areas: Some Theoretical Considerations. In A. Jackson (ed.) *Anthropology at Home*. London: Tavistock (ASA Monograph 25).
Asad, T. (1986) The Concept of Cultural Translation in British Social Anthropology. In J. Clifford and G. Marcus (eds) *Writing Culture. The Poetics and Politics of Ethnography*. Berkeley, Calif.: University of California Press.
Barth, F. (1987) *Cosmologies in the Making. A Generative Approach to Cultural Variations in Inner New Guinea*. Cambridge: Cambridge University Press.
Barthes, R. (1982) Authors and Writers. In Susan Sontag (ed.) *A Barthes Reader*. London: Jonathan Cape.
Boon, J. (1982) *Other Tribes, Other Scribes*. Cambridge: Cambridge University Press.
—— (1986) Between-the-Wars-Bali. Rereading the Relics. In G. W. Stocking (ed.) *Malinowski, Rivers, Benedict and Others. Essays on Culture and Personality*. Madison: University of Wisconsin Press.
Bourdieu, P. (1977) *Outline of a Theory of Practice*. Cambridge: Cambridge University Press.
Clifford, J. (1982) *Person and Myth. Maurice Leenhardt in the Melanesian World*. Berkeley, Calif.: University of California Press.
—— (1983a) On Ethnographic Authority. *Representations* vol. 1 (1983), pp. 118–46. Repr. in Clifford 1988.
—— (1983b) Power and Dialogue in Ethnography: Marcel Griaule's Initiation. In G. Stocking (ed.) *Observers Observed: Essays on Ethnographic Fieldwork*. Madison: University of Wisconsin Press. Repr. in Clifford 1988.
—— (1985) On Ethnographic Self-fashioning: Conrad and Malinowski. In T. C. Heller, M. Sosna and D. Wellberg (eds) *Reconstructing Individualism: Autonomy, Individuality, and the Self in Western Thought*. Stanford: Stanford University Press. Repr. in Clifford 1988.
—— (1986a) Introduction: Partial Truths. In J. Clifford and G. Marcus (eds) *Writing Culture. The Poetics and Politics of Ethnography*. Berkeley, Calif.: University of California Press.
—— (1986b) On Ethnographic Allegory. In J. Clifford and G. Marcus (eds) *Writing Culture. The Poetics and Politics of Ethnography*. Berkeley, Calif.: University of California Press.
—— (1988) *The Predicament of Culture. Twentieth-Century Ethnography, Literature, and Art*. Cambridge, Mass.: Harvard University Press.
—— and G. Marcus (eds) (1986) *Writing Culture. The Poetics and Politics of Ethnography*. Berkeley, Calif.: University of California Press.
Conaway, M. E. (1986) The Pretense of the Neutral Researcher. In T. L. Whitehead and M. E. Conaway (eds) *Self, Sex and Gender in Cross-cultural Fieldwork*. Urbana and Chicago: University of Illinois Press.

Crapanzano, V. (1977) On the Writing of Ethnography. *Dialectical Anthropology* 2: 69–73.

—— (1980) *Tuhami, Portrait of a Moroccan.* Chicago: Chicago University Press.

—— (1986) Hermes' Dilemma: The Masking of Subversion in Ethnographic Description. In J. Clifford and G. Marcus (eds) *Writing Culture. The Poetics and Politics of Ethnography.* Berkeley, Calif.: University of California Press.

Degénerando, J.-M. (1969/1800) *The Observation of Savage Peoples* (transl. and ed. by F. C. T. Moore, with a Preface by E. E. Evans-Pritchard). Berkeley and Los Angeles: University of California Press.

Dumont, J.-P. (1976) *Under the Rainbow: Nature and Supernature Among the Panare Indians.* Austin, Texas: University of Texas Press.

—— (1978) *The Headman and I. Ambiguity and Ambivalence in the Fieldworking Experience.* Austin, Texas: University of Texas Press.

Dumont, L. (1986) *Essays on Individualism. Modern Ideology in Anthropological Perspective.* Chicago: University of Chicago Press.

Dwyer, K. (1977) On the Dialogic of Field Work. *Dialectical Anthropology* 2: 143–51.

—— (1982) *Morrocan Dialogues. Anthropology in Question.* Baltimore and London: Johns Hopkins University Press.

Fabian, J. (1983) *Time and the Other. How Anthropology Makes its Object.* New York: Colombia University Press.

—— (1985) Culture, Time and the Object of Anthropology. *Berkshire Review* 20.

—— (1986) Presence and Representation: The Other and Anthropological writing.

Fernandez, J. W. (1985) Exploded Worlds – Text as Metaphor for Ethnography. *Dialectical Anthropology* 10: 15–26

—— (1986) *Persuasions and Performances. The Play of Tropes in Culture.* Bloomington: Indiana University Press.

Freilich, M. (1970) *Marginal Natives: Anthropologists at Work.* New York: Harper and Row.

Geertz, C. (1988) *Works and Lives. The Anthropologist as Author.* Stanford: Stanford University Press.

Griaule, M. (1957) *Méthode de l'ethnographie.* Paris: Presses Universitaires de France.

—— (1965) *Conversations with Ogotemmêlli.* Oxford: Oxford University Press.

Hastrup, K. (1986) Veracity and Visibility. The Problem of Authenticity in Anthropology. *Folk* 28.

—— (1987a) Fieldwork Among Friends. Ethnographic Exchange within the Northern Civilization. In A. Jackson (ed.) *Anthropology at Home.* London: Tavistock (ASA Monograph 25).

—— (1987b) The Reality of Anthropology. *Ethnos* 52: 3–4.

—— (1990) The Ethnographic Present: A Reinvention. *Cultural Anthropology* 5 (1).

—— (in press) Out of Anthropology. The Anthropologist as an Object of Dramatic Representation. *Cultural Anthropology.*

Lyotard, J.-F. (1984) *The Postmodern Condition: A Report on Knowledge.* Minneapolis: University of Minnesota Press.

Malinowski, B. (1922) *Argonauts of the Western Pacific* (Eighth impression). London: Routledge & Kegan Paul.

—— (1967) *A Diary in the Strict Sense of the Term.* London: Routledge & Kegan Paul.

Marcus, G. E. and Fisher, M. M. L. (1986) *Anthropology as Cultural Critique.* Chicago: University of Chicago Press.

Mauss, M. (1972) *Towards a General Theory of Magic*. London: Routledge & Kegan Paul.

Mead, M. (1977) *Letters from the Field, 1925–1975*. New York: Harper Colophon Books.

Moore, F. C. T. (ed.) (1969) *The Observation of Savage Peoples* (1800) J.-M. Degénerando. Berkeley and Los Angeles: University of California Press.

Myerhoff, B. (1978) *Number Our Days*. New York: Simon and Schuster.

Okely, J. (1975) The Self and Scientism. *Journal of the Anthropological Society of Oxford* **6** (3): 171–88.

—— (1978) Privileged, Schooled and Finished: Boarding Education for Girls. In S. Ardener (ed.) *Defining Females. The Nature of Women in Society*. London: Croom Helm.

Parkin, D. (1982) Introduction. In D. Parkin (ed.) *Semantic Anthropology*. London: Academic Press (ASA Monograph 22).

Pratt, M.-L. (1986) Fieldwork in Common Places. In J. Clifford and G. E. Marcus (eds) *Writing Culture. The Poetics and Politics of Ethnography*. Berkeley, Calif.: University of California Press

Rabinow, P. (1975) *Symbolic Domination. Cultural Form and Historical Change in Morocco*. Chicago: University of Chicago Press.

—— (1977) *Reflections on Fieldwork in Morocco*. Berkeley, Calif.: University of California Press.

—— (1985) Discourse and Power: On the Limits of Ethnographic Texts. *Dialectical Anthropology* **10**: 1–13.

—— (1986) Representations are Social Facts: Modernity and Post-modernity in Anthropology. In J. Clifford and G. E. Marcus (eds) *Writing Culture. The Poetics and Politics of Ethnography*. Berkeley, Calif.: University of California Press.

—— and Sullivan, W. M. (1979) *Interpretive Social Science. A Reader*. Berkeley, Calif.: University of California Press.

Radin, P. (1957) *Primitive Man as Philosopher*. New York: Dover.

Ricoeur, P. (1979) The Model of the Text: Meaningful Action Considered as a Text. In P. Rabinow and W. M. Sullivan (eds) *Interpretive Social Science. A Reader*. Berkeley, Calif.: University of California Press.

Rosaldo, R. (1980) *Ilongot Headhunting 1883–1977. A Study in Society and History*. Stanford: Stanford University Press.

—— (1984) Grief and the Headhunter's Rage. In J. Bruner (ed.) *Text, Play and Story*. Washington, DC: American Ethnological Society.

Sperber, D. (1985) *On Anthropological Knowledge*. Cambridge: Cambridge University Press.

Stocking, G. W. (1983) The Ethnographer's Magic: Fieldwork in British Anthropology from Tylor to Malinowski. In G. W. Stocking (ed.) *Observers Observed*. Madison: University of Wisconsin Press.

—— (1986) Anthropology and the Science of the Irrational: Malinowski's Encounter with Freudian Psychoanalysis. In G. W. Stocking (ed.) *Malinowski, Rivers, Benedict and Others. Essays on Culture and Personality*. Madison: University of Wisconsin Press.

Stoller, P. (1984) Eye, Mind and Word in Anthropology. *L'Homme* **xxiv**: 3–4.

Strathern, M. (1987) Out of Context: The Persuasive Fictions in Anthropology. *Current Anthropology* **28**: 251–82.

Tedlock, D. (1983) *The Spoken Word and the Work of Interpretation*. Philadelphia: University of Pennsylvania Press.

Turner, V. (1986) *The Anthropology of Performance*. New York: PAJ Publications.

Tyler, S. A. (1986) Post-modern Ethnography: From Document of the Occult to

Occult Document. In J. Clifford and G. E. Marcus (eds) *Writing Culture. The Poetics and Politics of Ethnography*. Berkeley, Calif.: University of California Press.

—— (1987) *The Unspeakable. Discourse, Dialogue and Rhetoric in the Postmodern World*. Madison: University of Wisconsin Press.

Wagner, R. (1975) *The Invention of Culture*. Englewood Cliff, NJ: Prentice-Hall.

Wax, R. H. (1971) *Doing Fieldwork. Warnings and Advice*. Chicago: Chicago University Press.

Chapter 8

Autobiography, anthropology and the experience of Indonesia

C. W. Watson

In a recent pyrotechnical display in which names were lobbed into the air like evanescent fireworks, Edward Said, in an address to the American Association of Anthropologists, argued that anthropology was complicit with imperialism (1989). He was not in this instance rehearsing the old debate about anthropology being the handmaid of colonialism, but, much more subtly, taking as his stalking horse recent developments in new American ethnography characterised by such works as *Writing Culture* and *Anthropology as Cultural Critique*, he demonstrated how even in these postmodernist texts the writing was not only grounded in the logic of an unequal relationship of power between writer and subject, but actively encouraged the perpetuation of that structure of inequality. He writes specifically of the way in which even the attempt to disclaim the authority of the discipline implicit in such self-deprecatory locutions as 'blurred genres' – one of Geertz's definitions of what ethnography might be – the problem of power is occluded.

That there is a great deal of substance in this charge is something which those of us who have watched the way in which the *obiter dicta* of anthropologists of the north become translated into the canonical orthodoxy of the south would not deny. The humorous anecdotes of the native informant going to the back of a room to extract the text definitive of the ethnography of his society in order to answer a difficult point on kinship hides a more disturbing picture of university curricula, student textbooks and a received tradition of western scholarship dictating what people should think of their own societies, and how they must reinterpret their own experience in terms of new anthropological categories. This is especially true of Indonesia.

Take for example the work of Clifford Geertz. His works on Indonesian society, in particular his works on Java, with their well-known categorisation of things Javanese, now translated into the Indonesian language articulate for Indonesian students, as much as for American ones, the regnant paradigms for an understanding of the Javanese. The stratification of the society, the tripartite division into *priyayi*, *abangan* and *santri*, the description of linguistic etiquette, notions of shared poverty, the conceptual division of *alus* and *kasar*, all now constitute an orthodoxy generated from, and entrenched within, a systematic imbalance in the creation of knowledge. It is an imbalance readily understood by perceptive intellectuals in Indonesia – as I learned to my cost, when on the occasion of a conversation I rashly defined myself as an anthropologist in answer to an enquiry. My answer brought about an instant change of mood in the informal conversational atmosphere and I listened to a bitter excoriation of anthropologists, in particular Geertz, who had done such damage first through failing to understand the nature of Islam in Java, and then through his works, leading others into the same errors of incomprehension. It was a subject which rankled. The lesson to draw from this was for me not so much the justice of the charge – the debate between Geertz and his critics on the accuracy of his perceptions is a never-ending one – but the vehemence and the passion which had sprung from the awareness of the inequality of academic intellectual exchange.

I recall the same attitude expressed not quite so vehemently, in the irritation of a senior civil servant in Indonesia caustically remarking that he was weary of hearing his colleagues say that in order to understand the contemporary political situation in Indonesia it was necessary to seek out the resident American political scientist currently doing research in Jakarta.

Let me take an example from my own work as a further illustration. In 1971 I published an article entitled 'Some Preliminary Remarks on the Antecedents of Modern Indonesian Literature.' It gained some notoriety among the handful of people interested in such things, since it called into question the received Dutch account of the origins of this literature which had emphasised the role played by the colonial government. In due course the article appeared on reading lists, and my revision of the periodisation was generally accepted. Just, however, as I was beginning to enjoy my modest – very modest – success, I was gently and properly put in my place by one of my radical Indonesian friends. He pointed out that my findings were not new, the research had already been done some years back, and that indeed my conclusions had been pre-empted by several publications in Indonesia in the early 1960s. It was only because I had published in English in an international journal that my work had been recognised, and the earlier Indonesian work had not. It was for him and for me a telling example of the structural inequalities which underlie the transmission of knowledge.

And yet, of course, one cannot let Said's point stand. It is far too glib, too facile, and even Said himself seems unsure what to do with it, since at the end of his piece, after both saluting and mildly chiding writers of recent ethnography who have attempted through a mixing of genres and new rhetorical strategies to offer more nuanced accounts of other cultures, he ends with a cautious suggestion that indeed the new ethnography may subvert the inequalities of power, if in no other way, at least by centrally and persistently acknowledging how inscribed they are within anthropology (Said: 225). Of course he is compelled to come to such a conclusion, since the alternative is silence, the end of anthropology, and although he toys with the idea, ultimately it is not acceptable to him, since he wishes to be seen not only as a champion of those who suffer from the iniquities of unequal access to power and the transmission of knowledge, but also as a profound humanist rejecting the extremes of a deconstructionist position of ineluctable relativism. Having recognised that we are condemned to think within the confines of a definitive set of paradigms, epistemes, tropes, we must neither surrender to despair, nor simply play rule-bound games, but recognise the constraints, and advance the analysis incrementally. Similarly, the awareness of how one's knowledge may be abused should not paralyse one into inaction, but should become incorporated creatively into the projects one defines for oneself.

It is precisely at this point that hermeneutics and the Diltheyan stress on autobiography offer such a helpful way forward for anthropology, since it allows for the inscription of reflexivity within the ethnographic enterprise. Hermeneutic interpretation is, as one knows, not without its pitfalls. Its self-referentiality, captured in the notion of the hermeneutic circle, leads sceptics to wonder whether it might not in fact be simply a refined mode of self-justification, a closed system, adequate unto itself and no use for anything else. The hermeneut, once he embarks on his task, is, then, like Sisyphus a condemned man, perpetually renewing an idle task, idle not simply because of the illusory self-referentiality but because of the refusal to acknowledge the confinement of his vision within the bounded set of epistemes which he cannot escape. There is no vantage point on which to stand and appraise: one is caught within a web of intellectual conceits, so much more insidious because the binding strands are invisible yet inescapable.

An example, not at the epistemological level, although *mutatis mutandis* the lesson to be drawn would apply there too, but at the level of narrative paradigm, with reference to Indonesia, shows how easy it is to become entrapped within an interpretive construction. In the 1930s, long before the debates on the social and epistemic constructions of knowledge had become commonplace, the Dutch historian van Leur commented on how the history of the East Indies had been written as though from the prow of a boat or the turret of a fortress. In other words, he was arguing that a Eurocentric vision had determined both what the historian chose to see and how he understood it. What was required, van Leur went on, was to see the historical phenomena from the perspective of the Indies. If one did, this would lead one, *inter alia*, to reconsider the significance of the European presence in the region in the sixteenth and seventeenth centuries. This was a view which, more than any other, contributed to a marked shift in the way in which historians of South-East Asia dealt with their subject.

Above all it was a view which appealed to nationalist historians after

Indonesia became independent in 1945, when a rewriting of the colonial textbooks became such a pressing task. And yet, in seeking to overturn the paradigmatic history the nationalist historians were inexorably caught within it, since that history conceived the experience of the previous three hundred years in adversarial terms: the Dutch confronting the indigenous population; and the nationalists adopted the same perspective: the indigenous population confronting the Dutch. It was not the historical interpretation nor the metaphorical structure which had changed but the attribution of qualities: now the Dutch were the villains and the indigenous population the heroes. The triviality of the example should not obscure for us the consequences of this version of Indonesian history, since its ultimate accomplishment, and the consequence of its argument, is the construction of a narrative – a story with a beginning, middle and end, teleologically plotted from the outset – with the success of nationalism being its triumphal conclusion. It is a narrative which thus rejects the moral evaluations of the colonial model and substitutes its own nationalist moral vision, but which structurally, like its colonial counterpart, leads to distortions and omissions in interpretation of the period. Nationalism as a narrative model for historical understanding is no more satisfactory than the notion of benign European colonialism. So much, then, for trying to think one's way through a hermeneutic circle to some fresh understanding!

And yet the task is not so aporistically hopeless as this might suggest. The very fact that we can come to some newer understanding of previous errors indicates progress of sorts. The trick, perhaps, is to appreciate that the project of interpretation does not promise a finite, total understanding: the object, the phenomenon, the other, can never be fully apprehended in itself, indeed it is an essentialist error to imagine that it even exists as such. Instead one works towards an increasingly refined and modified understanding which depends cumulatively on increasingly sharper perceptions generated by the dialectic of constantly reformulating a position by strategically juxtaposing it against alternatives.

However sceptical we may be of the claims of hermeneutics, we have all become familiar with its methods, particularly in the recent practice of what has become known as interpretive anthropology. Geertz, above all, has demonstrated the method in a number of seminal essays, such as 'From the Native's Point of View: On the Nature of Anthropological Understanding' (1983), 'Deep Play: Notes on the Balinese Cockfight' (1973) and my own favourite 'Found in Translation: On the Social History of the Moral Imagination' (1983). Borrowing from literary criticism and regarding social events as texts he proceeds to advocate a strategy of interpretation by means of 'thick description'. Essentially this thick description requires the constant intervention into ethnographic depiction of the event of the anthropologist trying to elicit the significance of actions for the participants, by juxtaposing her own understanding – drawn from prior experience, historical knowledge, logical assumptions – against a native understanding as it can be elicited from either behaviour or a native exegesis. In the same way as a literary critic works in this way on a text – Geertz's example is Spitzer constantly asking of himself in relation to Keats's 'Ode to a Grecian Urn', what does this mean? – so the anthropologist working on her 'text' will, if she is at all sensitive, arrive at a challenging and intellectually stimulating interpretation which will then become incorporated into the anthropological version of literary criticism, namely ethnography.

The analogy from literary criticism is deceptively appealing to those who have, like myself, come into anthropology by way of literary studies and have enjoyed the rewards of engaging with a text and exploring its meanings. Ultimately, however, as one stretches the analogy and reviews the myriad ways in which criticism is conducted and the debates over what is legitimate in critical strategies, the attractiveness of the analogy wanes, and one becomes more concerned with what Geertz makes of his own approach.

Looking closely at some of the seminal Geertzian texts, some of his American admirers (Clifford, Rabinow, Crapanzano) have drawn attention to the sleights of hand which he is guilty of and the way in which the deictic nature of the text collusively draws the reader of the essay into a dialogue with Geertz which effectively excludes the subjects of the essay, who remain almost as objectified (and as disempowered) in his account as they might have been in a conventional analysis. These lapses, and they are serious lapses, do not, however, invalidate the method – any more than the flawed nationalist inversion of values invalidates the possibility of the enterprise of subverting the colonial historical paradigm – but simply serve to caution us that, even in the hands of its most accomplished practitioner, the interpretive approach is open to pitfalls, and we must be careful how we employ it.

Geertz frequently poses the hermeneutic problem in terms of understanding the other who is at one and the same time familiar and strange. We are equally in error, he suggests, if we assume that the anthropological other is identical to us in the conceptualisation of experience or if we assume that there is no similarity whatsoever. The anthropologist's task of interpretation has as its intention the rendering of similarity and difference in a comprehensible form. And of these two aspects of the other it is on balance the difference which needs to be demonstrated, since the more common error is to assume similarity. He then gives accounts of Balinese, Javanese and Moroccan society to illustrate the importance of appreciating different concepts of human experience and behaviour.

Two linked features of the Geertzian project disturb me: the easy way in which Geertz sees the other in generic terms, the Balinese, the Javanese, etc.: one wonders if the English or the French could be so glibly characterised; and the emphasis on the alienness of th other's view: one wonders if in the last instance Geertz is not proposing an intellectual's version of the search for exotica. These points seem to me quite crucial. Consequently, what I want to do in the rest of this chapter is to argue from my objections to a position which holds that our difficulties in understanding other cultures will persist so long as we do continue to regard others as typical examples of a genus – *homo* Baliensis, *homo* Javanicus – and that, furthermore, however alien and exotic the phenomena are, they are inevitably explained in terms comprehensible to us – that is after all what being confined within an epistemic discourse condemns us to – and that the task of interpretation should be to enable us to see ourselves in that strangeness, rather than exclude us from it.

Certain cultures have acquired in the western imagination a very distinctive otherness which at one level immediately calls into question Geertz's suggestion that we too readily assume a universal similarity; but to be charitable, perhaps Geertz was not arguing about conceptions of other cultures and civilisations, as much as about conceptions of the way other people think and the way their behaviour should be interpreted – although the distinction is not an easy one to retain. Be that as it may, the exoticism of specific other cultures in the western imagination needs to be noted and I want to draw attention to what has been written about the western constructions of Bali and China, and then contrast these with the case of Indonesia.

Thanks to Geertz again, and to James Boon, we are familiar with the anthropological romance of Bali and the way in which a discourse drawn from the tropes of pastoral idyll and noble savage was imposed on the island turning it in successive versions of a tropical paradise, in imaginative forms appealing as much to globe-trotting hippies as to wandering artists and curious anthropologists. The details need not concern us here. The construction of China in western historical imagination occurs in a similar way, but it is a very different kind of otherness that is located there, serving the instrumental purpose of generating a consciousness of other aspects of the western self from those which 'Balis' elicit.

In a recent article Zhang (1988) very usefully summarises the history of western images of China showing precisely how at various junctures, and differing from one European society to another, the image of China was changed in order to adapt to changing notions of a European self. That the process still continues he shows by illustrating how even contemporary writers such as Foucault, very much alive to the way in which the other is manipulated to confirm an image of the self, still construct their own Chinas.

The point of principle to which Zhang is drawing attention by these examples is that of the process of differentiation, fundamental not only to the procedures of logic, but also to the construction of notions of self. There is, then, given this principle, an inevitability that we shall always be constructing our Chinas, our Balis, not simply out of our categories of knowledge, our episteme, but out of a view of ourselves. Zhang, however, refuses to accept the desperate inevitability of this, and argues again that hermeneutics offers a way out. In projecting how the enterprise might be carried out, he draws inspiration from Borges, the author whose comic reference to the ordering of things in a fabled Chinese encyclopedia had proved such an inspiration to Foucault. Borges, quoted by Zhang affirms that: 'We love over-emphasising our little differences, our hatreds, and that is wrong. If humanity is to be saved, we must focus on our affinities, the points of contact with all other human beings; by all means we must avoid accentuating our differences.' Zhang comments on this that: *Borges is particularly sensitive to the problematic of the Other, and the theme of double identities runs throughout his works. In other words, the Other often turns out to be no other than the Self* (Zhang: 113, emphasis in original). In other words what Borges is suggesting is a collapsing of that seemingly inevitable distinction between Self and Other, and Zhang taking him up proposes that the hermeneutic method lends itself to just that purpose.

There appear to be two stages in the way in which knowledge of the Other – and at this stage Zhang is thinking in terms of the other being cultures and civilisations such as Japan and China which are 'other' for the West – should be pursued. The first is a careful deconstruction of the myth of the Other, explaining how the myth has been created and what purposes it has served. This will not in itself prevent us from constructing our own myths – replacing ours for theirs – but it will make us more alert and sensitive to the strategies of myth-making, causing us to reflect on our own usages and manipulations. Above all, it will emphasise for us the need to pay attention to the voice of the Other, as far as possible letting it speak for itself. And this indeed is the second stage of the process: to create the conditions for a knowledge of the Other which so incorporates the Other as to change the Self, so that ultimately Other and Self are fused in a process which Zhang, borrowing from Hegel, describes as *Bildung*.

Now there is something almost mystical in this last part of Zhang's paper, and the process of *Bildung* is not sufficiently clearly described to avoid the charge that what is advocated is more a profession of faith, than any satisfactory method of 'transcending the Self-Other difference in the movement towards fusion'. None the less, the outlines are clear, and although the ultimate achievement of the aim may be in some doubt, the potential gains to the experience of what it is to be human in the hermeneutic attempt to dissolve Self into Other should surely encourage a serious engagement in the project.

Anthropology, like literary studies, is a particularly good place to start, since despite Said's reservations and the mutterings of complicity, it has always been, or at least it has during the last hundred years been, the task of anthropologists both to show the falsity of myths of other societies, and to work with ever-increasing sophistication to alternative constructions which do indeed have as their object letting the Other speak. And this has been true despite our awareness of how the alternative constructions have in turn become myths, and sometimes dangerous myths. In what follows, then, I want to examine the myths of Indonesia, and then suggest by reflexions on my own experience how we can from within anthropology circumnavigate the hermeneutic circle.

THEIR INDONESIA

A first observation is that Indonesia does not carry the same intellectual and imaginative currency as either Bali or China. There are, in other words, few recognised images of Indonesia. There are good historical reasons for this: as a nation-state Indonesia did not exist prior to 1945, and the former Dutch East Indies was never considered to constitute a geographical or a cultural unity. Thus one was familiar with Java, Sumatra, Bali, Borneo, each of which had acquired characteristics which were unique and distinctive – the head-hunters of Borneo, the dances of Bali, the giant rats of Sumatra and the formal ritual of the Javanese court – at the same time as collectively they represented the quintessential tropics where climate and geography caused people to live in a different relationship to nature than elsewhere, where consequently man could be paradoxically both noble and savage, and where the European self had as his duty the extirpation of the savagery without himself succumbing to it.

This image of a dangerous, but seductive alternative, appealing in many ways to what is understood to be the dark side of the European self changes dramatically in the post-war world, when geo-political journalism replaces both literary fiction and travel documentary. Indonesia is henceforward recognised as newly-independent nation, lurching madly from crisis to crisis, controlled by a mad dictator – Sukarno – obsessed by delusions of grandeur. It is an image fuelled by the Cold War but also feeding on labels such as under-developed country, Third World etc. Now, however, the wheel has come full circle: travel writing is again popular, the international political scene is quiescent and the television shows images of Buginese boat-builders in London, Lamahera whale-hunters, Balinese irrigation systems, tiger hunters in Sumatra and men wearing penis-sheaths in Irian: the exotic is once more fashionable – its identification being of course predicted on the comfort of the order and repose of the familiar.

Within specialist circles the images are more diverse – making one pause to reflect for a moment whether that diversity of imagination has not always been present in the conception of the Other: were there not always simultaneously different Chinas? The political science specialists continue to begin with the nation-state. Anthropologists quickly ignore Indonesia for the sake of the Minangkabau, the Batak, the Kerinci, the Nuaulu or the Javanese, although they often make their way to the latter through something identified as being the Indonesian language. There is a certain amount of inevitability in this selective vision: anthropologists prefer the bounded universe of a small cultural group with a long historical tradition to the amorphousness of the modern state which with its homogenising tendencies and assimilative power creates anew as well as calls into question the distinctiveness of the sub-culture.

To confine ourselves here to the apparently homogenous ethnic group, then, we can note the way in which Java has been variously constructed and deconstructed in recent years. One process of deconstruction has led to seeing how Javanese ideas of power are perceived within an indigenous tradition thereby calling into question the earlier paradigms of universal analytical categories seen to have derived from and been specific to western experience. A later analysis of such culturalist interpretations reveals, however, that the forms designated peculiar to Java have been doubly constructed by exegetes: first in a re-description of Java employing theosophical categories current in Dutch circles at the turn of the century, and, then in a reworking of that re-description which both ignores the earlier influence and foists its own interpretive scheme upon it. At every calling into question of the earlier interpretations a plea is made to let the Javanese speak with their own voice.

Part of the problem seems to lie in the form of the demand: let the Javanese speak for themselves. There is an assumption that the Javanese speak with one voice, and consequently the task is to identify that voice with representative sampling: a nineteenth-century text, a court ceremonial, sumptuary laws, the iconography of modern statuary. It is a method which in the hands of a skilled ethnographic craftsman can yield dazzling displays of other cultures, but of course at the great cost of keeping them at a distance, circumscribing and therefore containing them, as the method of conventional anthropology commits us to doing. One might ask, however, if there may not be other ways of letting others speak which begin not from a desire to control through a pretension to comprehensive knowledge, but from a desire to share experience.

A model for another kind of knowing which is not premised on a desire for totalisation is clearly friendship. The friend initially appears as other, as stranger (as etymologists frequently remind us), and becomes friend through a mutual exchange of personal knowledge, through direct disclosure in conversation and indirectly through behaviour. One learns to know a friend, but one never knows her completely – there would be an arrogance and an assumption of superiority and condescension to imagine or to behave as though one did – and there is no desire to appropriate. This, then, I am suggesting, is a different model of learning and knowing which has important implications for anthropology, but which seems at first sight at odds with it, since anthropological knowledge has after all always pretended to a systematic completeness.

The best example I know of a sudden shift in the anthropologist's perception of what sort of knowledge he should be trying to attain is to be found in Robert Jay's paper in the Dell Hymes collection 'Reinventing Anthropology'. Jay, an anthropologist who has written an excellent account of Javanese villagers, describes how he was graphically made aware by a question addressed to him at the end of a period of fieldwork that his work up till that point had been one of exploitation, that is, an intellectual exploitation of members of the society turned by his anthropological gaze into instruments for the production of his ethnography. The self-revelation shocked him into requiring of himself that in all future work he would treat relationships with others as inter-personal – with all the consequences of that attitude – before anything else.

Jay does not, however, indicate how his new attitude might lead to a change in anthropological praxis. At this point, therefore, the hard-nosed British anthropologist might well argue that the direction which Jay takes may lead to friendships but it will not lead to good ethnography. It is, consequently, important to show how the abandoning of completeness can be both beneficial to the growth of personal relationships and to the cause of anthropology. Again one must proceed by analogy. The writing of a novel or the making of a documentary have as their intention the partial description of a society: there is no pretence to completeness. The novelist and the film maker draw upon their experience in designing and crafting their work, and it is essentially an experience of living with and sharing common sentiments and affections with members of a society. Ultimately, in the course of creating their oeuvre a process of selection and focusing is involved, and when the final shape emerges, it is presented as a partial account. Even when the writer is not sympathetic to his subject, there is no implicit statement that the account is a totalising one. It sets itself up to be judged not only within the consistency and coherence of its own structure, but within the criteria which the reader and the viewer bring to it of their own experience. It is not therefore self-contained. The same procedures should govern the writing of ethnography. The starting point should be one of the sharing of inter-personal experience. The rest will follow naturally from that. By way of illustrating what may arise if the opportunities are taken, the following autobiographical comments relating to a twenty-year experience of Indonesia are offered not so much as a model but as an example of false starts and constant renewals in which anthropology continues to be implicated.

MY INDONESIA

Going out to Indonesia initially as a volunteer I was determined that I would learn the language, Indonesian, as well as possible, in order not simply to be able to communicate but to make close friendships. I knew little of Indonesia: I had read a couple of books, knew about the massacre of

Communists for which Muslims were, as far as I understood it, to blame. Unlike the anthropologist going to the country I was ignorant of the ethnic diversity of Indonesia. What I anticipated was an experience of Indonesia – I suppose I too saw it in generic terms then.

As the months went by and I became progressively fluent in Indonesian, I was brought up sharp by two observations which made it clear to me that although language was an essential pre-condition for understanding, more was required. My initial assumption had been the one that Geertz warns against, that ways of thinking and perceiving are identical the world over. I can only plead the callowness of youth. The two observations were not sudden illuminations; they came gradually. First of all, that matters of etiquette were not idiosyncratic forms of conventional behaviour which had degenerated into ritual, but were in fact indicative of social attitudes and evaluations of appropriate inter-personal behaviour which could not always be readily deduced from context, but which required a more systematic study. The second observation linked to this, was that among the group of people whom I called my friends there was a common sharing of what might be called an Indonesian experience – foremost, the experience of the traumatic political events of the previous ten years which they had witnessed together in Bandung – and yet at the same time there was a distinctive experience common only to those who shared membership of the same ethnic group. Again the placing and identifying of that ethnic experience was not always readily visible, but was revealed to me gradually.

Having made those observations I did not consciously set about trying to remedy my ignorance or acquire a knowledge of these phenomena in the same way as I had purposefully set about acquiring a knowledge of the language. Instead I continued to pursue an experience of Indonesia, to keep up with my friends. This became a matter of reading newspapers and magazines, discussing politics and religion, going to films, talking about sport and food. It also meant reading novels and poetry which very slowly gave me access to my friends' experience – they too had read the novels and the poetry, and we could compare our understandings. It also brought me to a better knowledge of one group of my friends, the Minangkabau, because, as it happens the early classics of the Indonesian novel are largely written by Minangkabau writers describing their culture.

When I left Indonesia after two years I wanted to know more, and the obvious avenue was to work through the novels, so I embarked on a research degree. Reading the novels was interesting, but the demands of writing a thesis meant that I had to accept an academic framework to which that reading had to be attached. I sometimes felt that I was being led in directions I had not intended to take. One of the corollaries of this academic exercise, however, was to have major consequences for me in that I became convinced that the form of the Indonesian novel, the narrative conventions which had become universally accepted, limited the experience which could be articulated in the novel. It was consequently a short step to a decision that if I wished to continue my quest for knowledge of the other – and I sometimes saw it in those terms – then I should become an anthropologist.

Eventually I set out to do fieldwork in central Sumatra, the culmination of years of planning. The experiences of fieldwork, the joys and the occasional irritations are not for recording here. The dawning of my self-doubts about the whole enterprise are of greater relevance. If Jay's moment of truth came when he was asked to share his knowledge with Malay villagers, mine came when I had an unhappy exchange collecting kinship terminology. I was trying to get some comparative data from villages in Kerinci which would throw light on the kinship in the village where I was working. After talking to a group of informants I had worked out the rules. I then asked an informant how he would address a certain relative. I had worked out that the term should be (classificatory) father. He said that the term was (classificatory) MB – he had a relative who fitted the specifications I had just given and this was how he addressed him. Not satisfied I pursued it, and eventually after a few minutes I browbeat him into conceding that I was right. Back home reflecting on the incident later that night I wondered what I had been playing at. If this was anthropology, then perhaps I should leave it alone. It was a doubt that continued to nag me, even after I had written my thesis.

Despite my doubts about the approach from literature and anthropology, doubts which arise from the way in which an academic framing of the subjects confines and limits what is available to me rather than from the nature of the insights derived from them, I still pursue both, for private satisfaction and for the sake of academic recognition. The ideal remains for me, however, that first privileged experience of friendship which in retrospect seems to represent exactly that fusion of self and other which should be the end of interpretation. It was, I recognise, an opportunity which is rare: encountering the Other not without pre-knowledge, but not with professional or academic presuppositions, and therefore being that much more open, that much more receptive to the voices of friends. Anthropologists going into the field in Indonesia today are perhaps less hampered by their intellectual baggage than they were twenty years ago. Part of the reason for this is their new self-awareness, and the reflexive consciousness of their discipline. They will be in an even more enviable position if they can convince themselves that axioms of amity apply as much to themselves as to those they meet, or if they feel that at the end of their fieldwork they can share Goethe's sentiment: *Man darf nur alt werden, um milder zu sein; ich sehe keinen Fehler begehen, den ich nicht auch begangen hatte.*

REFERENCES

Clifford, J. (1988) *The Predicament of Culture. Twentieth Century Ethnography, Literature and Art.* Cambridge, Mass. and London: Harvard University Press.

—— and G. E. Marcus (eds) (1986) *Writing Culture. The Poetics and Politics of Ethnography*. Berkeley, Calif., Los Angeles and London: University of California Press.

Crapanzano, V. (1986) Hermes' Dilemma: The Masking of Subversion in Ethnographic Description. In J. Clifford and G. E. Marcus (eds) *Writing Culture*. Berkeley, Calif., Los Angeles and London: University of California Press.

Geertz, C. (1983) *Local Knowledge. Further Essays: Interpretative Anthropology*. New York: Basic Books.

—— (1973) *The Interpretation of Cultures*. New York: Basic Books.

Jay, R. (1974) Personal and Extrapersonal Vision in Anthropology. In D. Hymes (ed.) *Reinventing Anthropology*. New York: Vintage Books.

Rabinow, P. (1986) Representations Are Social Facts: Modernity and Post-Modernity in Anthropology in J. Clifford and G. E. Marcus (eds) *Writing Culture*. Berkeley, Calif., Los Angeles and London: University of California Press.

Said, E. W. (1989) Representing the Colonized: Anthropology's Interlocutors. *Critical Inquiry* 15(2), Winter: 205–25.

Zhang L. (1988) The Myth of the Other: China in the Eyes of the West. *Critical Inquiry* 15(1), Autumn: 108–31.

Chapter 9

Changing places and altered perspectives

Research on a Greek island in the 1960s and in the 1980s

Margaret E. Kenna

INTRODUCTION

In this chapter I discuss fieldwork carried out in Greece in the 1960s, 70s and 80s. The first piece of research, sixteen months' doctoral fieldwork in 1966/7, concentrated on the inhabitants of a small island in the Aegean (to which I gave the pseudonym 'Nisos', the Greek for 'island', in my publications). A later research project, carried out in three months in the summer of 1973, focused on island migrants in the suburbs of Athens. Most recently, a year's research, from August 1987 to July 1988, was divided between the island and the migrant community. These places have changed and so have the people who live in them. Some have literally changed place, moving from the island to the city or in the opposite direction; others have changed through growing older, and through new experiences and opportunities. In the 1960s many islanders were moving permanently to the city or going there for seasonal work; in the 1980s this direction of movement reversed. Migrants were returning to Nisos, either permanently to work or retire, or temporarily, to seize opportunities offered by its tourist development. Paralleling these changes of place are alterations, which I will attempt to outline, in the mutual perceptions of islanders, migrants and anthropologist.

RETURN AND REVISIONS

This long-term association of mine with the same places and with people who regard themselves as in some sense members of the same community provides an opportunity to assess the significance of my own gender, age, stage in the life cycle, personal history, and other factors for my fieldwork and writing. Return visits enabled me to find out from islanders and migrants how they had seen me in the past, and how they would revise those definitions in the light of their current perceptions. These visits also made it easier for me to assess, from a later vantage point and with greater knowledge, the local and national significance, and effects of specific historical events (such as the Colonels' coup in April 1967), or of trends

Plate 9.1 Margaret Kenna with village children, Nisos, August 1966

whose significance could really only be evaluated with the passage of time (such as the combined effects of the growth of inflation, and curbs on migrant workers in other European countries on internal migration and investment strategies in Greece).

One way of assessing the influence of these fieldwork experiences in three decades is to ask: if I had not gone back, how would my perceptions of myself and of Nisiots in the 1960s be different and how would their views of me (or rather, my perceptions of their views of me) be different? What would certainly have remained constant is the effect of the first piece of fieldwork on my theoretical interests, particularly in kinship and religion. But later visits have prevented the first fieldwork from becoming selectively edited by memory and have helped me to remain aware of possible misinterpretations and lack of subtlety in the analysis of earlier material. For example, if I had not gone back in 1973 (just before the Athens Polytechnic Rising, the Turkish invasion of Cyprus and the end of the Colonels' regime), and in 1987/8 (when the socialist government was in considerable difficulties), my views of island politics would have remained as formulated in the 1960s: that national political parties were used as labels for local competition and conflict without any real understanding of the parties' political theories and policies. This misinterpretation resulted partly from my lack of

Plate 9.2 Margaret Kenna at the harbour, Nisos, May 1989. The young man in the foreground was the little boy on her knee in the 1966 photograph

understanding, not of the events of Greek political history, but of their meaning at local level, which I slowly began to comprehend as I read more and established deeper, long-term relationships. I had discovered when doing library research prior to fieldwork that Nisos was used as a place of political exile in the 1930s (it was used so again in the later 1960s), and noticed that few people were willing to talk to me about this period during the 1960s and 70s. However, towards the end of my most recent visit, in July 1988, I was shown mementoes and asked to listen to reminiscences of the 1930s (see Kenna 1991a). These gave me an insight into what must have been perceived earlier as the danger of such confidences, with their revelation of political allegiances, particularly to an ignorant outsider. I do not think that the twenty-two years which had passed since my first visit were necessarily a test of my trustworthiness and discretion. I believe that it was only when a socialist government had been in power for some time that people with left-wing backgrounds or associations felt able to talk about their pasts. It is from being able to make comparisons across time, and with the material of other fieldworkers, that I can now recognise the significance of certain silences, and recognise that what people did not talk about at all is as important as what they were willing to tell me.

EDUCATING RITA

For an anthropologist, first fieldwork inevitably involves making a fool of oneself, facing up to apparently overwhelming difficulties, and unravelling clues which lead to some sort of satisfactory explanation (Egan 1984: ix–x), and so it is no accident that it is the experiences of the novice which are so easily represented by standard fictional genres: the funny story, the fairy tale, the detective puzzle. Incidents of my 1960s fieldwork ('the night the well overflowed', 'how a hen pecked my bottom') have become set pieces to be retold to friends in Britain or in Greece, or used as illustrative anecdotes in lectures. Thinking carefully through these comic yarns later often revealed additional or alternative meanings to the incident, as well as showing that the stories excused or trivialised an experience which was then humiliating or painfully damaging to my self-regard, but which can now be understood, excused and forgiven from a position of greater experience and confidence. I do not have nearly so many tales of this type to tell about fieldwork in the 1970s and 80s, because on these visits, no longer a novice, I made fewer basic linguistic, postural and cultural errors of the kind which lead to farcical misunderstandings. Rather, my errors were of a more sophisticated kind and therefore less easily encapsulated in a revelatory punch-line genre. Learning fieldwork skills, I was also learning how to comport myself in a way which was acceptable to Nisiots as well as to my emerging view of myself.

During the 1960s fieldwork, I saw myself as being treated by the islanders as a young, uninfluential foreign woman, whose status was reflected in being addressed as 'Margarita' by everyone and referred to as *Margarita i Engleza* (English Margaret), to distinguish me from the many island women of the same name. This suited both my view of who I actually was, an inexperienced postgraduate anthropology student, and also a half-recognised romantic notion of myself as 'little friend of all the world', taken from reading Rudyard Kipling's *Kim*. I don't think that I really understood at that time the different ways in which the islanders could have interpreted my presence there: primarily as an outsider and a foreigner, whose gender was a complicating factor. In the 1970s, my short return visit as a recently married woman in the first years of a university teaching post gave rise to some perplexity. I was still using the same camera and tape-recorder as on my visit six years earlier, and I was not dressing or behaving as befitted my status as Greeks would define it. How could I work in a university if I did not even wear a gold watch? At that time I was still not prepared to make what I felt was a compromise, and dress in a way which in Greek terms would emphasise my status. During the 1980s visit, I noticed a much wider variation in modes of address and reference to me. As a middle-aged, married woman, now known (at least by migrants who had attended a talk I gave at one of the foreign archaeological schools in central Athens) to have some academic standing in Greece as well as in Britain, I was addressed formally, as *kiria Margarita* ('Mrs Margaret'), and described to others in terms which cast reflected glory on islanders and migrants. At the other extreme, my friends from the 1960s marked our intimacy by calling me *Rita*, or even *Ritouli*, an affectionate diminutive for which the nearest translation is probably 'Ritakins'.

This validation of my academic status on the one hand, and of long-term personal friendships on the other, proved a mixed blessing for fieldwork in the 1980s. Publicity, through the migrants' newsletter and an Athenian radio interview, meant that whatever I said was under scrutiny. I felt that I would be expected to conceal 'family secrets' and to portray islanders and migrants in a light of which they would approve, and, knowing something about cross-cutting factions among islanders and migrants, I knew it would be impossible to please everybody. Being taken seriously, albeit in situations whose terms were framed by others, was an experience I had not faced before. My education, both as 'Mrs Margaret' and as 'Rita', continues.

FIELDWORK IN THE 1960s

As a prospective fieldworker I saw myself as having an appropriate mix of insider and outsider characteristics in my own culture to qualify me for participant-observation. Born in Australia, with two years of my childhood in America, followed by permanent residence in Britain, I had been a solitary, bookish schoolgirl marked out for a degree course in English or Classics, from a politically liberal and tolerant family in which discussion and analysis of situations, character and motives were taken for granted. I was brought up to value scholarly achievement and community service, personal questioning and sensitivity to the needs of others. I can now see that this background produced a personality which was possibly the least likely to be able to deal with the members of a community who are brought up to impose their will on others, who are socialised both to conceal information and also to recognise the subtlest of cultural clues from which to infer it, and who try to establish their own sense of self through competing with others over definitions of situations (on fieldwork in Greece see Clark 1983; Friedl 1970; see also Dickson 1982).

When I arrived on Nisos in May 1966 I was single, twenty-four years old and spoke evening-school tourist Greek. I found a place to live below a café. My landlord, the café proprietor, cooked an evening meal for me, and this gave me good reason to be sitting in the café, normally a place where women do not go. In time I was accepted in other village cafés, although I was never able to hold a private conversation there, as any man I spoke to would raise his voice sufficiently to allow others to hear what we were talking about. This was frustrating and I interpreted it as a deliberate attempt to block my questioning about particular harvest yields, renting arrangements or whatever I was trying to investigate. With hindsight, I realised that the strategy of making the interchange public was a courtesy to me as a foreigner who did not understand that a quiet conversation between an unrelated man and woman could be interpreted as an attempt to arrange an assignation. Later, when I was able to visit people in their homes, my questions still met with what I felt were prevarications, noncommittal answers, obvious untruths, and promises that all would be revealed another time, a time which never came.

Collecting information was not only impeded by problems of gender but by what I now recognise to be, on my part, cultural, and probably class, assumptions about politeness, sincerity and respect for privacy which came up against very different Greek assumptions about knowledge as power, information as a valued resource, and secrecy and concealment as social skills. I was naïve enough not to realise that people would, and did, deliberately lie to me, and that this served both as a strategy of concealment in public situations (where others were being misled as well, but probably suspected it), and as a test of my perspicacity and of my ability to discover what I wanted to know by other means. I was initially taken aback by the range and depth of questions about myself, my family and my life. After a time I realised that I was being asked the same questions again and again, presumably to check up on my consistency. I see now that the islanders assumed that, if I would reveal so much so easily, these were either well-rehearsed lies, or there was still much more being concealed. In addition, if I was being so open about myself, there was no guarantee that I would not just as freely reveal to others the details of crops and livestock which I was trying to collect on private visits.

At this time, and during thesis-writing, before the development of feminist anthropology enabled me to feel a sense of positive achievement in presenting a picture of 'the world of women', I felt frustrated and disheartened at being excluded from 'the world of men' in island life, from the world of politics and administration in which, I was firmly told, women were not interested (hence my difficulties in understanding the links between local and national politics). I was never able to get a detailed picture of the founding and working of the island's agricultural cooperative, nor to attend meetings or read the minutes of the village council. I am inclined to wonder now whether the problem was entirely one of gender or was because of the political sensitivity of these areas, and doubts about the intentions and trustworthiness of any outsider, whether fellow-villager, Athenian, or foreigner.

As I have implied, my most intimate contacts on the island were with women, in their houses, at the grocery shops, in evening visiting groups and at church. Women, like men, asked me over and over again about my family. When I told them that I was an only child and that I had come to the island to collect information in order to write a thesis and gain the 'highest' of university qualifications, they were puzzled. If I was an only child, they reasoned, I was sole heir to my parents' property and therefore likely to make a very good marriage; but if my parents had allowed me to travel and live by myself, they either didn't care about my reputation and safety or they weren't going to give me a dowry. It was clear that I had to provide my own and find a husband who would tolerate my past. When I went back to Nisos in 1973 I had been awarded a Ph.D., had a university post, and was married, and thus their projected scenario appeared to have been confirmed.

There was another puzzle for them too which I found out about later in the first fieldwork period. I was talking to a woman about beliefs concerning conception and the mother's role in determining the sex of a child. She told me that sitting with the legs crossed at the knee twisted up the womb and prevented conception. Only prostitutes sat like that. But so did I. All the time I had been asserting the purely academic nature of my stay on the island, I had in terms of their body language been defining myself as having quite different interests. What had eventually outweighed this interpretation also created problems which I was not completely aware of until recently. In over-eagerness to conform to what I thought was the islanders' definition of proper conduct, I tried to live up to the model given by those women who had the most time to spend talking to me – middle-aged and elderly women. This model was based on expectations of young women when my informants themselves were young, and even then, probably as an ideal rather than a realistic prescription for everyday behaviour. So I turned myself into an anachronism without realising it and was then held up to young island women as a shining example. No wonder that many of them were shy with me and unwilling to confide.

MAIN THEMES OF FIRST FIELDWORK

Given the islanders' preoccupation with my dowry, it is not surprising that the main theme which emerged from my first research was related to things which women talked about much of the time: how children were named, what dowries would be given to daughters, how a family estate would be divided between sons, and the cost and organisation of memorial services for the souls of the recently dead. The thesis which I eventually wrote had as its central theme the systematic relationship which, I argued, existed between naming, inheritance and ritual obligations (summarised in Kenna 1976).

When I first suspected this relationship, I began to ask islanders about the various elements of the scheme: men as much as women described the pattern of naming and its recognised exceptions, gave hypothetical as well as actual accounts of how houses would be provided as dowry for all the daughters in a family, and of how family fields and other property would be allotted to sons according to the names which 'resurrected' either the mother's or the father's side, and of how heirs discharged their obligations by carrying out the cycle of memorial services. So my suspicion of a systematic relationship between kinship, property and ritual behaviour seemed to be confirmed. However, just as I had failed to notice that it was older women who had told me how to behave, so (I now think) I failed to realise that the most systematic accounts of these interconnections were given to me by those people whose family situation most closely fitted them. Despite writing that 'the ideal of land passing through a line of men and houses passing through a line of women is recognized explicitly' (1976: 30), I was not bold enough to state the implications of what I took to be an indigenous model of gender-linked property and of parallel, almost unilineal, lines of owners and heirs. I now think that even my tentative account of the model was too rigid, did not take into account the competing definitions of differently situated island families as to the appropriate parental provision for children, and was not set, as it should have been, in the context of a particular moment of Greek economic and political history. In part, this search for an unambiguous model, which could be validated by reference to informants' own accounts of it as well as to material which fitted it, resulted from the perceived necessity of finding a theme around which to organise my doctoral thesis. The rigidity of the model was a product of the nervous tyro's need for order. Recently, in comparing family organisation and economic activities on the island in the 1960s and 80s, I tried to be more critical of the 'farmer's model of self-sufficiency' and to set against it the strategies of shepherding and fishing households for achieving independence (see Kenna 1990: 152–3).

My theoretical orientations at the time of fieldwork were unsurprising for that particular phase in British social anthropology: the days of classic structural functionalism and its contemporary opponents were over. Ideas of conflict and change, the work of the Manchester School, the structuralist ideas of Lévi-Strauss, were filtering down to undergraduate level. Studies were being published which drew careful distinctions between actors' and observers' models, ethnographies were appearing which dealt with urban life, scattered populations and situations very different from those which could be investigated with assumptions of consistency and boundedness. Although I knew that a wealth of historical and statistical records existed for Nisos, I felt that participant-observation was the only valid method of investigation, particularly as experience soon taught me to distrust published figures and printed words. Instead of incorporating these into the analysis with comment, I simply left them out. Similarly, when visiting Athens to collect my grant and buy supplies, feeling like a country bumpkin with my dialect words and island accent, I regarded what went on in banks, offices and scholarly circles as irrelevant to my fieldwork concerns. As a novice, with a naïve confidence in myself as the only trustworthy source for collecting data, seeking anxiously for some clear structural principles on which to base a doctoral thesis, I hardly considered the possibility of a more complex situation, and of other sources of data.

FIELDWORKER'S BODYWORK

Occasionally I would be able to spend a whole day with a woman, perhaps helping her to bake the weekly batch of bread and trying to bring a range of topics into our casual conversations. I was exhausted by the unaccustomed and constant physical effort, and found writing fieldnotes after such a day almost impossible because of weariness. But the women, too, talked of the unremitting and draining hard work inevitably involved in island life, with one season's characteristic aches and pains replaced by the next. Perhaps this is why, when I was asked in 1988 by a Greek interviewer on an Athenian radio programme to evaluate the changes on Nisos, my first thought was that the routines of everyday life were now less exhausting for women.

What I remember most clearly about that first experience of fieldwork, and what was consciously omitted from all my writings, was its extremely physical nature. Fieldwork memories are nearly all bodily ones: painful sunburn from May to September, shivering in the clammy chill of the winter months when my landlord was in Athens, flea-bites, bruises on thighs from café chairs and wooden donkey saddles, prickly rash from sitting on horse-hair sofas, hay-fever at threshing time, period pains during long church services, split and bleeding feet, eye-strain from reading and typing by paraffin lamplight, and blisters from pulling up buckets of water every day. One of my father's heroes was Francis Galton, some of whose 'shifts and contrivances' I remembered and made use of (Galton 1872/1971), for example, turning one's sleeves up outside-in to prevent them unrolling. However long the catalogue of my physical miseries, it could never validly compare, I felt, with the dangers experienced by fieldworkers in Africa, South America, New Guinea, on whose texts I had been brought up as an undergraduate. I was conscious that being a Mediterraneanist was thought rather odd and not 'real fieldwork' by others, including my fellow students, some of whom carried out fieldwork in Africa (e.g. Eyben 1971; Gomm 1972; Heald 1982). It was not until later that I realised that the timing of my fieldwork in the Mediterranean was both too early and too late. Too late for me to be a real pioneer (Campbell 1964; Friedl 1962), but too soon to place my own work within a wider context of studies carried out in Greece. My assumptions were that such a context would have been provided by publications in English; my acquaintance with those in Greek was minimal. I don't recall being actively encouraged to read what Greek scholars had written, and at the doctoral student stage I would have been prevented from doing so by linguistic ineptitude, since such works were generally written in the convoluted formal Greek which characterised academic and scholarly publications. In addition, I believe I assumed their lack of relevance, because of what I took to be their authors' folkloristic orientation and patriotic fervour in linking modern Greek customs to Ancient Greek roots.

A great deal has been written about moments of mystical revelation on Greek islands; Durrell, Fowles and other authors are even read to orchestrate the traveller's experiences. I had no such moments, but my winter miseries in particular convinced me of the supreme value of friendship and confirmed in me the importance of the life of the mind – not necessarily the academic life – a life in which ideas are important and are critically discussed. What I had unreflectingly thought of as an ordinary view of life became subject to question. My relatively unformed and, by student standards of the 1960s, uncontroversial political views, were taken by islanders as daring and dangerous; my taken-for-granted ideas about standing up to cruelty and corruption and insisting on the right to express a point of view were reflected back to me as naïve and inconsiderate. I became self-conscious about my own historical and political situation at the same time as I began to realise something about the times which islanders had lived through, including the use of the island as a place of political exile during the 1930s. When the Colonels seized power in April 1967, I felt as vulnerable as many of the islanders because of the views I had expressed. It was then that I remembered being in California during the McCarthy era when I was seven years old, hearing my parents and their friends talking about the Loyalty Oath and being told that I must never repeat to others any of the conversations I overheard at home, an experience which would have struck a chord with many of the islanders. It seems possible that some of the opinions I expressed in the 1960s may have resulted in the confidences about left-wing sympathies and activism which I recently received.

URBAN FIELDWORK IN THE 1970s

My next piece of fieldwork was six years later, in the three months of the summer vacation of 1973. I had been a university lecturer for five years, married for three, and my doctoral thesis had been accepted two years earlier. The focus of this piece of research was the island migrants in Athens, their involvement in the building trade, and the role of their Association in their own and island affairs (Kenna 1974, 1983). This research made me feel that I had previously accepted too easily the islanders' description of themselves as 'far from God', and that I was now better able to see the close and complex ties which bound the two communities together. Looking back now, I think that I then made the assumption that ties of these types had been there before and that I just hadn't seen them. I distinguished between only two types of migration, that before 1940, which I characterised (following Brandes 1975: 14) as 'institutional in that it conformed to traditional expectations for men ... simply involving the exchange of one type of manual labour for another' (Kenna 1983: 266), and post-war 'transformational' migration which I interpreted as radically altering island life 'and even threatening the continued existence of a viable community' (op. cit.: 263). What I didn't realise was that there was a difference between migration within the post-war period, in the 1960s and 70s, because conditions in Athens had changed; there was still a huge demand for building labourers, but they were now much more strongly unionised, their position in the migrant community was changing and hence their influence on island affairs. Inflation and recession were soon to follow.

The islanders had, in a sense, dragged me with them to the city and not only forced me to realise the relevance of what I had previously regarded as 'sociological' material and theoretical treatments of migration, migrants' associations, unionisation etc., but also made me reconsider the relationship between anthropology and sociology as disciplines which had an absolutely crucial significance for me, and not just because I was teaching in a joint department.

During the weeks I was in Athens, investigating the life of the migrants, I became a pawn in a power struggle between two categories of migrant, now struggling for control of the Migrants' Association. The people I knew best in the migrant community were islanders who had recently migrated; many of them had been young and unmarried seven years before – just as I had been – and now had young families. The men were affluent building workers and wanted changes in the Association's programme of events and fund-raising projects to take account of their interests. The members of the Association's Committee, older men in mostly clerical and commercial white-collar jobs, who knew me only from their summer visits to the island, were impressed by my university status, and were eager to invite me to events which would enhance their own position and gain reflected glory from mine. Standing with them, but warmly greeting their political opponents, the recent migrants who were my old island friends, made for some socially awkward situations. The recent migrants enjoyed the discomforture of those who had previously been their patrons as well as their social and economic superiors, but were now earning much less than even unskilled building workers.

Returning to Nisos at the end of this second piece of fieldwork helped me to reassess as a married woman the extent to which I had earlier, when unmarried, been excluded from or included in women's discussions. At

Eastertime in 1967, I had been present during a baking session (after almost a year on the island), when views on methods of contraception and their impairment of women's sexual satisfaction were voiced (Kenna 1977). At the time I was quite surprised to be included in such a discussion, but contributed some information about the contraceptive pill, which (I later realised) probably implied personal rather than technical knowledge. Comments during my 1970s visit on my age at marriage, twenty-eight, late by their standards, inclined me to think that the women's reasoning in the 1960s was that because of my age (twenty-five in 1967) and freedom from parental constraints, I was bound to have had some sexual experience, even if I was not the loose woman they initially thought me to be, and that I would not be shocked by their talk.

Just as my women friends had been worried in the 1960s about my finding a husband, they were now worried that after three years of marriage I was still childless; I had lost a great deal of weight which meant, in Greek terms, that married life, particularly its physical side, was not satisfying. I was urged to make a pilgrimage to the miracle-working icon of the island's patron saint to set all these things right. To convince me, I was told many stories of miraculous cures, rescues and other demonstrations of the saint's power. Although I had, as I then thought, no reason to visit the saint's shrine as a pilgrim, these conversations rekindled an interest in icons, vows and pilgrimages which resulted in several years' library research (Kenna 1985), and still continues. However, soon after my return to Britain, I underwent several years' treatment for infertility.

THE BARREN YEARS

Following the 1973 visit, the Committee of the Migrants' Association made me its only non-Greek honorary member. It was to be ten years before I visited Greece again. During that time my university job involved me in a great deal of lecturing and teaching which left its mark on my writing style, turning it from tentatively suggestive to heavily expositorial. This didactic mode also discouraged me from thinking creatively about theoretical issues and from questioning my own fieldwork materials. (More recently I have been encouraged to try out new ways of writing by reading Becker 1986.) My department's decision to expand to single honours degree schemes involved teaching a larger number of courses, and reading for these channelled my efforts into rediscovering the classics rather than keeping up with developments in my own field. Having researched in a disciplinarily marginal place, I was now a member of a geographically marginal academic institution. Unincorporated into a network of reciprocal invitations to seminars and conferences, and almost cut off from the small peer group of other Mediterraneanist anthropologists, I began to lose interest in my own work and contact with current research, until a series of SSRC-sponsored

European seminars (see Grillo 1980) reintroduced me to it. Another highlight of these gloomy years was supervising an extremely lively and challenging postgraduate student (see Marvin 1988).

In the spring of 1983, I made a brief return visit to Greece, to maintain and re-establish ties with islanders and migrants. This visit was made not only with my husband but also with a four-year-old son. Soon after arriving back on the island, following island custom, I walked barefoot up the rocky path to the Monastery to hang a votive thank-offering on the icon. With a greater understanding than before of the connections which the Greek Orthodox Christian tradition perceives between outward form and inner meaning, I felt that this action appropriately expressed both my personal feelings and my respect for island customs without risk of misunderstanding or appearing hypocritical. Remembering one of C. P. Snow's characters defining himself as a 'reverent agnostic' I would now adapt the phrase to describe myself as an 'agnostic ritualist' to indicate both my personal convictions and also my doubts. My first fieldwork experiences of funerals, memorial services and exhumations had indicated the significance and power of ritual, and my own later personal experiences of bereavement had convinced me of its importance for grieving and mourning. Recently I have written about funerals, memorial services, graves and family vaults in an attempt to understand better the changes which have been taking place on the island (Kenna 1991b).

The brief return visit of 1983 provided material for a successful research proposal suggesting a restudy of the island, now with electricity, and with a small but significant number of returned migrants, some of whom were becoming involved in the tourist development of the island.

CHANGES IN THE 1980s

This most recent piece of fieldwork was carried out between August 1987 and July 1988 (see Kenna 1989, 1990). It was as tough in its way as my first experiences in the 1960s. I had to make difficult choices between professional obligations and domestic requirements, and once again the physical body impinged, its ailments now those of middle age. I had to form new relationships with island and migrant officials whose predecessors had retired or died, and I had more intimate experience than before of Greek bureaucracy, not least in attempts to obtain maps, statistical data and historical information. And, as on previous visits, my interpretations of the past altered, and Nisiots' views of me changed. This was partly because of the way the research was organised, with two main periods on the island at the beginning and end of the research year, and a middle section in Athens in the winter when the Migrants' Association put on its programme of social and fund-raising events. However, I also made a number of short visits to the island outside the tourist season. These comings and goings were more characteristic of a member of the migrant community than of an outsider, whether tourist or anthropologist (cf. Rapp 1986). In addition, the brevity of these visits set useful deadlines for people to look for material to show me, and to decide to trust me with confidences.

In the light of the influx of tourists on the island, varying from room-renting bird-watchers and wild-flower enthusiasts to nudist hippies and tattooed punks camping on the beaches, the islanders' assessments of my own appearance and behaviour since the 1960s were revised. At the Athenian end, my involvement in the activities of the scholarly community there, by giving talks and seminars to which I was able to invite some migrants, had unexpected repercussions. The migrants in the audience in the chandeliered reception rooms of the Canadian Archaeological Institute relayed to others, and to the islanders, the evidence that I had produced research which was known in these circles, and I was asked to show to the Migrants' Association and to the island's recently formed Cultural Society, a video-film which I had made,[1] using photos I had taken over the past twenty years. This gave me an opportunity to try to summarise and explain my various pieces of research to the people they most concerned, but who, until now, seemed to me either not to have been interested in them or to have misunderstood them.

If the making of the video-film, and its showing in Athens and on Nisos had been a carefully thought-out research strategy it could not have been more successful. Soon, almost everyone in the migrant and island community had heard about it and wanted copies. People were eagerly seeking me out, anxious to give me information to supplement my original research and to assist the current project. It was a novel experience.

CONCLUSION

When I first arrived in Greece, central aspects of my personal and academic socialisation, such as the value placed on sharing information and co-operating with others, were confronted by Greek cultural assumptions which emphasised that knowledge was power and hence encouraged the concealment of information. My socialisation as a novice anthropologist had taken place at a time in the history of the discipline and the profession when teaching was based on 'exotic' classics and when questions about the validity of Mediterranean countries, Europe and Britain itself as appropriate fields for research were ignored rather than argued. Reinforcing marginalities resulted in an attempt on my part to be unobtrusive rather than to argue or experiment. Institutional support, most notably in the area of supervision, was couched in the ethos of boys public schools: drop them in the deep end and see if they can swim. Gender was ignored as an obstacle to academic achievement, its significance in fieldwork was possibly more noticeable in contrast, although retrospectively it seems likely that its importance was over-emphasised and perhaps confused with the role of outsider. Peer group support depended on chance friendship rather than on arranged programmes (a notable exception being Bailey's at Sussex[2]).

Long-term association has modified this catalogue, bringing other kinds of restriction which result from intimacy as well as from publicity. Changes in age, status and stage in the life cycle have altered my own perspectives and affected both fieldwork experience and analysis. Each successive backward look offers a refocusing of its object. Autobiography, like history, is constantly being rewritten.

ACKNOWLEGEMENTS

The pieces of fieldwork referred to in this chapter were made possible by grants from the following bodies: 1966–7, Mediterranean Committee (LSE/UKC/SOAS); 1973, SSRC Social Anthropology Committee; 1983, University College of Swansea Research and Fieldwork Committee; 1987–8, ESRC Social Affairs Committee.

NOTES

1 The video was made with the technical advice and assistance of Dave Fresco of University College Swansea's CCTV Centre (now the Media Resources Centre).
2 At Sussex in the mid to late 1960s, a group of postgraduate students went through pre-fieldwork training together and then carried out research in different parts of Europe (France, Spain, Austria, Italy etc.). They sent in regular field reports to Bailey, who not only wrote back to them about their own and each other's findings (e.g. all of them sent in graphic accounts of pig-killing and sausage-making in November of the fieldwork year), but also visited them in the field. In addition, all the students met together with Bailey for a mid-fieldwork discussion, and, on their return to the UK, wrote up their doctoral theses and contributed to edited collections on the themes of political entrepreneurship and local development (see Bailey 1971, 1973; see also Silverman 1974). To my knowledge, no account of the organisational aspects or the implications for postgraduate training of this innovative scheme has been published.

REFERENCES

Bailey, F. G. (ed.) 1971. *Gifts and Poison: The Politics of Reputation.* Oxford: Basil Blackwell.
—— (1973) *Debate and Compromise: The Politics of Innovation.* Oxford: Basil Blackwell.
Becker, H. (1986) *How to Start and Finish your Book, Thesis or Article: Writing for Social Scientists.* Chicago: University of Chicago Press.
Brandes, S. H. (1975) *Migration, Kinship and Community: Tradition and Transition in a Spanish Village.* London: Academic Press.
Campbell, J. K. (1964) *Honour, Family, and Patronage: A Study of Institutions and Moral Values in a Greek Mountain Community.* Oxford: Clarendon Press.

Clark, M. H. (1983) Variations on Themes of Male and Female: Reflections on Gender Bias in Fieldwork in Rural Greece. *Women's Studies* 10: 117–33.

Dickson, A. (1982) *A Woman in Your Own Right: Assertiveness and You.* London: Quartet Books.

Egan, S. (1984) *Patterns of Experience in Autobiography.* Chapel Hill and London: University of North Carolina Press.

Eyben, R. (1971) Social Organization in Neighbourhoods in Central Burundi. Unpublished Ph.D. thesis, University of London.

Friedl, E. (1962) *Vasilika: A Village in Modern Greece.* New York: Holt, Rinehart and Winston.

—— (1970) Fieldwork in a Greek Village. In P. Golde (ed.) *Women in the Field: Anthropological Experiences:* 195–217. Chicago: Aldine Publishing Company.

Galton, F. (1872/1971) *Francis Galton's Art of Travel: A Reprint of 'The art of travel, or shifts and contrivances available in wild countries'.* Newton Abbot: David and Charles.

Golde, P. (1970) *Women in the Field: Anthropological Experiences.* Chicago: Aldine Publishing Company.

Gomm, R. (1972) Harlots and Bachelors: Marital Instability Among the Coastal Digo. *Man* 7: 95–113.

Grillo, R. D. (ed.) (1980) *'Nation' and 'State' in Europe: Anthropological Perspectives.* London: Academic Press.

Harris, C. C. (ed.) (1990) *Family, Economy and Community.* Cardiff: University of Wales Press.

Heald, S. (1982) The Making of Men: The Relevance of Vernacular Psychology to the Interpretation of a Gisu Ritual. *Africa* 52: 15–35.

Kenna, M. E. (1974) *A Study of Permanent and Temporary Migrants to Athens.* Final report to SSRC Social Anthropology Committee on project HR 2445/2, lodged in British Library Lending Division.

—— (1976) Houses, Fields and Graves: Property and Ritual Obligations on a Greek Island. *Ethnology* 15: 21–34.

—— (1977) Melitera: Greek Island Cheesecakes. In J. Kuper (ed.) *The Anthropologists' Cookbook*: 34–6. London: Routledge & Kegan Paul.

—— (1983) Institutional and Transformational Migration and the Politics of Community: Greek Internal Migrants and their Migrants' Association. *European Journal of Sociology* 24: 263–87.

—— (1985) Icons in Theory and Practice: an Orthodox Christian Example. *History of Religions* 24: 345–368.

—— (1989) *Islanders, Migrants, and Tourists: Changing Relationships on a Greek Island.* Final report to ESRC Social Affairs Committee on project G00 232341, lodged in British Library Document Supply Centre.

—— (1990) Family and Economic Life in a Greek Island Community. In C. C. Harris (ed.) *Family, Economy and Community*: 143–63. Cardiff: University of Wales Press.

—— (1991a) The Social Organization of Exile: The Everyday Life of Political Exiles in the Cyclades in the 1930s. *Journal of Modern Greek Studies* 9 (1): 63–81.

—— (1991b) The Power of the Dead: Changes in the Construction and Care of Graves and Family Vaults on a Small Greek Island. *Journal of Mediterranean Studies* 1(1): 101–19.

Kuper, J. (ed.) (1977) *The Anthropologists' Cookbook.* London: Routledge and Kegan Paul.

Marvin, G. (1988) *Bullfight.* Oxford: Basil Blackwell.

Rapp, R. (1986) Ritual of Reversion: On Fieldwork and Festivity in Haute Provence. *Critique of Anthropology* 6: 35–48.

Silverman, S. (1974) Bailey's Politics (Review). *Journal of Peasant Studies* 2: 111–20.

Chapter 10

The paradox of friendship in the field

Analysis of a long-term Anglo–Japanese relationship[1]

Joy Hendry

INTRODUCTION

The theoretical concern of this chapter is with the role of 'friendship' in ethnographic enquiry. The analysis would appear to demonstrate both a fundamental incompatibility in the roles of 'friend' and 'informant', and the benefits of combining these roles. Several personal accounts of fieldwork mention 'friends' made in the field (e.g. Foster 1979: 180–1; Rabinow 1977; Smith Bowen 1954), some, like Powdermaker (1966; cf. Watson, this volume[2]), emphasising their overall importance for the work. On the other hand, a practical manual of advice for ethnographic research positively advises against turning friends into informants, largely because of the confusion of roles which is thought to arise (Spradley 1979: 26–8).

There is, of course, a wide range of meaning in the term 'friend', even only in the English language, and Rabinow discusses this problem directly, eventually opting to classify only one man, who refuses to become an informant, as a true 'friend' in the field (op. cit.: 29, 46–9, 142). Crick's contribution to this volume finds it 'odd' to speak of friendship with an informant, whereas Foster (1979: 181) felt able to compare long-term friendships with his Mexican informants with those he holds with his colleagues at Berkeley, despite differences in wealth and power. The problem is of course compounded when there is a notion approximating 'friendship' amongst the people with whom an ethnographer chooses to carry out research, so that each side has preconceived, often deeply held ideas about what the relationship should involve.

This chapter approaches the issue by focusing on a relationship of just this sort, which now spans nearly two decades, between the author and a member of the society where research has been carried out several times. The association started out as friendship, moved into a more or less cooperative venture in ethnographic enquiry, but eventually turned quite sour. The tale illustrates the advantages and dilemmas for the anthropologist of turning a friend into an informant, but it also exposes problems for the informant of having an anthropologist as a 'friend'. Ultimately, professional enquiry can only benefit, in a depth not possible with shorter-term, less intense

Plate 10.1 Joy Hendry, far left, with the tennis group between matches. Tateyama, Chiba, Japan, November 1986

relationships (cf. Foster 1979; Caplan, this volume), but in exposing the feelings and expectations of the individuals involved, the chapter raises the issue of the personal cost of the knowledge acquired.

Again, we are concerned with the 'self' of the anthropologist, but also with the 'self' of the 'other', and the way each 'self' acting in pursuit of professional enquiry may come into conflict with the interests of their personal 'selves'. The problems of the anthropologist in this respect have been much discussed, but they are, after all, problems which we bring upon ourselves in our choice of profession. The difficulties imposed upon an informant, particularly one who is initially acting in good faith as a 'friend', have been less well documented. In this case, an unexpected rupture in personal relations actually contributed to anthropological knowledge, which posed a new dilemma for the ethnographer.

An important difference between this and many other accounts of ethnographic enquiry is that the 'substantial inequalities of wealth and power which normally separate anthropologist and informant' (Crick, present volume) were not applicable, except possibly in favour of the informant. The inequality of academic exchange, noted by Watson in another chapter in this volume, was also less evident, and it was possibly through an intellectual balance too even and open to adjustment that some of the conflicts arose. The informant also had almost as much experience of the social home of the anthropologist as the anthropologist had of the informant's milieu, making it possible for power and equality to be quite negotiable.

It was also quite dangerously possible to blur the cultural context of daily interaction, a problem which would seem generally to characterise the interactions ethnographers describe as 'friendships' in the field. Perhaps in our efforts to find solace in an endlessly alien environment, we may fall back on our own expectations at unguarded times, a relapse made easier when the 'alien' has earthly experience! Powdermaker, in her aptly entitled *Stranger and Friend: The Way of an Anthropologist*, has a telling way of finding 'friends' among Italians, Melanesians and Africans, but makes no mention of friendship during her forays into urban black or Hollywood America.

AN ANGLO–JAPANESE FRIENDSHIP

The relationship to be considered here spans eighteen years. It began before I even became an ethnographer in any formal sense. My initial encounter with Japan took place earlier in the same year I was to take up social anthropology. It was a carefree six months, spent learning Japanese, trying to teach English, and absorbing the experience with few preconceptions about social analysis. I was keen to immerse myself in Japan, and Sachiko,[3] whom I met through the English teaching, was keen to make contact with the western world. We worked together, and she invited me to stay with her family. A few months after I returned to England, she found an *au pair* position with a family in Oxford.

Over the years our friendship deepened. Sachiko stayed in England for about two years and we shared many experiences. By the time I went to Japan to do my first fieldwork, she had returned and married, and we visited one another in our respective Japanese homes. Later, after my own marriage, she travelled to England with her husband, and came to stay with my family. Letters and cards kept us sporadically, but surely, in touch; proximity of age and position in the life cycle repeatedly brought us into situations we found interesting to compare. When I decided to embark upon research related to one of these situations – the rearing of small children – Sachiko offered to find me a field location in the town where she was living. Thanks entirely to her, my children and I found ourselves suitably installed in a house attached to a kindergarten.

At first, my research activities were separate from my friendship with Sachiko. We lived fifteen minutes' drive apart and visited one other for relaxation. With two small children of her own, however, she was naturally interested in the topic and we spent many a long hour chatting informally about our respective methods of childcare. Previously, I had thought of

Sachiko as very westernised, but she surprised me constantly in her approach to her task as a Japanese mother, and I gradually realised that she was an excellent informant. She also helped me to locate, and read, books and pamphlets on the subject. Indeed, she worked so hard for the project that eventually I suggested that we claim a research assistant's fee from the Foundation which was supporting the research.[4] She demurred at first, but finally agreed on the condition that we spend her fee having fun together.

A few years later, Sachiko brought her children to England for two months. I had completed my research on child rearing, and was beginning to read around a new subject, namely Japanese forms of politeness. Sachiko again showed interest, and together we mapped out plans for research. On her return to Japan, Sachiko posted Japanese books on the subject, and wrote to me about her ideas. To avoid some of the possible distorting effects a foreign researcher would have on the polite behaviour of Japanese informants, I proposed employing Sachiko and a Japanese anthropologist, who had trained in Oxford, as part-time research assistants. A grant for the project was eventually forthcoming[5] and Sachiko was able to arrange accommodation for us in a house close to her own.

THE POLITENESS PROJECT

The inspiration for this project came from my experience at the kindergarten, a private establishment where the head teacher placed great store by the language she and her employees used. Emphasising the importance of using speech levels correctly, she schooled her teachers in the art of addressing parents and other visitors. The families associated with this (rather expensive) kindergarten also formed something of an élite in the town, and the use of speech levels is one way in which they demonstrate their perceived edge over their fellow mortals, as elsewhere (see Hendry 1985). My association with this establishment made clear that women's language, in particular, can be more flexible and open to manipulation than suggested by textbooks, which usually focus on the language of men. This study would thus open up an area as yet little discussed in western publications.

During my first visit to the kindergarten, I had worked with many of the families in the parents' association, and I had sometimes discussed them with Sachiko, who knew them only through me. We had also talked about the relative advantages and disadvantages of this kindergarten over some of the public ones, which I had also visited, and I had expressed my own views much more frankly with Sachiko, as a friend with children as yet too young for entry, than I had with mothers involved in the system. By the time of our return, however, Sachiko's elder daughter had been through the private kindergarten and her younger one was still there. Sachiko had thus become involved herself with the élite mothers of the private establishment, some of them my previous informants with whom I hoped to work again.

Since politeness and speech levels are used to some extent self-consciously, at least part of the investigation had to be carried out covertly to avoid the danger of people adjusting their language in my presence. Sachiko agreed with this principle, but it was, of course, difficult for her to engage in deception with her close friends, so we decided to include her *nakama*, or 'inside group' in the part of the project designed to discuss the use of speech levels in an open and analytical way. Sachiko proposed including me in activities of her group so that I could observe the language and behaviour used at close quarters over a prolonged period, and she could alert me about the effect of my presence, if any.

We did indeed meet often and some members of the group came to our house for English lessons with Linda, a former student of mine accompanying us to help with my children. People gradually drop polite levels of speech as they become better acquainted, so amongst these closer relations I was able to observe more intimate forms of address. By meeting these women in a variety of different circumstances, I was also able to observe the way in which the use of polite language varies contextually. At formal kindergarten events, for example, particularly within earshot of the headmistress, language reached a peak of politeness; on the tennis court, with a young and somewhat rakish tennis coach, the women's language was at times barely distinguishable from that of their school-age daughters.

A PERSONAL RIFT, BUT REVEALING TO RESEARCH

During this time, Sachiko and I created specific times to discuss the research, although I was pursuing the more covert side of my investigations in a number of housewifely activities which did not involve her. Many of our domestic activities, such as shopping and marketing, were carried out together, however, as well as events involving the school, attended by her elder daughter and my two children, the neighbourhood, and Sachiko's *nakama*. Few days therefore passed without some sort of interaction between us.

About three weeks after we moved into the house, I began to detect some unease in the relationship. Sachiko also taught some English, and although she and I usually spoke Japanese together, she switched to English when my student was present. On the pretext of feeling sorry for Linda, who in fact was greatly enjoying her life, Sachiko began to invite her on certain *nakama* outings, which would have been quite beneficial to my research. Since the conversation was then largely in English, there was little point in my going along – even if I had been specifically invited, which often enough I was not. I knew that Sachiko enjoyed using her English, and I had no desire to interfere with Linda's enjoyment, so, with something of a heavy heart, I found alternative ways of continuing my work.

The payment of Sachiko's research fee posed another difficulty. We had agreed at the outset what proportion of her time she would devote to the project, and I had applied for and received rates on the Burnham scale, according to her age and qualifications, which included a masters degree in education. With the yen so strong, the fee seemed derisory, but I solemnly wrapped it, in the fashion I understood to be appropriate, and presented it to Sachiko every month with a polite phrase of thanks. I suspect, with hindsight, that I made the transaction too formal. The same approach worked for my other research assistant, but she was younger than I and several years my junior at the same institute in Oxford – both factors which create an automatic inbalance in relations in Japan entirely inappropriate for friends.

The first real dissonance arose on the annual neighbourhood sports day which I looked forward to as an opportunity to get to know people. Sachiko was the local representative for registering children who wanted to participate, but she claimed when I mentioned it that it was too late for mine to join in. They therefore went off to alternative events with football and baseball groups, and I went along with Linda. We were warmly welcomed, but almost everyone we encountered expressed disappointment that the children were not with us. Of course they could have participated, they reassured me. When Sachiko herself appeared, her children were indeed permitted to take part. What was she doing? This occurrence almost began to smack of sabotage.

Little by little, Sachiko became 'too busy' to help me with my project. Her life was filled with sewing and knitting, coffee-drinking with her friends, and various activities associated with the PTA of the kindergarten, where I was also pursuing my research interests with other parents and members of the staff. We still went shopping at the weekly cooperative together, we still attended cooking and tennis classes for which we had enrolled, and school matters brought us into contact. Meetings for the specific purpose of research became increasingly difficult for her to accommodate, however, and she began to postpone or cancel even those arranged in advance.

Calls at her house were also being met with some frost, interestingly enough expressed through the use of precisely the polite language we had been discussing. Whereas previously we had used informal language with each other, often finding it unnecessary to make explicit much of our communication, now I was being greeted with respectful expressions of welcome, which actually carried the meaning of rebuffs. Here was a practical example of something I had read: when a person wants to put the brakes on in a relationship, she reverts to the type of polite language used with strangers. Now I was able to experience the contradictory signals of a formal invitation to enter, with non-verbal cues such as posture and body position barring my way. Relations with Sachiko were clearly deteriorating, but her personal behaviour was most revealing for the research.

Some time later, a second incident occurred when I asked Sachiko to record a kindergarten parents' meeting for analysis of the type of language used. Since she had originally agreed to take on such tasks, and some of the parents had already cooperated with me, I didn't anticipate any problems. Sachiko was reluctant, however, and the tape, when she returned it, was little use. She claimed that the other parents had not liked the idea, but when I played it back, it was she who had expressed reservations, right there on tape. I felt that if I were not careful, she would soon prejudice not only the cooperation of the neighbours, but perhaps also my longer standing relations with the kindergarten parents.

Soon after this incident, matters came to a head. On an extremely stormy morning, Sachiko (unusually) drove the other three children in the neighbourhood to school, leaving mine to battle their way on foot through the wind and rain. We emerged from our house to see her returning, and my face must have registered some shock, for while I was accompanying my own children, Sachiko came to ask Linda whether I was cross. With true British understatement, Linda reported that she thought I was pretty upset. Later that day, when Sachiko appeared with an apology, we had our first open discussion about the turn our relations had taken.

She explained that she had not realised the burden it would be living so close and, for example, my constantly enquiring about her private affairs. One particular occasion she mentioned was when I had asked her about the destination of some plants she was preparing to give away. She had not said anything directly because she was reluctant to spoil our fifteen-year friendship. Instead, she had been trying to put distance between us, hence her barrier-building strategy. Neither did she like accepting money from me, since that made her feel obliged to help, although she assured me that she was still interested in contributing to the project. I thought it best to terminate the financial agreement, and Sachiko seemed relieved. The conversation cleared the air, and it made me feel on safer ground, but it did little immediately to improve relations.

We tried to avoid bothering Sachiko as much as possible after this, and her attitude gradually improved. Interestingly, however, several further examples of non-verbal communication (see Hendry 1990) occurred, which were distinctly useful to the study (as she herself may have realised). For example, we exchanged small gifts of food and flowers rather frequently during the rest of our stay, a recognised means of maintaining communication with neighbours. Sharing a gift received, or a batch of home-baked cakes or other food is a friendly way to do this, offering an opportunity to exchange pleasantries. A gift left in one's absence expresses the relationship, but is less congenial. Nevertheless, the very act of participating helps to heal old wounds. Our families also occasionally went out to dinner together.

After we left Japan, Sachiko and I resumed a rather sporadic correspondence only after a good few months had elapsed. A year later I visited her, but relations were still a little cool, although in the interim she did try to communicate her side of the situation through a third party. For a while, her cards and letters started with apologies, going on to speak of hopes for our 'recovered' friendship. Her last letter includes an idea she has had for how the rift might have been avoided (see below). My feeling is that our friendship will, indeed, recover. In our dotage, with our children grown and gone, we may even come to laugh over our anthropological experiences together. But why should this rift in our relations have come about?

A CASE OF ROLE CONFLICT

Sachiko's own explanations are interesting. Through the third party, another western anthropologist, she expressed some resentment that, by carrying out research with her *nakama*, I was treating this middle-to-upper-class group in the same way that I had treated the country people I had previously worked with in southern Japan. This was true, in the sense that both groups were 'being studied', although I had, with her guidance, adopted a different approach, and she had not objected during the first period of research when she had been involved more in an analytical capacity. In her latest letter, she discusses in some detail the way her house of the time (in comparison with her present residence) offered very little private space away from the public gaze.

In both cases, Sachiko expresses a feeling of vulnerability in being the object of study. This was something she had not anticipated, since she had agreed at the planning stage that a good way for me to learn about the use of speech levels would be to accompany one person, in practice herself, into a variety of different situations. In some unconscious way, then, I, by being an ethnographer, was communicating the very inequalities which Crick, Watson and others have discussed, but which I had felt were absent. This was undoubtedly compounded by Japanese hierarchical notions which Sachiko entertained about the country folk I had worked with in the past. Nor is she unaware of the abundance of anthropological work on pre-literate societies.

This sense of inequality was quite incompatible with friendship in a Japanese view. Confucian ideology characterises friendship as a relationship of equality, indeed, the only dyad in the Confucian order of things characterised in this way. The business of 'employment' therefore probably did not help either. The receipt of money – demeaning, meagre sums which she certainly did not need – put Sachiko in a position of obligation which she found increasingly difficult to fulfil. She had given up full-time work to attend to her children, and, perhaps also to her *nakama*, and this new arrangement could well also have been undermining the relations, and the new role she had chosen for herself.

There was also undoubtedly a tension based on the incompatibility of our respective social and professional positions. Here the word 'professional' refers also to Sachiko's choice of 'housewife' as a profession. A direct translation of the word is used in this context in Japanese, and the occupation is highly regarded. While we had originally met through an interest in each other's cultures, our paths had drawn apart in the way we had pursued that interest. We had also chosen different responses to the less culture-specific problem, for women, of resolving the conflicting demands of the 'modern world', on the one hand, and the expectations with which we had been socialised, on the other. Differences of opinion based on our reciprocal analyses of each other's chosen worlds may also have upset the balance of equality necessary for 'friendship' in a Japanese view.

More central to this volume, however, is the conflict of interests imposed by the anthropologist on her 'friend'. During the first field trip to the area, my research activities had for the most part been separate from my relationship with Sachiko, and although she had introduced me to her neighbours so that we could discuss their attitudes to childcare, she had always remained entirely in control of these meetings. She was, to me, a friend who was helping out by introducing people in informal circumstances; to her neighbours I believe she gained some kudos through having close contacts with the cosmopolitan world, reinforced by further relations established with some local English teachers. She played a mediating role in which she could interpret each of the parties involved to the other, and my presence did not threaten her good relations with her neighbours. Nevertheless, from a Japanese point of view, too much contact with the outside world can spell danger, and by the time of my second visit, Sachiko had already surprised, perhaps shocked, her associates by spending two months away from her husband staying with me in England. She had also built up friendships with other mothers whose children attended the private kindergarten, and my return to the area, possibly to re-establish old relationships with kindergarten contacts, may have seemed threatening. After all, if Sachiko had a reputation for knowledge about foreigners and their habits, it was important that we should not destroy the images she portrayed.

The *nakama*, or 'inside group', is a particularly important unit. Sachiko once explained to me that, since childhood, she had always been afraid of being ostracised by her *nakama*. This confession had surprised me a little, for in more youthful times, she had struck me as something of a rebel. Indeed, she and her husband had belonged to a rebellious student organisation. On reflection, however, I realised that this group had been her *nakama* of the time. Now her interests were quite different, and she had recently decided quite deliberately to give up her full-time teacher's job to concentrate on raising her children. Her relations with other mothers were now a priority, therefore, and her generous offer to share her *nakama* for the purpose of my research, may soon have caused her some regret.

The problem might have been less tricky had she chosen to send her children to the local city kindergarten, where parents coincided with those of the school our children now shared. A certain antagonism existed among some of these parents for others who appeared to set themselves up as an élite. Indeed, my original discussions with Sachiko about this phenomenon had formed part of the whole basis of the research project. Now, Sachiko, herself, had become part of this 'élite', and she was treading a proverbial tightrope in trying to maintain good relations with the parents of other children who attended the local school. Our arrival in the same neighbourhood, an apparently undiscerning anthropologist with two unruly children, all of us carrying previous relations amongst 'the élite', may well have undermined her sense of control.

Perhaps the greatest stress on our friendship stemmed from differences of opinion which had arisen between us, largely based on the different directions we had chosen in our lives. In some ways, I could not help being impressed by the total dedication of Sachiko and her friends to their families and the education of their children. On the other hand, the life of tennis, sewing, knitting and chatting, struck me as a waste of the high level of education most of these women had attained. As always, Sachiko and I expressed our opinions freely to one another on these subjects and many others. Under the circumstances, particularly from my side, more prudence would probably have been wise.

In Japan, a friend is one of the few people likely to hear one's true opinions on a subject, one's *honne* as opposed to the *tatemae*, or polite front, more commonly presented to the world at large. For the anthropologist, it is vital to have such friends, but reciprocity depends on a fair measure of agreement. In general, during fieldwork, it might be thought better to avoid expressing negative opinions about matters close to the hearts of informants. In other words, one can really only pretend to be a friend.[6] Nevertheless, like Jean Briggs (1970: 25) acting out the role of dutiful daughter,[7] I sometimes grew tired of the role I was playing, and made the mistake of revealing this to my host, as friend, rather than as informant. As with Briggs, however, my mistake actually led to a deeper understanding of the people I was investigating.

Another example of such a beneficial error is described by Annette Weiner (1984: 166–8) during fieldwork with the Trobriand Islanders. All three peoples – Utkuhiksalingmiut, Trobrianders, and the Japanese – prefer not to confront one another in open expression of irritation (cf. Briggs 1970: 26–7), and Sachiko carefully chose non-verbal ways to convey her dissatisfaction. I had to learn their meanings the hard way. I then learned more about the subject than I would have, had I been more prudent in the first place. Indeed, the lapse of prudence deepened my understanding of the subject of my research, although the increased knowledge was gained only at the cost of a good relationship.

I thus bring home better ethnography with which to impress my anthropological *nakama*, and I leave Sachiko to continue her life. At least for the time being, my long-term professional support of intercultural goodwill would seem to override the shorter-term, personal expressions of it. With a further period in the field, I can possibly use my new-found knowledge to put things right again. On the other hand, perhaps it is my own expectations of friendship which need revising?

NOTES

1 I would like to thank Lola Martinez and Helen Callaway for their helpful comments on drafts of this chapter.
2 Watson maintains, after considerable discussion, 'that first privileged experience of friendship which in retrospect seems to represent exactly that fusion of self and other which should be the end of interpretation' remains his ideal.
3 The name of the individual has been changed.
4 The research was supported by a Japan Foundation Fellowship which includes provision for the employment of a research assistant.
5 The project was funded by the Economic and Social Research Council (UK), reference number: G0023 2254/1.
6 Smith Bowen discussed a similar problem when she noted that many of her moral dilemmas in the field 'had sprung from the very nature of my work, which had made me a trickster: one who seems to be what he is not ...'.
7 A major difference with Jean Briggs's case is that her two roles of daughter and ethnographer sometimes came into direct conflict when being a good daughter would mean neglecting the notes she needed to write up.

REFERENCES

Agar, M. H. (1980) *The Professional Stranger: An Informal Introduction to Ethnography*. New York: Academic Press.
Briggs, J. (1970) Kapluna Daughter. In P. Golde (ed.) *Women in the Field: Anthropological Experiences*. Chicago: Aldine Publishing Company.
Foster, G. M. (1979) *Long-term Field Research in Social Anthropology*. New York: Academic Press.
Hendry, J. (1985) The Use and Abuse of Politeness Formulae. *Proceedings of the British Association of Japanese Studies* 10: 85–91
—— (1987) Respect, Solidarity or Contempt: Politeness and Communication in Modern Japan. In Ian Nish (ed.) *Contemporary European Writing on Japan: Scholarly Views from Eastern and Western Europe*. Ashford: Paul Norbury.
—— (1990) To Wrap or not to Wrap: Politeness and Penetration in Ethnographic Inquiry. *Man* (N.S.) 24: 620–35.
Okely, J. (1975) The Self and Scientism. *Journal of the Anthropological Society of Oxford* 6 (3): 171–88.
Powdermaker, H. (1966) *Stranger and Friend: The Way of an Anthropologist*. London: Secker and Warburg.

Rabinow, P. (1977) *Reflections on Fieldwork in Morocco.* Berkeley, Calif.: University of California Press.

Smith Bowen, E. (1954) *Return to Laughter.* London: Victor Gollancz; Berkeley and Los Angeles: University of California Press.

Spradley, J. P. (1979) *The Ethnographic Interview.* New York: Holt, Rinehart and Winston.

Weiner, A. B. (1984) From Words to Objects to Magic: 'Hard Words' and the Boundaries of Social Interaction. In D. L. Brenneis and F. R. Myers (eds). *Dangerous Words: Language and Politics in the Pacific.* New York and London: New York University Press.

Chapter 11

Ali and me

An essay in street-corner anthropology

Malcolm Crick

'an anagram made flesh' (Fowles 1977: 656)

The importance of the 'self' in the processes of fieldwork and interpretation should be obvious to anyone who takes the semantic dimension of anthropology half seriously. If the 'self' is the research instrument, any piece of research is suitable for an exercise in the sociology of knowledge (Gould 1975: 64–5): why *this* research problem, why *this* interpretive frame, why *this* chief informant? If participant observation is ultimately grounded in human inter-subjectivity (Adler and Adler 1987: 31), we clearly need to understand our ethnographic products in terms of the producers and the production process, that is to say in terms of ourselves, our informants and the specific contexts in which encounters have taken place (Dumont 1978: 96, 199). If much that we call 'method' has characteristics of a 'reaction formation' designed to protect the investigator from anxiety in the face of social phenomena (Devereux 1967), then clearly a most important kind of ethnographic data is what is going on *inside* the researcher. If anthropology is about 'otherness', any definition of our subject matter necessarily involves a corresponding self-definition. The fact that anthropology has always been implicitly about 'ourselves' is now clear; what is required is that the implicit become explicit (Crick 1976: 153, 1982: 288, 307–8). We require that our 'selves' become objects for scrutiny in the same way that our research has rendered 'objects' those other selves with whom we have interacted in the field.

Valuable work has recently been done on gender aspects of the self in fieldwork, but there are many other dimensions to the 'self' – something of a catch-all term for pieces of cultural baggage, personality traits, values, psychological defences and so on – that still require unpacking. The 'self' may be 'simultaneously enabling and disabling' (Peshkin 1985: 278), but this means that we have two good reasons for paying it due attention rather than dismissing it as an unfortunate, complicating factor in our work. In any case, since we cannot shed the self, we must give it a focal place in our writings

(Cesara 1982: 2, 7). Some 'ethnographic facts', after all, may be little more than temporary agreements on meaning between anthropologist and informant in a transient relationship, both involved in a liminal mode of communication, which inevitably produces only partial comprehension. This being so, it is vital that our work preserves a strong sense of its fragile, inter-subjective origins, instead, as has been the case, despite the importance of 'being there' to the fieldwork tradition, of a textual product in which the presence and individuality of both ethnographer and informant are obliterated (Crapanzano 1976).

In any relationship, 'self' and 'other' are both performers and audience to one another (Berreman 1972: xxxiii). The definitions of 'self' of both parties are partly constitutive of and constituted by the ever-changing bond. Not only can one never be fully aware of who one is in a relationship, since the self is less a thing than a process, one can never be entirely sure what definition of 'self', situation or relationship the 'other' has created. On top of conscious impression management about what one conceals and reveals, there is the unconscious side, which means that one can never describe with full confidence the basis of the relationship. And, given that ethnography normally ties people of different cultural traditions, we have the fact that the two parties will certainly not share exactly the same communicative rules or understanding of each other's role (Fabian 1979). There is, indeed, something a little unnatural in the almost forced exchanges in this marginal realm, and it is perhaps a sensing of this that may lead to a reluctance fearlessly to explore the nature of the ties created for fear that this will lead to a 'rupture' and thus an exposure of the shaky grounds of ethnography (Rabinow 1977: 28, 30, 39, 45, 47, 114).

The field situation is thus inevitably 'ironic' in that ethnographer and informant conspire with one another, are part of a 'working fiction' that they have a shared world of meaning, while in reality, at any time, their agreement could fall apart and they could be exposed as inhabiting separate, mutually uncomprehending worlds (Geertz 1968: 151–4). This is a 'peculiar species of good faith between ethnographer and informant which verge[s] on bad faith' (Webster 1982: 93). With the substantial inequalities of wealth and power which normally separate anthropologist and informant, combined with the researcher's professional reasons for being in the field, speaking of 'friendship', as we often do, is somewhat odd. It is but a strategy, 'sop behaviour' (Bleek 1979: 202–4) that is merely part of the extraction of information. The term 'rapport', much used in discussions of fieldwork, thus acquires something of a phoney 'romantic' quality, since the communication for which the ethnographer strives is equally part of his/her professional self-definition. The relations between ethnographer and informant are more accurately seen, perhaps, as mutual exploitation. Both parties risk and exchange information; and one of the risks is necessarily the relationship itself between them (Lundberg 1968; Agar 1980: 86). While the ethnographer clearly has the accomplishment of professional work as a central motivation, in the case of informants a range of motivations is possible. But because a mutual dependency grows up, the durability of the relationship may involve leaving certain stones undisturbed. Too thorough an investigation of the presenting selves might prove destructive because it might reveal the mismatch of intentions. In the ethnographic situation, then, as in others, two parties, dependent perhaps to different degrees, may hold on to deliberately hazy images of their relationship, which allows them to reach a sufficient number of personal goals for it to be worth persisting with (Crapanzano 1980: ix).

This chapter concerns the relationship between myself and a pavement hawker in Kandy, whom I shall call Ali. Ali was of considerable importance during my seven months of fieldwork in Sri Lanka during 1982 when I was studying international tourism. That research involved observation, relationships with a number of people on the streets of Kandy, library research, interviews, essays written by local schoolchildren, a seminar in the Kandy Town Hall – in other words, a host of methods – but the relationship with Ali was crucial to my overall experience of the field situation. As in any relationship, a dimension of my bond with Ali was unconscious, and insights continue to dawn years after leaving the field. I have never been sure how to label my relationship with him. I always referred to him by his first name, and, in fact, he only once told me his full name. He, on the other hand, always called me 'Doctor'. This difference in mode of address no doubt well expresses the asymmetrical character of our situation. If I call Ali a 'friend' or 'informant', both labels would say too much and also leave something important out. After half a century of our fieldwork tradition, we are still not really happy with our lexicon for the 'other': natives, locals, informants, collaborators, respondents, subjects – all are to varying degrees embarrassing or inappropriate (Whittaker 1981: 439, n. 2). If the terms 'research assistant' or 'key informant' imply specific duties, payment for service and an almost contractual arrangement about how much time would be made available, Ali was neither. Since English is the language used in the informal tourism arena in Kandy, I did not need an interpreter. I am also sure that my own meanness would have inhibited my hiring a research assistant in any case. I was also determined to remain free to follow my interests wherever they led, and I was aware of how possessive a research assistant can become (Rabinow 1977: 75). None the less, the street corner where Ali sold his goods became the most important of the 'observation posts' I set up in Kandy.

Over seven months, Ali and I had numerous conversations, some about tourism, some about life in general. Only on one or two occasions did I follow a pre-determined line of questioning with him in any formal kind of setting, preferring information to flow haphazardly from the more casual context of the street corner itself, where I could watch what was going on, and he could get on with his business. I certainly paid Ali for specific jobs he did for me, such as translating essays written by Tamil schoolchildren. We often shared afternoon tea or a more substantial meal, and I got to know the rest of his family quite well. Occasionally I would go to a new guesthouse with him as my guide, and we often went shopping together, both in Kandy and in the villages nearby where I was not known. I did not pay Ali for his time because he was collecting commission. The deal was that he had to tell me how much he had been given, so that I could learn more about the relationships between guesthouse proprietors, shopkeepers and street guides. He sometimes offered me the commissions back, but I always told him to keep them. I was also able to direct other business his way. Since I spent so much time on his corner, many tourists arriving in Kandy asked me about accommodation, and I would fix them up, sending Ali in advance to certain establishments so that he could claim a cut from the rent. Towards the end of my stay, the owner of the guesthouse where I was staying informed me that he wanted to stop 'catching the tourists' himself, and so needed a reliable guide to do the work for him. I suggested Ali to him, and Ali was engaged – unfortunately, though, for only a limited period of time, since he found the work in Colombo too difficult.

If there were several ways in which I helped Ali, on occasions he was invaluable to me, for instance when I wanted to talk to the prostitutes in the slum area near where he lived about their relationships with tourists. I would never have embarked on these enquiries alone. Such incidents suggest that my relationship with Ali was not quite like that which exists between tourists and locals. Commissions for guides normally raise prices for tourists without their suspecting anything, but there was I with Ali, deliberately having him accompany me in order to find out what the level of 'kick back' was. I was also frequently drawn into the bargaining which went on at his corner between Ali, other vendors and the tourists passing through. The fact that I did not side with the foreigners, but invariably pointed out that the amount of money they were haggling over was a small amount to the tourist but might represent a substantial difference in the daily income of the vendor, gained me the reputation as a stranger with a difference, since the pavement hawkers there had not seen a foreigner adopting such a role before.

Ali was a Muslim of deep religious convictions. Apart from the daily observances, he also knew something of the philosophical literature of Islam. He told me how if he ever cheated anyone it would rebound on him, because he would in turn be robbed. He also told me of a recurring nightmare of an experience he had had early in life of seeing a very rich man dying slowly, and in extreme agony. Ali had actually been educated at Kandy's most prestigious private school, though he did not like other people knowing this.

Though now working on the streets, he came from a very wealthy family. His father had been a very rich merchant, and his brothers were all wealthy shopkeepers, in Kandy and elsewhere. Ali had originally wished to study medicine at university but he had left school instead, to help out in his father's business. Since that time there had been a succession of entrepreneurial, clerical and supervisory positions. A fire had destroyed most of his possessions and he was then forced to sell goods in the streets to earn a small income. He now lived with his mother and one of his younger brothers. Despite having ended up on the streets after a privileged start in life, he was generous with the little money he had. He donated a proportion of his income to the poor, and he also told me that a small pension he received was paid directly into a local children's welfare association. There was something noble about Ali, even amidst the obvious colossal fall that had taken place in his life. He waxed lyrical about life in the 1940s under the British, as the son of a wealthy merchant attending an exclusive private school. He was proud of having met Lord Mountbatten during the war and of mixing easily, so he told me, with white women in the armed services. I was very aware of having heard only snippets of Ali's life. He never told me, for instance, why he married so late in life, and I never discussed the drinking problem which others told me he had. With one afflicted by so many troubles I was always on the look out for 'tall stories'. None the less, I felt that Ali was a benign soul, which could certainly not have been said of too many of the others on the streets of Kandy in 1982 who, I felt, would have been only too ready to trick me.

The first time I saw Ali selling a range of goods on the pavement, I actually walked straight past him. I was on my way to the central market at the end of my first week in Kandy, and he was shouting out the wares he had for sale. I did not stop to inspect his goods, but later that afternoon I passed the same spot on my way home to my guesthouse and Ali remembered me from the morning and said: 'Oh, I see you have bought yourself something. Can I have a look at it?'. Ali's good command of English, plus his hesitant, polite curiosity, caught my attention. I informed him that I was in Kandy to write a book about tourism, and he told me that he knew something about the subject and was willing to help. He added that he would not tell me anything about drugs, because if he did, he would be killed. He also asked a number of searching questions in those early days in regard to the sort of book that I wanted to write. Would it be critical of tourism? Would it stop Australian tourists from coming to Sri Lanka? Would the street guides in Kandy suffer if I published my findings? I told Ali that I had a number of criticisms to make about international tourism in general, but I said that I would try to be fair. I also stressed that it would not be a 'guide book' but an academic work, which tourists would not read. This last remark, though true, was, I am sure, my effort to gloss over the misgivings I had about international tourism in the Third World. I could hardly reveal their full extent and then expect Ali, who earned money from tourism, to say anything very revealing to me. I also made a habit of telling people that I was Australian. Again, factually correct, but I was also hiding the fact that I had been born in England, for fear that 'English' was a marked category in Sri Lanka, given its colonial past, which might affect how people responded to me. Like other anthropologists, my 'opening remarks' were a strategic combination of revelations and concealments (Georges and Jones 1980: 54).

Given my own awareness of the ways in which I fell short of complete honesty, I was the more curious as to why Ali was so willing to help me. Was his gesture on a par with the offers of 'help' with which tourists are regularly bombarded? I was wondering, in other words, what Ali's definition of the situation was. We need to be aware of the extent to which our ethnographic subjects are themselves indigenous ethnographers (Clifford 1983: 139; Marcus 1980; McKean 1976: 12). But we have also to be aware of the large range of pragmatic motives that might attract an informant to such a strange identity as an anthropologist; we need to be aware, in other words, of how the informant is 'reading' the anthropologist (Goldkind 1970; Herzfeld 1983: 162). Informants are 'culture brokers' who are innovative in their interaction with field researchers; their motives might be altruism, curiosity, ego-enhancement, or sheer financial profit (Kirk and Miller 1986: 64). Obviously one must be wary of 'professional stranger-handlers' and approaches made early in one's field period (Agar 1980: 85–6, 117), but in the touristic arena, nearly everyone is some kind of stranger handler. There is, indeed, the so-called 'touree' (van den Berghe 1980: 378–9), who comes into being purely because tourists exist, and whose rules for operation may not correspond to other areas of cultural life. Having been approached by one professional con-man during my first week in Kandy, I was wary of overtures in general. No matter how clear the evidence is at the overall systems level as to who benefits most from international tourism (Crick 1988: 44–9), at street level, the tourist is frequently the victim. I certainly experienced the tourist arena very much as a predatory niche.

I had a string of very good reasons for starting up and continuing a relationship with Ali. He spoke three languages. His street corner was near the cafés, hotels and banks in Kandy, and on the route most tourists took to get from the bus and railway stations to the hotels or guesthouses. There was a sense of dependability; I knew that he would always be there. Also, Ali was a 'marginal' man, like many prized informants. He was not, in fact, an experienced street guide, so was on the periphery of even the 'informal' tourist arena (tourist activities not licensed by the Ceylon Tourist Board). Whilst he occasionally did some guiding, he was mainly a pavement hawker, and therefore, for the most part, had to deal with the other street guides as a business man. I regarded this as an advantage, for Ali was not confined to either an internal or an external view of tourism in Kandy. It was noticeable how sometimes when Ali spoke to me about tourism he did so as a guide, and at other times he spoke as someone who simply observed those involved in tourism, as if he too were a streetcorner anthropologist. Ali was one of the few people who understood the sort of book I wanted to write. Other people, including hotel managers and guesthouse proprietors, presumed that I was planning a 'guide book' which would make recommendations about particular establishments, no matter how much I explained what my real interests were. Ali was also the only person I met in Kandy who was willing to put any of his ideas on tape, others being too fearful that what they said would be used against them. Like many an informant too, he had that often crucial combination of significant experience of westerners and a series of personal tragedies (Agar 1980: 87, n. 3). We also had what I felt to be common interests. I was in Kandy to learn about tourism, and because his business activities were not going very well, he was thinking of abandoning his hawking and becoming a tourist guide instead. So he wanted to learn more about tourism himself. We were, in that sense, learning about tourism together.

I am conscious that while all of the above reasons for the relationship are very rational, they are silent as to my deeper, emotional needs, and presumably those of Ali too. I was in Sri Lanka for seven months, for most of that time on my own, and non-threatening human contact was vital. Also, apart from the journey from England to Australia in 1977 to take up a lecturing position, I had never been overseas. In that sense, I was more naïve and ignorant than most tourists in Asia. In addition, because of other writing commitments, I had to embark on my fieldwork with very little preparation (Crick 1989), making me feel even more uncomfortable. It has been said that the experience of other cultures may reawaken long-repressed memories (Cesara 1982: 3, 7), and I had always hated holidays and found them meaningless. But there I was, having produced a library-based doctoral thesis in the quiet confines of Oxford, on a street corner with touts, prostitutes, con-men, pickpockets, studying people having their holidays. Faced with my nagging sense of unpreparedness, a feeling that my personality was less than worthless for research on this particular topic, combined with a professional responsibility to write about tourism without prejudice, I was frequently bored by my chosen topic, and the possibility of simply spending time on Ali's corner, talking to him about anything under the sun, was not a luxury, but vital for my own emotional survival.

To cap it all, of course, there was guilt, stemming from the feeling that the time I spent on Ali's corner, with my overbearing need for information, would adversely affect his business activities. The normal opening line in the 'tactics talk' of the much maligned touts on the streets of Kandy was 'Hello, friend'; but there was I, essentially touting in public for data. Ali told me that my being there did not affect what he did, but to say that my presence on the street corner made no difference would be inaccurate. For a start, because I became an object of attention and gossip, Ali too became an object of close scrutiny. When I appeared frequently on that street corner, people were asking what kind of business I was up to, and naturally asked Ali what was going on. When he explained that I was just studying tourism, many of the guides became very jealous of him, wondering what qualities he possessed which meant that he, rather than they, had been able to 'catch' me. This jealousy extended even to his guide friends. At one time Ali and his friend Felix, a young guide, were both quite vigorously competing with each other as to the quality of their insights and rubbishing each other to such an extent that I did not know how to return the situation to what it had been before I arrived. What made things worse was that several people watching me did not believe that I was really studying tourism at all but was involved in some nefarious activity. All manner of speculation as to what I was doing was growing up, from the idea that I was a drug courier to the thought that I might be a plain-clothes police officer. Rumours about me apart, Ali's own tentative forays into tourism were beginning to cause him trouble. One day a thug threatened him with violence if he did not hand over some money. On another occasion when I arrived, Ali was looking very glum, and Felix told me: 'there are things in his life that you do not know about'. I guessed – correctly – that he had been warned by some of the rougher guides to stay out of tourism or to face the consequences. Ali displayed much bravado over this incident, showing me a solid silver belt which he wore around his waist which he said he would use to defend himself. He added that most guides were 'all mouth'.

Through the seven months that I was in Kandy Ali persisted with his dual occupations of selling goods from the pavement and trying to catch tourists. Actually both activities were 'doing the tourism' since the goods he had on display were almost entirely purchased by foreigners. Because tourism was bad in Kandy in 1982, both sources of income were drying up. Everyone was saying that there were fewer tourists in the streets, and there was even a feeling that tourism had peaked in Sri Lanka. Occasionally when Ali found a tourist who wanted lodgings, he would pack up his wares and disappear for the afternoon. Sometimes he would be gone for just an hour or so leaving me or a shoe repairer to watch his goods. Very occasionally he would be absent for several days if he had been lucky enough to interest a tourist in a longer trip.

Despite my efforts to remain marginal, over time my ties with Ali took on a significance I could not have envisaged. I realised this most clearly when he told me he was thinking about moving away from Kandy to try some other means of making an income, either working on the nearby Mahaweli dam project or else supervising a coconut plantation for one of his brothers. I realised that if this happened I would lose an important part of my research routine and also an important companion. In a way the realisation of my own research plans depended upon Ali's failure to find a way out of his predicament. Given the large number of street guides in Kandy during 1982 and also the relative scarcity of tourists, catching a tourist became very difficult and making substantial gains an increasingly rare occurrence. Weeks, indeed months, went by with Ali on the street corner for seven hours a day without a single sale. He began notching up marks on a pole to record the number of days without any business. Given that he lived with relatives he always had enough to eat, but it hurt his pride when he could not contribute to the household. Things were made worse in the wet season with the daily need to gather up his wares and rush for cover to escape the early afternoon downpour; on some days when the weather looked too unsettled he disappeared at noon and did not return. And precisely because things were tough that year, many of the guides were driving very hard bargains. They would arrive with a tourist, negotiate a commission for themselves which, given what Ali told me was his normal profit margin, meant either selling his goods at cost, or else pushing his prices up to retain a profit margin but at the same time making his goods that much less attractive. If Ali refused to deal under these conditions, the street guides would just tell the tourist that they could find much better quality goods in the market or elsewhere. In the worst months, Ali, simply to gain some income, did, in fact, sell some goods below what he told me were cost price.

A growing sense of desperation in the guides was clearly evident, which produced intense frustration for the tourists. Many tourists newly arrived in Kandy, tired from the journey and angry at the number of guides they had to pass by to get into the town, were exasperated by the time they got to Ali's corner. They would walk fiercely straight past his display of goods, neither looking at him nor acknowledging his presence when he spoke to them. Even his quite exceptional English and jocular behaviour failed to gain him attention. 'Hello. Welcome to Kandy. So nice to see you here. Look, real banana skin wallets. I am so sorry to have troubled you. I would really like to own your knapsack' – nothing was making the tourists stop and look. Despite the run of bad luck and the increasingly uncivil atmosphere in the streets, only twice did Ali lose his temper in my presence. He was sad and resigned rather than angry with those passing by. He once did get hostile with an arrogant Indian tourist who offered a ridiculously low price for one of his items, and likewise with a German whom Ali asked, in desperation 'Do you think we are babies?'.

It would have been easy to have become embroiled in Ali's financial predicament. But, apart from occasionally bailing him out not constituting a long-term solution to his problems, I was determined not to set any precedents which might lead to him or anyone else continually asking me for money. I did once make a very specific small loan, but requested that it be paid back, which he was able to do a few days later. It was a different matter when Ali announced one day that his young wife was very ill, and that she and his son had had to return to her village, followed by her being admitted to hospital. Although Ali did not ask directly, I simply could not refuse to help, but, again, making it perfectly clear that this would not be the thin end of the wedge. Ali told me how in a public hospital, unless the doctors and nurses were given gifts, a patient simply would not get adequate care and attention. The sums involved were quite beyond Ali's reach unless he took out a loan or humbled himself by asking relatives, but they were not substantial to me. I had to make a judgement about our entire relationship. Was his wife really ill? Did one really have to give money to staff in a hospital to ensure good care? Was giving Ali money here simply the only decent thing to do given our respective circumstances? Can an anthropologist create relationships and then refuse the ensuing involvement (Dumont 1978: 91)? Or was involving myself in this way with his troubles a way of assuaging the guilt I felt over the exploitative role playing that I was up to (Gans 1968: 56–60)? Or, was this an archetypal instance of a tourist being taken for a ride?

My need to feel that I was not tied up in a network of deceptions was enhanced by the fact that I was reading *The Magus* (Fowles 1977) at the time, a novel I had chanced to see at the airport on my way to Sri Lanka. As I made my way through the streets of Kandy each day, hoping for occurrences or encounters which might suggest patterns in the events I was witnessing, this book took on a special significance. The reader's efforts to comprehend what goes on in the book parallels, it seemed to me, the struggle of Nicholas in the text itself to make some sense out of the curious string of events in which he was involved. From chapter to chapter, as contexts changed, characters would appear and disappear; some relationships would become firmer and others more enigmatic. One interpretation would be adopted which would bring to the fore its own particular set of fairly solid landmarks and supporting evidence; a shift of stance, or reliance on another person's account, and other patterns emerged, with the previous markers losing their value. In anthropological research there is a constant shifting of stance in an effort to reach a firm view. What at one stage looks like a productive framework for linking the events suddenly loses its appeal. Evidence suddenly loses its compelling quality as new insights emerge out of the flux of events. At bottom, the ethnographer, like the reader of *The Magus*, and like Nicholas, have to decide where, if anywhere, to place their trust. Is it possible to occupy a position where reliable patterns will come to light? Are there any informants on whose testimony one can place such weight that, in the light of it, one can proceed to build a picture of the whole in which the details will make sense? Studying tourism may perhaps not involve the semantic complexity involved in some other anthropological topics, but the matter of trust is crucial all the same. I was in a niche where officials, guesthouse owners, shopkeepers and street guides would contradict each other's accounts of what was going on. Furthermore, the guides would actively try to discredit each other's information, even when they told me that they were friends. This is clearly a situation where the possibility of systematic deception is an ever-constant worry. Whatever the seemingly increasingly popular ideology of the international tourism industry that tourism is a wonderful opportunity for learning about other cultures, at street level, information is less in evidence than money-making, deception and harrassment. Indeed, many people's personal interests in tourism are quite incompatible with the provision of reliable information.

The field experience is one where culture shock and being away from the normal contexts which support one's definition of self can mean that one can become a stranger to oneself (Pouwer 1973: 2). Stress in the face of ambiguity obviously enhances one's need for some stable reference point (Agar 1980: 50). This is a period when just as one may learn something about oneself, so anxiety may lead to a 'freezing' of one's personality (Crapanzano 1980: 137), which lessens the likelihood of one experimenting with potentially difficult relationships. Because so many of the events in fieldwork can be ego-dystonic, since one may experience nagging feelings of failure and incompetence, the need to have oneself confirmed by a significant 'other' is vital (Wax 1960: 174). For me, Ali was this significant 'other', a man whom I hoped was a safe reference point. Referred to as 'uncle' by some of the younger street guides in Kandy, he liked to keep an avuncular eye on them lest they get themselves into real trouble. Although the idea of the fieldworker 'as a child' has limited validity, something of my relationship with Ali, a man in his fifties with me in my early thirties, was in this avuncular mould. As the months went by, the link acquired several other strands, and when I went to Katunayake airport to leave Sri Lanka in October 1982, Ali was with me. I was clutching my bag full of fieldnotes and he was full of tears, thanking me for what I had done for him and his family.

I would like to think that something that could be called 'friendship' had grown up, but I am conscious that the only reason I was in Sri Lanka was to get material for a book. Given that ultimate purpose behind all the relationships I forged, it was possibly my own sense of guilt (Golde 1970: 91) that I was using people, that produced my lingering sense that perhaps everyone was using me. Perhaps, therefore, even an uncle might be a master magician? A certain amount of doubt is, of course, useful when appraising information gained in the field; the doubt creates the distance in which analytical work can be accomplished. But as the anthropologist, pretending to be more knowledgeable than a mere tourist, watches the touts catching the ignorant foreigners, perhaps he is in reality not much more than a sophisticated tourist who gets caught by a sophisticated con-man? Anthropologists want more lengthy stories than tourists, perhaps they simply get spellbound and tricked by more masterful tellers of tales? The question therefore poses itself: did Ali regard me just as some complex type of tourist? Was our relationship similar to that he had with other foreigners in Kandy? I have often wondered, for there were very few occasions on which I explicitly talked to him about our relationship, and even in some of those I

was oblique, asking about the meaning of the Sinhala term *yaluva* (friend),
customary Sri Lankan mores as regards hospitality and so on. For the most
part, I was content not to examine too closely what it was that kept our
relationship going. Was Ali, like Doc in *Street Corner Society* (Whyte 1955),
more a research collaborator than an informant? Were we less like anthropologist and informant than two people mutually producing understanding
for one another (Cesara 1982: 2, 7)? Or was I being 'taken for a ride' in the
same way as many tourists are?

Anyone's field research is bound up, to a certain degree, with the identity
of the chief informants one obtains. They affect not only what one does, but
how one interprets, to whom one has access, etc. It is also clear that for both
conscious and unconscious reasons one seeks out certain people and avoids
others. While it may be correct to say that it is laziness and disadvantageous
to cling to 'easy' relationships in the field (Hammersley and Atkinson 1983:
104), it is not easy to evaluate the overall benefits and drawbacks of any
relationship, because one does not know how one's research would have
gone if one had done things differently. There is a 'wager' character to
anthropological interpretation in general (Dwyer 1982: 280, 286), but there
is also clearly a gamble element in regard to the relationships one sets up.
One does not know what benefits will accrue, and one certainly cannot keep
withdrawing from ties in a state of distrust just after creating them, since one
would then never get anything under way. Some act of trust – albeit keeping
one's wits about one – has to be made. One may have specific research
objectives, but again, the ethnographer–informant link, like any relationship, is unpredictable. It unfolds in ways which neither party planned,
and may require evolving definitions of selves and changing boundaries as
to what is shared and what remains private (Georges and Jones 1980: 64;
Adler and Adler 1987: 16–17). What is clear is that a strong mutual
dependence may grow up. The mutuality here must be stressed, for while
the anthropologist has the resources upon which the informant depends, the
anthropologist depends on the supply of information. The anthropologist
may even unconsciously have chosen his or her informants for their
dependent traits, assuming that these will secure the bond and guarantee the
information it yields. But the researcher may then become dependent upon
the informant's dependence. I quickly assessed Ali as an informant having a
strong intelligence and reflexive distance from his own culture. I also saw
that he also had deep personal needs to be met, perhaps to compensate for
the areas of failure in his life. He, I judged, wanted to talk, wanted to be
listened to and wanted to be valued. My needs were the same. I know only
too well what value Ali put on the information he gave me. When making
tapes together, he went out of his way to give me a balanced view of the
issues we discussed, despite the fact that I had emphasised the tapes were to
present an individual voice. I also know how disappointed he was when I
informed him that when I wrote my book I would have to give fictitious

names to all the characters in it in order to protect them. He desperately
wanted me to use his real name.

Mutual dependency may produce a strong bond in a relationship, but it
invariably entails a deep ambivalence and a smouldering explosive potential
as well (Georges and Jones 1980: 66). There were several times during my
seven months in Kandy when I backed off probing Ali's world lest I come
face to face with facts I would rather not acknowledge. One such occasion
concerned some gifts I wished Ali to make for me to bring back to Australia
as a memento of our time spent together. Ali was happy to do so, and I gave
him a large sum of money to buy the raw materials. I was then considerably
perturbed one day when one of Ali's friends told me that Ali did not actually
make any of the goods he sold. This information, I felt, went to the heart of
the issue of trust in our relationship, because Ali knew that the gifts were
very special to me since he would be making them himself. If he could
deceive me over this, what about everything else he had told me? Some days
later I raised with him the general issue of the goods he sold, their cost price
and so on, and I told him that a street guide had informed me that he simply
sold things on behalf of others. He was visibly hurt, showing me the
callouses on his hands resulting from the manufacturing process. He told me
that he used his brother's workshop late in the evening, after the female
employees had gone home. I could have asked to see the workshop, I
suppose, but that would not have removed all my doubts, so I dropped the
matter altogether. I had not been able to be brave enough to raise the issue at
all in regard to the gifts themselves.

One can never really know another person's motivations. One can know a
person to a certain degree, but there is always a hidden core of individuality
which one must respect in others, just as one wishes it to be respected in
oneself (Crapanzano 1980: 136–7, 152). I enjoyed Ali's company, but I
am not really sure why he tolerated me. Was Ali treating me like a
tourist? Were my suspicions, even if emotionally very real, formulated in
an anthropologically appropriate manner? How many different types of
stranger did local people lump together as 'tourists' of some kind? After all,
my own originally intended Sri Lankan research on Buddhist notions of
social action had shifted to tourism when I was mistaken for a hippie by a
novice monk (Crick 1989). Besides, if 'self' and 'other' make meaning
equally in the ethnographic encounter, there being no privileged position as
regards the definition of the situation (Rabinow 1977: 151), my suspicions
about Ali were tantamount to denying him any say in defining our
encounter. Anthropologists have a time-honoured tradition of distancing
themselves from other kinds of Europeans in the Third World, whether they
be missionaries, traders, administrators and so on. But the fact is that
whatever their individual outlook, their discipline is sustained by the same

structures of economic and political inequality that made possible the presence of these others. The anthropologist, in this sense, is a metonym of the western world (Dumont 1978: 44). But so, in this day and age, is the tourist. Quite apart from Ali's right to bring his own set of meanings to our relationship, then, perhaps we have some painstaking comparative work to do when construing the anthropological 'self'. To put it pointedly, is an anthropologist an 'in-depth tourist or an entirely different breed of sensation seeker?' (van den Berghe 1980: 376). If Ali regarded me as a kind of tourist, perhaps he was right (Brewer 1984: 499).

A number of anthropologists have made passing remarks about the similarities between tourists and anthropologists, but they seldom dwell on the matter long enough for us to be able to derive much self-knowledge. But field researchers and tourists are overlapping identities (Crick 1985: 76–83), no matter how much we acknowledge that there are different types of research, as indeed there are different types of tourist, and no matter how many very obvious differences exist between what anthropologists and tourists do. Can we be so confident that our motives for being in other cultures are totally different to those of tourists? If it is our relationship with our informants which converts us from tourists into anthropologists (Richardson 1975: 520, 527), do our relationships really rest on a completely different basis? If the tourist–local link is a parody of a human relationship (van den Berghe 1980: 378), and if there is an overlap between ethnographers and tourists, perhaps further scrutiny here may throw some light on the shadow side of our anthropological selves. MacCannell suggests that we are very different from tourists because mystification is fundamental to tourism whereas we are clear about our motives (1976: 179). This may sound commonsensical enough, but we must not exaggerate the extent to which tourists are mystified, nor can we afford to exaggerate the level of reflexive insight we have attained.

Both anthropologists and international tourists are temporary strangers in another culture and their reasons for being there are very much more to do with our culture rather than the interests of the 'other'. What for one is the 'pleasure periphery' visiting which gains one kudos, for the other is the 'ethnographic periphery' where one gets data to build a career. At the end of the stay, tourists leave clutching what they prize - photos, souvenirs etc. – and anthropologists leave clutching notes (and, no doubt, photos and souvenirs as well). What for one is a matter of conspicuous consumption, for the other is conspicuous production (of data, and later publications). While in the field both rely on a range of local 'culture brokers' who know what they want – tourist guides in the one case, and interpreters, research assistants, and the like, in the other – their guides and our informants may not be dissimilar in their motivations. If we look somewhat askance at the brief, instrumental relations established with locals by tourists trying to get what they want, behind our own myths of 'rapport' and 'immersion', we actually engage our energies in entrepreneurially forging links which will deliver the goods we are after. As tourists move on, failing to keep promises about sending gifts or writing, so many anthropologists let relationships fade once back in the writing environment and with a different audience; the anthropologist is also free to 'pick up and go' (Mintz 1977: 56–9). If the tourist is 'at play' while we are 'at work', we must recognise that for the anthropologist, the field is a rest from normal routine academic duties (Gonzalez 1986: 97). Fieldwork is also very much like playing a game. The irony of the field situation, its ethical ambiguity, are very much to do with the fact that participant observation is like 'playing at' being a member of another culture (Karp and Kendall 1982: 257). Let us, finally, not forget that though academics, we are not in a totally different universe to tourists, sightseers and spectacle hunters: etymologically, the terms 'theory' and 'theorist' derive from the Greek for sightseer and spectacle (Abbeele 1980: 13). We are, in other words, intellectual tourists. If these suggested similarities between anthropologists and tourists seem unpalatable, others writing in the reflexive mode have recently found other identities to compare us to – conmen, double agents, shamans, tricksters, among others (Schechner 1982: 81; Boon 1982: x, 6).

We need to look again at the interactive, dialogical basis from which much of our anthropological knowledge ultimately derives. On a street corner in Kandy stood an ethnographer and an informant. But we have only to ask what kind of an ethnographer the informant is, and what kind of a tourist the anthropologist is, in order to see very differently the identities of 'self' and 'other' involved. Did I not spend much time reading novels, being bored, hating the place I was in, and having very mixed feelings about the people I was with, just like most tourists (Barley 1983: 20, 97)? And did Ali's very livelihood not depend upon his knowledge of human nature, his understanding of what people from other cultures were after, and his ability to act quickly in social situations – in short a well-developed anthropological sensibility? And if Ali did regard me as some kind of tourist, employing the same rules in our relationship as he did in those with other tourists, does this undo the value of his testimony anyway? After all, if our relationship was between a tourist and a local, it was exactly such relationships that I had come to Kandy to explore.

Such a view highlights the irony of the field situation. It is obvious that 'participant observation' coexists with a series of sometimes painful contradictions – stranger/friend, involvement/detachment and so on. One of these ever-present tensions is that between having insight and being in the dark, and sometimes, indeed, not being able to recognise the difference. This is a familiar existential situation for ethnographers in terms of the relationships they create in the field, just as for everyone else. Perhaps we have to accept that to the extent that our fieldwork is reflexive, it must be ambiguous (Karp and Kendall 1982: 250). Even if it were theoretically possible to remove the uncertainties in my relationship with Ali, the possibility of even commencing the task is not there for me at present. Kandy has not escaped the escalating violence in Sri Lanka over the past few years, a violence which has severely crippled the tourism industry in that country. The relative calm which made mass tourism possible also made my stay, and thus my relationship with Ali, possible. I have left the place I call 'the field', but Ali is still there. It says something about the courage of one anthropological self, that while the occasional tourist will still, no doubt, be passing Ali's corner, the threat of violence notwithstanding, I am only prepared to risk myself to the extent of writing papers, from a very safe distance, about my experiences there.

REFERENCES

Abbeele, G. van den (1980) Sightseers. The Tourist as Theorist. *Diacritics* 10, December: 2–14.
Adler, P. A. and Adler, P. (1987) *Membership Roles in Field Research*. Beverly Hills: Sage.
Agar, M. (1980) *The Professional Stranger. An Informal Introduction to Ethnography*. New York: Academic Press.
—— (1986) *Speaking of Ethnography*. Beverly Hills: Sage.
Barley, N. (1983) *The Innocent Anthropologist. Notes from a Mud Hut*. London: Colonnade Books/British Museum Publications Ltd.
Berghe, P. L. van den (1980) Tourism as Ethnic Relations: A Case Study of Cuzco, Peru. *Ethnic and Racial Studies* 3: 375–92.
Berreman, G. D. (1972) Behind Many Masks: Ethnography and Impression Management. In G. D. Berreman *Hindus of the Himalayas. Ethnography and Change*. Berkeley: University of California Press.
Bleek, W. (1979) Envy and Inequality in Fieldwork: An Example from Ghana. *Human Organization* 38: 200–5.
Boon, J. (1982) *Other Tribes, Other Scribes. Symbolic Anthropology in the Comparative Study of Cultures, History, Religion, and Texts*. Cambridge: Cambridge University Press.
Brewer, J. D. (1984) Tourism and Ethnic Stereotypes. Variations in a Mexican Town. *Annals of Tourism Research* 11: 487–501.
Cesara, M. (1982) *Reflections of a Woman Anthropologist. No Hiding Place*. London: Academic Press.
Clifford, J. (1983) On Ethnographic Authority. *Representations* 1: 118–45.
Crapanzano, V. (1976) On the Writing of Ethnography. *Dialectical Anthropology* 2: 169–73.
—— (1980) *Tuhami. Portrait of a Moroccan*. Chicago: Chicago University Press.
Crick, M. (1976) *Explorations in Language and Meaning. Towards a Semantic Anthropology*. London: Malaby Press.
—— (1982) Anthropology of Knowledge. *Annual Review of Anthropology* 11: 287–313.
—— (1985) 'Tracing' the Anthropological Self: Quizzical Reflections on Field Work, Tourism and the Ludic. *Social Analysis* 17: 71–92.
—— (1988) Sun, Sex, Sights, Savings and Servility. Representations of International Tourism in the Social Sciences. *Criticism, Heresy and Interpretation* 1: 37–76.
—— (1989) Shifting Identities in the Research Process: An Essay in Personal

Anthropology. In J. Perry (ed.) *Doing Fieldwork: Eight Personal Accounts of Social Research*. Geelong: Deakin University Press.

Devereux, G. (1967) *From Anxiety to Method in the Behavioural Sciences*. The Hague: Mouton.

Dumont, J.-P. (1978) *The Headman and I. Ambiguity and Ambivalence in the Fieldwork Experience*. Austin, Texas: University of Texas Press.

Dwyer, K. (1979) The Dialogic of Ethnology. *Dialogical Anthropology* 4(3): 205–24.

—— (1982) *Moroccan Dialogues. Anthropology in Question*. Baltimore: Johns Hopkins University Press.

Fabian, J. (1979) Rule and process. Thoughts on Ethnography as Communication. *Philosophy of the Social Sciences* 9: 1–26.

Fowles, J. (1977) *The Magus*. A revised edition. London: Triad/Granada.

Gans, H. J. (1968) The Participant Observer as a Human Being: Observations on the Personal Aspects of Fieldwork. In R. G. Burgess (ed.) (1982) *Field Research. A Sourcebook and Field Manual*. London: George Allen and Unwin.

Geertz, C. (1968) Thinking as a Moral Act. Ethical Dimensions of Anthropological Fieldwork in the New States. *Antioch Review*: 139–58.

Georges, R. A. and Jones, M. O. (1980) *People Studying People. The Human Element in Fieldwork*. Berkeley, Calif.: University of California Press.

Golde, P. (1970) Odyssey of Encounter. In P. Golde (ed.) (1970) *Women in the Field. Anthropological Experiences*. Chicago: Aldine Publishing Company.

Goldkind, V. (1970) Anthropologists, Informants and the Achievement of Power in Chan Kom. *Sociologus* 20(1): 17–41.

Gonzalez, N. L. (1986) The anthropologist as female head of household. In T. L. Whitehead and M. E. Conaway (eds) (1986) *Self, Sex and Gender in Cross-Cultural Fieldwork*. Urbana: University of Illinois Press.

Gould, H. A. (1975) Two Decades of Fieldwork in India. Some Reflections. In A. Beteille and I. N. Madan (eds) (1975) *Encounter and Experience. Personal Accounts of Fieldwork*. Delhi: Vikas Publishing House.

Hammersley, M. and Atkinson, P. (1983) *Ethnography. Principles in Practice*. London: Tavistock Publications.

Herzfeld, M. (1983) Looking Both Ways. The Ethnographer in the Text. *Semiotica* 46: 151–66.

Karp, I. and Kendall, M. B. (1982) Reflexivity in fieldwork. In P. Secord (ed.) (1982) *Explaining Human Behaviour*. Beverly Hills: Sage.

Kirk, J. and Miller, M. (1986) *Reliability and Validity in Qualitative Research*. Beverly Hills: Sage.

Lundberg, C. (1968) A Transactional Conception of Fieldwork. *Human Organisation* 27: 45–9.

MacCannell, D. (1976) *The Tourist. A New Theory of the Leisure Class*. New York: Schocken Books.

Marcus, G. E. (1980) The Ethnographic Subject as Ethnographer: A Neglected Dimension of Anthropological Research. *Rice University Studies* 66 (1): 55–68.

McKean, F. (1976) An Anthropological Analysis of the Culture-brokers of Bali: Guides, Tourists and Balinese. Paris: UNESCO/IBRD.

Mintz, S. (1977) Infant, Victim, and Tourist. The Anthropologist in the Field. *Johns Hopkins Magazine* 27(5): 55–60.

Peshkin, A. (1985) Virtuous Subjectivity. In the Participant Observer's I's. In D. N. Berg and K. K. Smith (eds) (1985) *Exploring Clinical Methods for Social Research*. Beverly Hills: Sage.

Pouwer, J. 1973. Signification in Fieldwork. *Journal of Symbolic Anthropology* 1: 1–13.

Rabinow, P. (1977) *Reflections on Fieldwork in Morocco*. Berkeley, Calif.: University of California Press.

Richardson, M. (1975) Anthropologist – The Myth Teller. *American Ethnologist* **2**: 517–33.

Schechner, R. (1982) Collective Reflexivity: Restoration of Behaviour. In J. Ruby (ed.) *A Crack in the Mirror. Reflexive Perspectives in Anthropology*. Philadelphia: University of Pennsylvania Press.

Wax, R. H. (1960) Twelve Years After. An Analysis of a Fieldwork Experience. In R. N. Adams and J. J. Preiss (eds) *Human Organisation. Field Relations and Techniques*. Homewood: Dorsey Press.

Webster, S. (1982) Dialogue and Fiction in Ethnography. *Dialectical Anthropology* **7**: 91–114.

Whittaker, E. (1981) Anthropological Ethics, Fieldwork and Epistemological Disjunctures. *Philosophy of the Social Sciences* **11**: 437–51.

Whyte, W. H. (1955) *Street-Corner Society. The Social Structure of an Italian Slum*. Chicago: Chicago University Press.

Chapter 12

From affect to analysis

The biography of an interaction in an English village

Nigel Rapport

[A]ny history or description of a social situation is an exercise of psychological knowledge. (Simmel 1908a)

THE INTERACTION

It is late afternoon in Cedar High farmyard, located on the edge of the village of Wanet in the Yorkshire Dales National Park. Doris and Nigel are loading up Doris's Vauxhall estate with dairy goods in preparation for the morning milk-round. Sid has just driven up the farm lane in his beaten-up Bedford van and is now leaning on the gate outside the cold-store room, smoking, while he watches Nigel doing the hefting. In anxious voice, Doris says, 'I just been on the phone to that Mr Park Warden you know Sid, and I'm still no better off now. I wanted to know if the building can start yet, right, but I couldn't get a straight answer. I don't know ... Fred'll have to phone again later and speak to his senior.'

'Nay. Those pencil-pushers want burning,' Sid sympathises. 'They want taking to the Strasbourg International Court, because I doubt what they're doing is legal.' Then his voice mellows, 'But you know, with all due respect, folks round here worry too much about them twined, narrow-backed buggers. Best thing is just to act dumb and ignore them; pretend you don't know, and ask their advice and then they're real! I mean all these offcomers think farming folk are unskilled, and lowest of the low – lower than an ant's armpit, right – so you just gotta beat them at their own game; act dumb, cos they're fine if they think they're telling you something.'

Nigel grins as he passes Sid with a load of yoghurts, but Doris's tired tones continue from the dairy. 'I'm almost sorry we began the new building at all ... But me and Fred've not had a lot yet, the farm's still bibs and bobs and you got to work like this at some stage of your life haven't you, to get what you want for family and house and that ... But I get so angry, them all coming round and telling us what to do. There's like a bubble of anger inside me wanting to explode.' Doris stops her sorting and looks toward Sid for emphasis, 'Ooh, and that woman in the planning department with the thick Scottish accent: I just wanted to throw her through the window. You'll have to speak to her next time she's here, Nigel,' she concludes, as Nigel returns from the last of the ferrying trips to the car-boot. Nigel laughs. 'Right,' he says, and heads over to where Fred has now finished the milking to help muck-out the shippon.

This was the kind of exchange in which Doris, Nigel and Sid would habitually engage; for in the early 1980s they were all living as neighbours in Wanet. Doris was treating Nigel (me) as apprentice farm-boy on the farm she ran with husband Fred, and had recently hired Sid to build the concrete walls of a large new cowshed for their expanding Friesian dairy herd. Sid was self-employed and a jack-of-all-trades, as well as being Doris's brother-in-law. He, Joanna (his wife), and Doris and Fred would quite often relax together over a dinner outside Wanet, enjoying the change of air. Doris, Nigel and Sid would also regularly bump into one another in one of the dale's pubs, especially on a darts-and-domino league night.

More significantly, Doris thought Sid was a braggart, two-faced and a fool. But then it was always good to talk out your troubles, and she could lead Sid into making the most hare-brained suggestions or into releasing the latest revealing titbit about his menagerie of a family and rocky marriage. At least she was better off than some!

Sid recognised in Doris the simplistic grasp of business matters that he expected in women. The least he could do when he came to Cedar High Farm to see two of his closest friends was to seem to take her silly worries seriously, and remind her there were always solutions to be found if locals stuck together.

Neither Doris nor Sid expected much verbal return from Nigel. He was a city kid who had come to Wanet to do some college project, only to find local work more rewarding. Doris sometimes found him 'underneath' or the wrong side out, but this was probably the after-effects of another night 'on the pop' up the pub; she had known other youngsters who were 'deep', not thinking much about anything at all beyond their own fantasy worlds. Sid, meanwhile, found Nigel's reticence more suspect, coming as it did from an 'offcomer' without history or connexions; not just an unskilled pup, living off the backs of working people, but a 'mystery-man', come to Wanet happen to report on real country characters like himself. But now with Nigel as his builder's mate, at least Sid could work him so hard that he had little time to chitter or faff about.

Nigel was working with Doris and Sid because he was engaged in anthropological participant-observation. Having them take him in hand, he could legitimately keep quiet while memorising more of their words and actions. By being quiescent he hoped to direct conversation and impressions as little as possible, to appear less of a threat, to differentiate himself from the presumptuousness of other offcomers – the tourists, second-home owners and retired who were coming into Wanet from off-aways – and to have local people construct him in their image.

THE ARGUMENT

I have begun to describe the relations between myself, as ethnographer in an English village, and two of my acquaintances in the field. It has become an anthropological commonplace in recent years that 'ethnographic reality is actively constructed, not to say invented' (Dumont, 1978: 66). Anthropologists make meaning in those environments in which they work, anticipating and accounting for events, as do their informants. However, not only are anthropologists social actors managing meanings through habitual interaction with others, they are also social actors engaged in interaction which, at least for them, is radically new. And here is the key to the anthropological enterprise: the opportunity to compare. Ethnographic data derive, firstly, from a comparison of meanings construed by anthropologists outside the field with those inside, and secondly, from a comparison of their own meanings with those they learn from their informants. What is involved is a cognitive shuttling between different constructions of experience and a juxtaposition of these (such juxtaposition remaining significant even when it is admitted that informants' meanings are of necessity empathetic constructions by anthropologists, dimensions and refractions of how they manage themselves).

The specific interactions in which the anthropologists' interpretations of ethnographic reality take place are critical to the whole exercise therefore, and such specificity should be revealed in reported accounts. This is so, I would contend, not only in the interests of intellectual scrupulousness regarding the route taken from observation to conclusion – although this is undoubtedly true – nor yet because the particular chemistry and circumstance of meetings between particular actors will eventuate in particular informations – although this is equally true – but because close focusing on the construction of meaning by individuals in interaction highlights important features of the constitutive dynamics of social life which might otherwise be lost, and certainly in the past have been obscured.

Hence, my course in this chapter is to further contextualise the interaction between Doris, Sid and Nigel with which I opened in terms of the individual biographies through whose juxtaposition it came to take place. I argue that regular relations between these three, in the form of routine meetings of words and actions such as this, occurred as a result of, and in the service of, their biographical diversities: the sameness of the common behaviours publicly exchanged, verbal and other, being a veneer covering diverse private intent. Indeed, to record such routine forms of cultural relations without reporting on the particular individuals who regularly used them in interaction would be to denude the forms of the purposes and process by which they were habitually brought to life.

First I recount the biographies of the three speakers; then I detail their conceptions of the relationships maintained by this particular interaction.[1]

THE BIOGRAPHIES

Doris is in her late thirties. She married young, to a local farmer, and had two children before he died of a freak heart attack. Doris inherited the farm, since her husband had been an only child, but, distraught with grief, she could put her mind to little for over a year. Then she met Fred, a local joiner but brought up on a farm (which his elder brother had inherited), and together they began to put Cedar High Farm on the map. Now she and Fred have been married a number of years, have two more children, and a farm edging up into the Wanet 'big league'. However, it has been a hard slog. Farming, after all, calls for more intelligence, stamina and learning than other professions because there is responsibility for so much life, and you can never wholly prepare for tomorrow. But then Doris is no skiver from hard work; she prides herslf that between them she and Fred coordinate an efficient business. None the less, she is bitter. It seems folk prefer to pity your misfortune and offer you charity than see you improve your position in life: now that Cedar High Farm has begun to prove itself, one-time sympathisers prove fickle. They want to take control of her farm and her life, have her and Fred as their dependants. But then having Fred's support makes all the difference. When he's working outside Doris feels protected, even when she's emotional and feels weak: he's predictable, and aggressive when it's necessary. She also has Polly, her former mother-in-law, and like a mother to her now that her own has died and her father become senile; Polly has long been someone to look up to. Doris's father was only a farm-manager and when she married on to Cedar High it was Polly who first taught her how to act more posh: how to respect property and the law; be sportsmanlike; emulate the upper classes who are better educated and better spoken; despise those vulgar members of the lower classes who wilfully refuse higher principles, who riot and rebel when thwarted in their search for short-term gain. Now Doris feels she is slowly making gains.

When Doris is fed up, of course, she also has girlfriends her own age. Relaxing with them over a drink in the pub she can forget the workaday world. She does not booze to excess, needless to say, since she is not saddled with the immoderateness of youth or the laxity of old age, and Fred is always there in case the drink breaks through her female defences. So it is nice sometimes to be chaperoned outside the farm.

But then again, Doris does not like leaving her children too long alone.

She should have learnt that it's no good caring too much about someone or something because then they just seem to die, but she cannot help herself: she was born soft. She was also born stupid, but one thing she was born good at was organising, and she is determined to organise a good family. So Craig (nine), Jessica (twelve), Karen (fifteen) and Keith (nineteen) (when home from the army) all know their role in the farm's smooth running. A close, happy family, Doris believes to be the source of the greatest happiness, and her farm is its material base. Indeed, Cedar High is the embodiment of their familial reputation, and if her children were ever to do something which besmirched it she has told them she could kill them – if she did not die of shame first.

Maintaining the farm sanctuary, however, is increasingly difficult. For other parents quiz her children in order to dig up dirt, and have their children teach hers bad habits. Moreover, this seems to be part of a general trend in Wanet. There used to be a traditional way of life here: hard but happy; people were bred to it and all pulled together. Then it became adulterated by the arrival of more and more city folk: offcomers who were stupid, thieving and effeminate – but rich. And now, locals seem to be copying them. Instead of standing united, neighbours helping their inter-dependent businesses in the harsh world of the market, they compete with one another, curry individual favours from offcomer visitors and dictatorial officials, and act quarrelsome and soft. It is all part of a national disease, Doris feels. Travel and cross-breeding have upset the natural rhythms of life; rhythms which have bred certain characteristics for certain habitats: English rhythms for England, urban rhythms for the city, Dale rhythms for Wanet. The cure is for foreigners to leave England to the English race, and offcomers to leave Wanet to its locals; maybe if the cities were improved, city folk would not want to leave them. Meanwhile, Doris sits it out with Fred and tries to uphold traditional ways. She would really like to remind people how offcomer stock just does not belong, but she bites her lip. When neighbours can do anything against you, your family, your animals and your business, and everyone seems to take offence so easily, its best to try and avoid possibly antagonising anyone.

Sid is in his mid thirties and has two sons, Dennis (sixteen) and Christopher (thirteen), and a daughter, Helen (fifteen). But his marriage to Joanna has not been a happy one and at various stages they have gone their separate ways. At the moment he is back with her again, but now makes sure he has room to breathe. He gives Joanna her housekeeping, eats her meals, sleeps with her, escorts her to the pub, even shows her new sites he is working, but he also likes to be off with his mates and he teases her if at these times she gets too close. But then it's only right for men to be together for a bit, working or boozing, betting, playing darts, scrapping and comparing notes about women. Sometimes Sid thinks women were the worst animal created;

always acting contrarily, they seem intent on weakening men or else ruining their friendships. So he always jokes about Joanna – she's frigid, she's bad-tempered, she's a miserable cook – and warns snoopers off.

Joanna gets occasional work as a daily maid, but Sid sees himself as a master-craftsman. He can build (lay bricks, plaster, paint, weld, roof, wall and fence); he can drive an HGV; he can manage a farm (run a dairy, handle sheep, work dogs and operate farm machinery). Mastery over all these skills, Sid is proud to say, earns him an independent living on the open market. The dole will never catch him; he could never be like these immoral people content to live off other taxpayers, off government hand-outs. And this is natural enough after all: those who will not work are sick animals who should be put out of their misery. Moreover, Sid's expertise came from years of apprenticeship and hard graft: no book-learning and paper diplomas for him. And this is how it should be: the unskilled learning from the skilled, the child from the adult, gradually and by imitation.

Sid's childhood was a happy time. His father was a cowman and often on the move around Wanet, taking his wife and three children from job to job. But even though poor, those years were ones of warmth and security. His parents were patient, his pals loyal, his teachers strict but fair. Thus protected both from sadistic coppers and from mean employers, Sid slowly left his naïve childhood world, gained concentration and self-control, and began to respect his parents' achievements and copy their ways.

Adolescence, however, brought upheaval when his father's retirement to a council house some miles outside Wanet estranged Sid from his pals. The strength of his parents was ebbing and he was left at the mercy of vicious, foreign gangs with which he was not popular. He could not really settle. But he did learn the ways of working a wider world, building up, indeed, a national network of job-contacts. Then, as soon as he could, Sid returned to Wanet to live.

Marrying Joanna in his late teens was the start of another blissful period. With her sister Doris and (then) husband Dick living on Cedar High Farm round the corner, it was like a reconvening of childhood associations. As newly-weds they struggled together to bring up families on meagre incomes. They worked and relaxed together, shared, bolstered each other up. In those days it was great living in an old village like Wanet. Everyone saw and said a lot of everyone else. Everyone was happy to practise old-fashioned skills in traditional ways.

But now the whole world has changed. For a start, children grow up too 'cute' by half. In a society without discipline, they become argumentative, ungrateful and always after the quick killing. Then, hard work is not respected; people put up with shoddy workmanship while the true crafts-man finds it hard to make ends meet. Next, these selfish and workshy, albeit silver-tongued, outsiders start prancing around Wanet as if they owned it; buying up property with their easy money, sticking their oars into every local committee, assured of support from forked-tongued offcomers in government. Finally, Sid even finds old pals in Wanet turning against him; like Doris and Fred, doing quite nicely on Cedar High Farm now, and forgetting those real friends who always stuck by them in the past.

Sometimes Sid feels like just sitting back and watching the world explode. At other times, he looks forward to a civil war when he can help the army and its allies rid the country of the radicals, students, perverts and Blacks who are now in command; jealous of England's glorious past and unique character, they just want to make it as uncivilised as everywhere else. Sid does what he can in Wanet anyhow. He curses offcomers, reminds young people about Wanet tradition, and shows their parents, by example, how to get the better of outside institutions. He'll stay 'tricky' and on the move, until the day locals unite and physically purge their dale.

Nigel is in his mid twenties. Single, he comes from a close-knit Jewish family in Cardiff. Both his parents come from religiously orthodox backgrounds, but their families have been in Britain since escaping from Eastern European pogroms in the 1880s and now feel well established. Initially, they set themselves up in business – clothing and wholesaling – first in London, then in Manchester and Cardiff, but both families have since come to boast their 'doctors and lawyers'. In particular Nigel's parents were eager that their children should have the educational opportunities which, growing up during the Second World War, peripatetic and Jewish, had escaped them. So they sent him and his young sister away to public schools in Bristol; then she went on to practise Fine Art and he went up to Cambridge.

Above all, Nigel's parents impressed upon him and his sister that they were special: Jewish in a country which had enabled them to become well-off. Now they had privileges their forebears did not. Therefore, they should be proud of their Jewishness and its traditions, but also appreciate the idiosyncrasies of the country around them: its liberalism, literature, history, security and beauty. They should use this wealth and succeed in terms of it; neither become parochial Welshmen nor isolationist Jews, but climb to the top of their chosen tree. That famous day would redeem all former sacrifice – their own, their parents', their religious group's.

Nigel felt great ambivalence about all of this. Sometimes he felt proud of his family name and looked forward to his own renown. At other times all he wanted was to be the same as everyone else: not saddled with difference but able to accept mediocrity and belong. He used to sing, or at least hum, the Welsh national anthem crossing the Severn bridge from school (then university) to home; one day he would change his name and become anonymous. But mostly he found himself standing outside himself, hearing his biography being read, or watching it filmed, and recounting his activities in the third person, even as he lived through them. It was a way of distancing himself from daily tests, and postponing the decision about whether his progress was happening to him or somebody else. Besides, these days did not need to be lived to the full because they were only steps along the way to his becoming, and they would be redeemed later: there was always higher and better ahead. The same went for relationships. Friends could, with relief, be sloughed off when a new grade had been achieved, and a better self could be built among those who did not know the weaknesses of the old. Only parents and sister knew Nigel's whole story, and they were backstage with him.

Recovering on a kibbutz from Finals, Nigel discovered something of a mediation. For here was a society of both heroic individualism and great familial care, of intellectuality and physicality, of life lived too immediately, even desperately, to be simultaneously reflected upon; and where, moreover, Jewishness was routine and an emblematic Star of David not something embarrassing, faintly obscene. So Nigel decided to go to Manchester, home of Gluckman's Israeli researches: a Ph.D. from living on a kibbutz would seem a happy compromise. Social anthropology, which he had originally stumbled on as an adjunct to archaeology, continued with because, as it turned out, the Comanches were more congenial then Mousterian cores, would finally be pursued as the path toward coming to terms with himself.

Manchester, however, had moved on. To do something significant, the new professor advised, was not to work in Israel: try 'patronage' in Spain; or, yes, England would also do. Thus Nigel redefined his feelings for Israel as 'holiday romance' and went north – the Lakes, the Dales – to find a village research location, and accommodation. This did not prove easy. Tourism had killed off the cheap rent, and second- or retirement-homes had taken over some villages completely. In Wanet, however, Nigel took up a vague invitation to visit a woman his mother had once met on a coach; they had spent a pleasant hour comparing children. The woman had been impressed by his mother's gentility and she soon appreciated Nigel's own polite company; she also knew of a cottage for rent over the winter.

Before he left for the field, Nigel was advised that fieldwork in Britain was, to a Briton, like nowhere else: local people would not appreciate being studied and may grant the newcomer no licence for oddness or naïvety. So be discreet, play down 'anthropology' and the accoutrements of formal sociological research, and avoid tourists! Nigel looked forward to his research, nevertheless. It would be something of a dream ticket: passage to a doctorate (and membership of an academic community) and passage to genuine Britishness at the same time.

Having settled into Wanet, however, moved from the cottage into a caravan on Cedar High Farm and achieved the surety of local work and local statuses, Nigel is not so sure. Far from 'solving' his ambivalence, far from finding values that he respects and would like to own, as his fieldwork progresses so Nigel discovers people leading petty lives, tied within narrow borders to stultifying pasts, entailing the depreciation of all the cosmo-politan virtues on which his self-esteem is based. It is fortunate too that

'Rapport' can be taken as French in origin not 'Jewy', and that most people just know him as 'Nigel from Cedar High'. Either he is worthless (like they say) and these eminently practical Dalesmen are the true descendants of English renaissance man, or else 'cultured', caring and liberal Britain is elsewhere. But then more likely still is that in their prejudices and the particularity of their values, he merely sees the counterparts of his own.

THE BIOGRAPHIES INTERRELATED

It is these biographies which I would relate together in order to ground this interaction, to explain why talking-relations between the three were maintained.

Thus, Doris saw in Sid cheap farm labour, even if a close watch had to be kept on him. For he had little ability or consistency and no desire to better himself. Indeed, if you let Sid be, he was idle, bossy, and disruptive of farm schedules and order, while boastful off Cedar High of his efforts, and her and Fred's helplessness. But at least she and Fred knew his measure: he could not say worse about them than he already had. So, they didn't mind helping him out by giving him odd jobs for back-pocket money and being neighbourly: it was not worth having Sid bearing grudges.

Sid saw in Doris, meanwhile, a good woman and long-time friend, upholding many traditional kindnesses and local skills. He liked paying frequent calls to Cedar High Farm, showing an interest in latest developments, because farm news was good local news. Cedar High Farm was like a joint asset that could help ensure the survival of a Wanet way of life, and the group of childhood pals who ran it. Sometimes, it was true, Doris forgot he was one of her most loyal friends, showing little respect for his skills and acting the interfering female. At these times he really felt like walking out and leaving Fred to give her a real talking-to. But then they all usually made it up with a good boozing session, and managed to keep the long-haired 'Arabs' off the pub dartboard for an entire evening.

In Nigel, Doris saw a stray who needed help building a pathway for himself in this harsh world. Furthermore, even though Nigel was bred with the urban traits of weakness, short-sightedness and ignorance, it was good for Fred to have an extra pair of hands around the place because crafting the cowshed was making him look tired. All Nigel had to be wary of was not becoming a liability; he had to beware giving anything away to nosy adults such as Sid. If Nigel kept farm secrets, then she would be equally silent about his faults and quirks, and her kindness in correcting them.

When Sid first met Nigel he was duly chary. He informed Nigel about 'phonecalls' he had made to check up on him, and that he was in Wanet on sufferance – so long as he esteemed the right people. Nigel, however, turned out to be no threat; you could feed him all manner of tall tales and still extricate just what you wanted to know. A few months mixing cement and carrying concrete at the rate Sid demanded and Nigel would not know whether to shit or shiver. Meanwhile, he would learn all about Sid's prowess – which women's holes Sid had filled or was going to, and which men's gobs.

Nigel was quite attracted to Doris: she was friendly and spunky. But then he also found her duplicitous with guests and affectionate to her besotted children only to the extent that they did their duty by the farm. Him she regularly caught in a number of infuriating double-binds: if she found him lazy, for example, it was the typical behaviour of an offcomer student; but if he worked too hard it was an attempt to take over the farm. Sid meanwhile – bitter, macho, reactionary and insecure, yet highly witty and astute – Nigel was drawn to as if the essential embodiment of his fieldwork experience. If he could win Sid over, or at least achieve a *modus vivendi*, it would feel as if the whole enterprise were a success. What was more, if their fates had been otherwise, a liminal figure like Sid (scrabbling for money and respect; toying with local traditions for which he wanted to feel nostalgia and yet which he had stepped irreversibly beyond) could have been conducting anthropological enquiry on him.

Nigel was pleased to have acquired regular relations with Sid and Doris, none the less, and would do whatever was necessary to maintain them. Fieldnotes were what mattered, and mailing more out of the dale felt like more capital secured. Meanwhile, he was providing free labour, as well as a butt for the free unloading of local anger and scorn; he was determined not to flaunt the extraneous experiences of an outside self.

THE ANALYSIS OF FORM AND MEANING

There is a complex overlap of definitions, then, as Doris, Sid and Nigel meet in the conversation with which this chapter began. Moreover, as was mentioned, the interaction is a routine one: Doris's, Sid's and Nigel's world-views habitually meet, influence and fulfil one another in this fashion. In Devereux's terminology (1978: 126–9), the interaction is an example of 'ego-syntonism': an enactment of forms of behaviour (confiding in a neighbour, reassuring a woman, instructing an apprentice, criticising offcomers, enjoy-ing a smoke at a sister-in-law's, loading up a vehicle for a milk-round) which all consider appropriate but which are used for the expression and gratifica-tion of a variety of meanings and motivations, instrumental and expressive. These may conceive of, inform, and be served by the enactment in different ways and to different extents, but they need not become harmonised, homogenised, or even more similar as the collective act proceeds or is repeated. The conversational meeting can be routine and yet remain an aggregation of diversity (Rapport, 1986: *passim*). Indeed, I would go further and say that diversity is the constitutive force: that it is through the variegated world-views that the collective act is maintained. Doris, Sid and Nigel regularly engage in interactions like this because of the personal ends they have to pursue and, in the name of neighbourliness, apprenticeship, traditionalism and so on, are easily able to do. These broadly public concepts and common behavioural forms are built upon far narrower personal bases, in short, and kept alive through possibly highly idiosyncratic use.

That is, I find the interaction pervaded by a significant dialectic: the tension between common forms and diverse meanings, between individual lives and cultural relations. Individuals 'consume' cultural artefacts, as Simmel envisioned it, in order to create and develop themselves (1971b: 351). Here, relations between Doris, Sid and Nigel represent superficial overlaps between separate and often rather different lives: alignments of individual lines of action for the achievement of often contradictory ends. Nevertheless, the three engage in their self-constructions side-by-side (by interacting with one another in public), and therefore the cultural artefacts they incorporate must be common ones, and exchanged in common ways. Indeed, were it not for the ready availability and legitimacy of the set of common behaviours, their limited number, their durability, their malleability and ambiguity, Doris, Sid and Nigel would be unable to maintain and further their biographies: to impart meaning to actions – others' and their own – and express this before one another as participants in, witnesses to, and audiences of, their daily constructed events. The collective behaviours can be said to represent a fund of clichés into which Doris, Sid and Nigel routinely dip, a socially accepted currency which they have all learnt how to use and agreed regularly to exchange; they do this, however, in personal and possibly non-consensually construed ways (Rapport, 1987: 185). Hence we reach the fundamental dualism that to understand the maintenance of cultural relations is to appreciate the specificity of the individual meanings that live through them: without individuals with diverse biographies to extend, there would be no relationships, and without common behavioral forms in which these could be lived and made flesh, no individual biographies.[2]

NOTES

1.

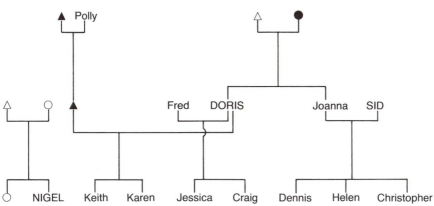

2. For comment and criticism, my thanks to Emanuel Marx, Moshe Schwartz, Gideon Kressel, Frank Stewart and Anthony Cohen.

REFERENCES

Devereux, G. (1978) *Ethnopsychoanalysis*. Berkeley, Calif.: University of California Press.
Dumont, J.-P. (1978) *The Headman and I*. Austin, Texas: University of Texas Press.
Rapport, N. J. (1986) Cedar High Farm: Ambiguous Symbolic Boundary. An Essay in Anthropological Intuition. In A. P. Cohen (ed.) *Symbolising Boundaries*. Manchester: Manchester University Press.
—— (1987) *Talking Violence. An Anthropological Interpretation of Conversation in the City*. St John's: ISER Books.
Simmel, G. (1971/1908a) The Problem of Sociology. In D. Levine (ed.) *Georg Simmel*. Chicago: Chicago University Press.
—— (1971/1908b) Social Forms and Inner Needs. In D. Levine (ed.) *Georg Simmel*. Chicago: Chicago University Press.

Chapter 13

Tense in ethnography
Some practical considerations

John Davis

We can use a variety of tenses when we write ethnography, and we choose one rather than another by conventions which are generally available to ordinary writers of English (and, so far as I am aware, French, Italian, German, Dutch, Danish, Spanish). We sometimes describe ourselves as using 'the ethnographic present'; but in my view that is misleading. Anthropologists do not use the present in ways which are exclusive to them, nor even in ways which they invented and which are now more widely diffused. And in any case, they use the present tenses so variously, with such different implications, that to refer to them as *the* ethnographic present conveys a wrong impression.

It is sensible to examine conventions from time to time, to see if they need revision in the light of experience and needs. Indeed, in the last few years textualist critics, 'meta-anthropologists' (Rabinow 1986: 43) have thought to undertake the task for us, no doubt considering we were too unreflective. I am not sure, however, that their efforts can have much practical consequence. First because they are predicated on the assumption that a text has meaning independent of its writer: 'the ability of a text to make sense in a coherent way depends less on the willed intentions of an originating author than on the creative activity of a reader' (Clifford 1983: 141). It would be surprising if their texts were much use to practical writers. Secondly, at least some of their texts exhibit the defects which they attribute to ethnography. We are criticised, for instance, for using the 'distancing' present tense,[1] which is conventional also in literary criticism. So, while Evans-Pritchard wrote *Nuer Religion* fifty years ago, Rosaldo among others discusses its intricacies in the present tense (Rosaldo 1986). You may not quarrel particularly with that; but in my role as a creative reader I think I am entitled to register that the prose used to analyse our prose and ethics exhibits many of the characteristics we are attacked for: the distancing present, the attribution of latent meanings beyond our purposeful control are both the object and the means of attack. How often too, our latent meanings 'betray' themselves; and they are nearly always vices, imputed through the device of 'it is no coincidence that ...'. 'Anthropology' becomes an anthology of the unselfconsciously betrayed intellectual and ethical failings of various notable practitioners. Extracted and combined they constitute such a pettily monstrous discipline, it becomes hard to understand why anyone should want to make the meta- of it. And you may begin to feel resentful that the tribe we belong to has such censoriously functionalist ethnographers: Clifford, perhaps, has an affection for us; but in general they lack the abundant geniality and wonder of Malinowski, or the meticulous sympathy of Evans-Pritchard, the linguistic subtlety of Ardener, the constructive fantasy of Leach; or even, I think I dare add, the intellectual rigour of Mair.

It was she who once said of a colleague with whom she found herself momentarily but still reluctantly in agreement, that it was a very rare gift to be completely wrong all the time. And it is in that spirit that I want to discuss tense in ethnography. That is one area in which textual critics have not been completely wrong, although the issues seem to me to be more complex than they have often said; and are essentially practical issues, not ones of principle.

In brief, I wish to justify the following assertions:

In English we have at our disposal a repertoire of eight uses of the present tense. The ethnographic present has been any of those, singly or in combination.

We have sometimes shifted among uses of the present tenses without clearly marking that we have done so; and that has been misleading.

We have always mixed the present tenses with past tenses.

We could consider using the past tenses more often.

WRITINGS IN THE PRESENT TENSES

People write eight kinds of thing exclusively in the present tense.

> On a dark night in Seville, Leporello is keeping watch, grumbling, outside a house in which his master Don Giovanni is engaged in his latest amorous pursuit. His target is Donna Anna ... (Salter, undated)

That is a *synopsis*, written for people who are about to witness a performance usually of an opera, where the action and language may not be immediately intelligible. An example in anthropology is Lévi-Strauss's summary of the story of Asdiwal, which is entirely in the present tense[2] (Lévi-Strauss 1967: 4–7).

Liturgical instructions are usually[3] in the present tense:

> The choir, clergy and family meet the body at the South Door. When they reach the screen, all stand, and these sentences are said by the Dean ... (King's College 1989)

And they are very similar to *stage directions*:

> THE DARK LADY, dressed in mourning, stands immobile at the foot of the stairs; THE CARETAKER is sweeping the front step ... After a few moments, enter THE MILKMAID from a side street ... (Strindberg 1960)

The common characteristic of all these is that they are participatory: they describe performances which you are about to join in, as an actor or as a member of an audience. They are about what to do, as a synopsis is not. But even the directions for a ritual performance and for a drama use the present tense in slightly different ways: apart from the conventional quasi-imperative 'Enter THE MILKMAID', the Ghost Sonata is firmly placed and dated: 'The action of the play passes in a Swedish provincial town, during the early spring of 1907'; and that information is given to the audience at each performance. Any present performance is a representation of that, even though you can assume that it is put on because the director thinks it has something of timeless interest to say, about humanity, or about Strindberg or both. The Order of Service, on the other hand, had no location and time other than the here-and-now, and was a bespoke version of a ritual for a category of recurrent unique events. So drama and ritual make essentially different references to the permanent, or 'eternal'; for even those rituals which have known origins (e.g. Eucharist, the Martyrdom of Hussain) do not begin with a notice ('The action of the Last Supper passes at Jerusalem in the early spring of 0032'); and when they do include a reference to the origin that is an explanation of why the participants commemorate it, as the prefatory notice to the Ghost Sonata is not. I think that some anthropological accounts of rituals are 'liturgical', or almost so: Malinowski's account of garden magic, for instance, reads sometimes like a synopsis, sometimes like a set of liturgical instructions (Malinowski 1965/1935: e.g. 143). And Evans-Pritchard's account of Nuer sacrifice, like the more generalised account in Hubert and Mauss, is also 'liturgical' in its structure (Evans-Pritchard 1956; Hubert and Mauss 1964/1899). Although the dialogue in Evans-Pritchard has potential, I don't know of any anthropological work which uses stage directions.[4] But I have included them here for completeness and to show that they are different from liturgical ones, even though drama and ritual are often enough loosely associated.

If those three kinds of text are written for participants, the next are clearly written for observers:

> ... the Infanta has come to watch Velàzquez at work. While one of her maids of honour offers her a glass of water, the King and Queen enter the room and are reflected in the mirror on the opposite wall. Several of the figures look towards them and out of the picture. Velàzquez is painting neither the Infanta, nor the King and Queen, but the greatest picture he ever made: The Maids of Honour ... (Luca da Tena and Mena 1987)

We also use the present tense to discuss photographs and maps. The characteristic of all these kinds of artefact is that they are permanent and continuous. Anyone can see them, and comment appropriately in the present tense. The artefacts themselves all claim also to represent in some way the real world: a map, for example the Mappa Mundi, a world which is itself fixed and continuous; photographs and paintings apparently capture real instants to make them fixed.[5] And we say 'It shows Jerusalem at the centre of the world', or 'One of the bowing Trobrianders may be seen to be looking at the camera' (Clifford 1983: 120). In that sense the Velàzquez is 'faked' since the painting represents a reality which is physically impossible: the eyes which see the scene are those of the King and Queen; and they see Velàzquez who is portrayed in the picture, painting what they see. But we are not indignant as we are when photographs are faked: two pictures can be combined; people can be blotted out; particular lenses and focal lengths can distort perspectives, for instance, to present quietly and without comment to the beholder, what his eye could see only in a photograph. The central claim of the photograph is that 'the photographer had to be there' (Barthes 1982: 209): it purports to be a mechanical representation, 'a message without a code' (ibid.: 196), and we may be uncomfortable when the photographer claims to be an artist after all. Anthropology has actual maps and photographs; and the case-histories and significant incidents we offer are analogous to photographs. We write them in the past tense ('I was there', with possibly an implicit claim that they are uncoded) and discuss them in the present.

Here are two further cases in which the present tenses are habitually used: a statement which is *true by definition*:

> In any normal distribution, 68 per cent of the observations fall within one standard deviation of the mean.

The present tense, in this case, implies 'did, does and always will', and is used also of those Laws which have been demonstrated *true by induction and experience*:

> If a quantity of heat Q is supplied to any substance at a constant temperature t, the work dW obtainable from Q by an ideal reversible engine working in a cycle of range dt must be proportional to Qdt multiplied by some function of the temperature, f't, which must be the same for all substances. (Carnot's Principle – the Second Law of Thermodynamics)

In summary: eight kinds of text are conventionally written in the present tenses. Three of them are 'participatory', three are 'observational' and two are 'scientific'. Each implies a different relation to reality. They are each part of a general English repertoire, and anthropologists have used nearly all of them. I think (but am not sure) that we have not used any other version of the present tenses.

THE PRESENT AND THE PAST

Anthropologists do not write exclusively in the present tenses. At a minimum, we generally use the past for our relevant autobiography, for the history of the people we study and for some case histories. Nearly all of us have written accounts of our fieldwork, how we came to be there, what we did, in the past tenses: our autobiography demonstrates that we were there, and can allow a reader to judge how good our representations may be.

Textual analysts say that this is a method for establishing authority:[6] authors attempt to guarantee their texts. No doubt; but you should also note that it would be odd if they didn't. For, unlike photographs, literary representations do not certify that someone was ever there (and in fact there are senses in which anthropologists who reconstructed past conditions of society were never there). The implied criticism is of two kinds. At a naïve level it assumes an equivalence of being an authority and having authority, and that having authority is reprehensible. At a more sophisticated level, it attacks the claim that such authority is personal, and asserts that this is an expropriation of a collaborative effort (Lewis 1973).

Although this second criticism seems to me applicable to some of us, they both rely almost exclusively on the effects which such texts have on (a certain kind of) reader, and they pay little attention to what the writer intended. One *locus classicus* for an authority-establishing past-tense introduction, used many times as an example, is Evans-Pritchard's account of how he came to do fieldwork with the Nuer.[7] Rosaldo, for instance, argues that even though Evans-Pritchard's account of how he did his fieldwork reads a bit bleakly, that is a characteristically British style – 'tongue-in-cheek understatement', perhaps even a deliberate attempt to exaggerate the over-whelmingness of the odds against producing such a fine book (Rosaldo 1986: 89). The facts can sustain another interpretation. For Evans-Pritchard used six pages to describe the circumstances of his research: he had done twelve months' fieldwork in four visits of between seven weeks and five-and-a-half months over seven years, and in different areas of Nuerland (Evans-Pritchard 1940: 7–15). By contrast in *Witchcraft, Oracles and Magic* perhaps half a page, a page, is devoted to the topic – and most of it was written by Seligman (Evans-Pritchard 1937. Evans-Pritchard wrote pp vii–viii, and Seligman contributed pp xv–xxv). It is difficult to know what the author's intentions were; but you could argue that he intended to issue a caveat: *The Nuer* was based on more doubtful evidence than *Witchcraft*, his authority was *less* secure.

In fact, it is quite difficult to come to any general conclusion about the purpose of those introductory passages in the past tense. I think that many anthropologists wanted to acknowledge funding agencies, to qualify the claims to authority which could have been attributed to them, to allow the reader to form an independent judgement about their procedures: it was an opportunity to put cards on the table. If it turns out that in the end we all deceived ourselves, and our readers simply found claims to authority, that is a pity; but it says something about the readers, too.

Case-histories, illustrative incident, are the photographs of ethnography: we have generally written them in the past tenses and discussed them in the present.

> Then he wailed aloud, as is the custom, jumped from a palm some sixty feet high and was killed on the spot ... The exogamous prohibition is one of the cornerstones of totemism ... It is an axiom of Anthropology that nothing arouses a greater horror than the breach of this prohibition ... Nor is this axiom devoid of foundation in fact. If you were to inquire ... you would find that ... the natives express horror at violating the rules of exogamy ... When it comes to the application of morality and ideals to real life, however, things take on a different complexion ... Public opinion was neither outraged ... nor did it react directly. (Malinowski 1926: 78–9)

This is Malinowski as Houdini: he has wrapped the facts (in the past tense) in Trobriand self-righteousness (Custom is) and tied them both up with high-falutin' theory (the axiom is); and invited us to watch as the facts break out of the parcel – and they do so in the past tense: Public opinion was not outraged. The passage leads to a formulation of a new more realistic account of social life: the operation of supernatural sanctions is not automatic; people have traditional ways of circumventing laws (ibid.: 81). And it leads too to a generalisation about procedure: 'the relation of actual life to the ideal state of affairs ... is very instructive' (ibid.: 84). In this passage, as very often elsewhere, Malinowski used the past tense for the particular events (in this case a suicide which he did not in fact witness), and two modes of the present. 'Custom is', 'the natives express' are generalised observation, as if to say 'from many instances I will not bother you with I can assert that this is generally the case'. And he used a scientific mode to express the Axiom of anthropology, and the importance of observing any divergence between ideal and actual action.

This combination of past and present is usually quite straightforward and understandable.

> It is an obvious truism that you can only carry on an argument with a man who understands what you say. The Kachins of Hpalang understood one another's arguments very well; the language in which they expressed these arguments was the language of ritual and mythology. (Leach 1954: 101)

In fact Leach distinguished very carefully between description and analysis, using different tenses, and occasionally a synopsis mode. He wrote Chapters V and VI of *Political Systems* chiefly in the present tense, and prefaced them with remarks to indicate that he was abstracting or generalising: 'I am trying to demonstrate the system of gumsa Kachin ideology, as if it were an integrated coherent set of ideas. I am talking about an ideal system ...' (ibid.: 107). He wrote the other chapters, drawing on written sources and personal experience, chiefly in the past tense.

That is all quite clear, even more straightforward than Malinowski: we conventionally generalise in an 'observational' present, using the past tenses to recount events. But we can create problems when we use more than one kind of present tense together with the historic past. Consider this passage from *The Nuer*:

> For the first time a single person symbolised ... the unity of a tribe, for prophets are tribal figures. But they have a further significance, for their influence extended over tribal boundaries. (Evans-Pritchard 1940: 189)

The past tense of 'symbolised' is history; it was then that prophets became tribal figures and their influence was extended. 'Prophets are tribal figures' is observational present – but is presumably also true of the period in the past, and could be written 'Prophets were tribal figures in the period before my fieldwork and still are (in 1930–6) in the sense that people talk about them a lot'. However, 'have a further significance' is a theoretical or analytic remark; did Evans-Pritchard intend they had a further significance to Nuer before 1930? Or in the period 1930–6? Or did he mean something like 'To us anthropologists (whenever it may be that we read about Nuer prophets) they are even more significant than I have described already'? Probably, I guess, all three: and it is an instance of the way in which our usage of tenses can conflate different meanings which arguably might be kept separate.

That instance is fairly trivial. The next case concerns the definition of Nuer tribes, and is in my view less so:

> (a) A tribe is the largest group the members of which consider it their duty to combine for raiding and for defensive action. The younger men ... went, till recently, on joint expeditions against the Dinka and waged war against other Nuer tribes ... In theory a tribe was regarded as a military unit. (Evans-Pritchard 1940: 120)

(The first 'is' is scientific; 'consider' is observational. The next two sentences indicate a recent change in the definition. The sense is: 'Warfare used to define Nuer tribes'.)

> (b) ... Another defining characteristic of a tribe is that within it there is *cut*. (*ibid.*: 121)

(The first 'is' is scientific; the second 'is' is observational, and contrasts with the 'was' of (a). Read: 'Even though warfare was no longer a defining characteristic, payment of compensation was'.)

> (c) A tribe has been defined (in the proceedings pages) by ... (4) a moral obligation to unite in war ... (ibid.: 122)

(Well: has it? Nuer did not in fact fight in 1930–6. So perhaps they were not then morally obliged; or they were morally obliged, but the occasion never arose; or they were only morally obliged, and so did not go to war.)

(d) Adjacent tribes are opposed to one another and fight one another ... (ibid.: 122)

Evans-Pritchard used this last passage as an introduction to his description of moderately amiable relations among Nuer of different tribes who lived near to each other: that is in the observational present; but the 'fight' of (d) is not observation at all: the present tense previously used was 'scientific-definition', but because of its context it now passes for description. So we get the perplexing progression: No warfare now (observation), to Moral obligation to warfare (definition), to Warfare now (observation). And then later (in definitional mode):

Between tribes there can only be war, and through war, the memory of war and the potentiality of war the relations between tribes are defined and expressed. (Evans-Pritchard. 1940: 161)

I think that this illustrates fairly clearly what is a common enough effect: we get into the habit of using the present tenses, and we can lose sight of which mode we are in. The rhetoric takes over. I should say that I think I understand Evans-Pritchard's reasons for using the present tense so generally in the Nuer. Apart from the conventions of ethnographic writing, he saved himself and the reader considerable effort by using the present. For the past tenses can seem to require greater specification of time and place, and if you write 'did', 'was', 'had been', one effect is to prompt the question 'Well, when, exactly?'. In an extended text, some specification becomes inescapable; but a text which is cluttered up with specifications of four field trips becomes unwieldy: writable, but scarcely readable, and in any case unsuited to an account of 'relations, defined in terms of social situation, and relations between those relations' (Evans-Pritchard 1940: 266). Also, the government of the Anglo-Egyptian Sudan wanted to know more about the Nuer, why they were recalcitrant. In these circumstances, which were those of many British and French anthropologists until the 1960s, it was a reasonable choice to write in the present tenses as a matter of course: the works were, in part, an answer to the question 'what on earth are these people like?' and a past tense account would have been inapt as a persuasive device for that part of the audience which could send in troops, or refrain from doing so. So I think that Evans-Pritchard was concerned among other things with tactical and strategic problems of rhetoric when he decided to write his observations in the present tenses. And if I have nevertheless used these passages to illustrate the uncertainties which the rhetoric can cause in all our minds, that is because his work illustrates more effectively what the dangers are. I could have used my own work to similar effect; but apart from the egotism of that, you are more likely to be persuaded that it is a pervasive danger, when you read of Evans-Pritchard's lapses.

The extent to which anthropologists have used the present tenses, and the ways they have combined them varies very much from person to person, even from one person's monograph to another. Model-builders, as Evans-Pritchard in *The Nuer* and Leach in Chapters V and VI of *Political Systems*, tend to use the present, in a mixture of mainly observational and generalising modes, with doses of 'scientific' present. People who have reconstructed past societies have also mainly used the present tenses, though the work of Maurice Freedman is a notable exception (Freedman 1966). That is partly because they have fewer incidents and case-histories to present: they were *not* there, and had to rely on documents or the memories of informants. No doubt it is also because their ethnography is very difficult to date: what old Rifians tell you is not very precise, chronologically, and it is more easily re-told in the present tenses:

> Le terme 'traditionnel' est utilisé ici pour désigner un état de société existant avant la colonisation espagnole (1912). Notre reconstitution est fondée essentiellement sur l'analyse des récits fournis par des vieux informateurs. (Jamous, 1981: 1)

In Jamous's work on the Iqar'iyen the present of the text is a composite of the rather imprecisely defined periods before 1912. It was created in the 1970s – the present of the fieldwork – from the memories of old men, presumably speaking in the past tense. It seems moderately complex, especially since Jamous does not tell us how he insulated his reconstruction from the present of his fieldwork. Gellner, model-builder and reconstructor, adopted a technique which is the mirror-image of Jamous's: his present tense refers to 'the period of 1954–61' when he was in Morocco, collecting the information which allowed him to model the period before French conquest in the 1930s (Gellner 1969: xxii). But in fact he scarcely used the past tenses at all, except for case-histories and history; so in his case too, the relation between past and present is not marked by linguistic shift. It is arguable that the distinction between the model and the present of fieldwork would have been clearer if he had used different tenses, especially since the quarter century between French conquest and his fieldwork was one in which government attempted to introduce many changes in social organisation. It should be said that Gellner (unlike Jamous) has helpfully indicated what many of those changes were.

Peters is the curious case of a model-builder taken for a reconstructor. He wrote mostly in the present tense, and emphasised that his information was from the period 1948–50; in 1967 he insisted that no one should 'assume that social relations as I observed them are present today or that they were the same at any time in the past either' (Peters 1967: 280). Of course, many of the facts were what people in 1948–50 said then about previous marriages, feuds, clients; and in some senses they were therefore old facts. But you may agree it is legitimate to imply something on the lines of 'this is how the Bedouin of 1950 interpreted their society', and to use the present tenses. Nevertheless, it is perhaps a surprise to find Peters's accounts used to modify the classic account of segmentary lineages. Those Bedouin, after all, had emerged from a thirty-year colonial war, from the brief and tenuous *pax italica*, the battles of the North Africa campaign which were fought over the tribes' territories, and from some years of British Military Administration: after such traumatising (Peters's word) experiences they were scarcely in a position to be constituted as the refutation of the classic model. Perhaps Hildred Geertz, or Roy Behnke Jr, for instance, have thought of Peters as a reconstructor; and have taken his virtual silence on the twentieth-century history of Libya to mean he was writing about some earlier period (Peters, 1960, 1970: 377; Geertz 1979: 377, n. 1; Behnke Jr 1980: 1–2). You might agree that the confusion could have been avoided if it had been conventional to use different tenses for reconstruction and 'the present'.

In summary: anthropologists have always mixed the present tenses with past ones, to varying degrees. Reconstructors and modellers have characteristically used the present tense. We have always written autobiography and case-histories, and histories in the past. Textualists have argued that autobiographical passages in the past tense have the effect of establishing authority; but it may be sensible also to try to imagine the intentions of writers: at any rate some of them may have been trying to come clean, to explain the defects or limitations of their work. When we have mixed present tenses, or mixed present and past, we have sometimes confused readers, perhaps even ourselves, about the status of our statements.

SOME PRACTICAL CONSIDERATIONS

Our textualist critics have emphasised the latent functions of text: the purposes of anthropologists are of minor importance compared to the effects of what they write. I suppose that could be true; and in any case they have clearly had fun by assuming that it is. We could wish that some of them had been less formulaic, and had been as careful readers as anthropologists are. But as writers it is our destiny to be concerned with our conscious purposes, rather than our unintended consequences. I think we can accept that we are not primarily literary stylists, and that our intended effects do not always come off; and that we belong to cultures with a repertoire of conventional rhetorics which we do not always question or experiment with as much as we could. The rhetorics are persuasive devices which we can deploy to create the effects we wish (within the limits of our skills); and that is a practical matter, with moral and political consequences as well as intellectual ones. In these circumstances we should be sure that we do in fact exploit the repertoire self-consciously.

In effect when we write ethnography we do three kinds of thing: we describe our experiences; we represent other people's descriptions of things we have not experienced, and we compare, abstract and generalise (in no required order). The tenses we use are one element in the battery of literary devices at our disposal to make our ethnography useful to others (as well as to propagate an image of ourselves, settle academic and other disputes, and do all the variety of things which follow from our having mixed motives).

I think that particular tenses have no intrinsic force. They are not, for instance, differentially persuasive: it is difficult to maintain that (say) the present tense is more vivid, draws the reader into events more than the past tenses do.[8] Rather, our choices have signalled what kind of thing we are doing, and what kind of audience we wrote for.

Anthropologists used to write partly for audiences which had a direct administrative and political concern in the people described. It was sensible to write descriptions in the present tenses because the audience would include people who would be taking decisions in ten or twenty years' time: some major part of the account would still be true, or held in memory as true, and it was important to maintain immediacy. I guess that the same rhetorical considerations apply for those of us who write reports as part of impact studies, advice for development agencies, or who want among other things to influence policy. Okely, for instance, could have written her account of Traveller-Gypsies in the past, describing them as they were in 1971–3 (Okely 1983). But that would not have been so persuasive for an official in the 1980s or 1990s; and since her information and analysis contain enduring truths, it seems sensible that they should not be lost in the past.

The case for writing abstraction in the present tense is also a strong one. First, because it is conventional to do so: that is what readers recognise statements of general principle by. That is the scientific mode of the present tense. It carries all the risks of pretension, but its value as a marker is really quite high – provided of course, that it is a marker. Loizos is the only contemporary anthropologist I know of who has written his statements of general principle in the past tense.

In his first book on Cyprus Loizos used the past tense for events, case-history, incidents; and he used the present tenses for his end-of-chapter summaries, which are the generalisations he extracted from the descriptions he had given (Loizos 1975: e.g. 61–81, 81–3). In his second book, written after the villagers of Argaki had become refugees, he used the present tense scarcely at all, except in reported speech (Loizos 1981). That was at least in part because he wished to analyse the stages of refugeehood, to record the phases of a sense of loss which changed in the first eighteen months after the Turkish invasion. Clearly, in this kind of anthropology, concerned with a long process which has several phases, the past tenses are appropriate for description. But Loizos also uses them for his analysis and generalisation, which broke new ground where there was not much general principle. In the past tense, generalisations seem to be more tentative, less detached from the events they are derived from, than they would be in a scientific present. It seems reasonable to take Loizos as a model, at any rate in describing those social processes which may have non-repetitive stages.

But is there also a case for writing our generalised descriptions in the past, instead of in the observational present? We have usually written accounts of particular weddings, of particular presentations, 'I came, ... I saw, ... I counted', and then continued 'labour is recruited so, ... urigubu consists of such, ... weddings take place after harvest ...'. Why have we switched tenses between kinds of description? Partly because particular descriptions demand the past tense. It would read oddly to say 'the team assembles in March 1929 to mend the chief's canoe'. But why have we not continued in the past tense? It may be because such descriptions are distilled from a variety of sources: we make them from what we have witnessed on several occasions, no doubt with slight variations; and from what we have heard from different people in different conversations. And to these we can add texts we have taken from dictation. The resulting account is often very removed from any particular instance: it is presented as the general framework which channels people's actions from day to day, and it can be useful to signal its status by a shift of tense. Moreover, we do have a sense that the framework is something which endures, and is not tied to a particular time and place.

It might still be sensible to consider using a past tense. It would fix the description in a particular time, and that has value for future academic readers (perhaps not, if it is administrators you wish to persuade). For our impression is that contemporary social changes are in many cases definitive and extensive, and it is inconvenient to suggest in a text which may have a life of twenty or thirty years, that the social arrangements of say 1990 will endure until 2020. The past tenses place a society; and they also serve to mark the text as belonging to a particular period: I think that the theoretical world we live in is less stable than it may have seemed forty to fifty years ago (though that appearance is no doubt partly an effect of hind-blindness, smoothing out controversies which were impassioning then, and which no longer excite us). The past tense may locate our texts more clearly in our current theoretical preoccupations, which could be a service to our students' students.

It should be possible to mark those aspects of social life which we consider to be fundamental, in other ways than by shifts of tense. We could write, for instance, that we consider them fundamental, and that we think they will endure more than others will. That not only introduces the future tense, but encourages us to discriminate among social forms as we do not always do at the moment.

We might likely suffer some interim incomprehension if we were to write more in the past tense. Consider, for example, the review by R. Fernea of a book which was written very carefully in the past tense: 'With no slight intended, perhaps this might be called "ethnographic journalism", a convergence of discursive styles' (Fernea 1989). Of course, he may have had additional reasons; but I guess the past tenses weighed heavily among them. Leach maintained on more than one occasion that ethnography is a kind of fiction, and if that were true I suppose we might want to make it clear that we were not *trying* to write novels. In any case, maintaining the present tenses would not be the only way to make our intentions plain. Finally, our present tenses are a way in which we distinguish ourselves from historians and social historians. Some of us would welcome an assimilation; and even those who would not, can scarcely claim that 'the' ethnographic present is the necessary literary diacritic: it is too varied, too implicit, too liable to cause confusion in our texts.

It is not required to come to a world-changing conclusion in a discussion which is essentially concerned with practical matters. What I have tried to suggest is that the radical critique by textualist meta-anthropologists is beside the point: people are going to go on doing anthropology even if anthropology is logically impossible, even if in doing so they unconsciously 'betray' the impossibility of finding a language which is both neutral and participatory. The ethnographic present is not in fact a single voice, but several – it could be as many as eight, each with their own significance and use. If we confuse them, we can mislead our readers, and that is a good enough reason for marking our different kinds of statement, among other ways with shifts of tense, perhaps using the past tenses more than some of our predecessors have done. But in all cases that is a practical matter, offering no guarantees of perfection. Indeed the textualist critic is never done; but new conventions may betray new inadequacies to him. We may have the sense that, however much we change our literary underwear, the postmodernist bus will get us in the end. Nevertheless, it would be interesting if conscious decisions to change our style really did invite a new critique, for that would suggest that our practical intentions are not wholly irrelevant.

NOTES

1 'Distancing' was the term used by Rosaldo (1986: 94). It is partly a moral judgement: the ethnographic present implies a conversation between you and me, about 'them'. For present tense discourse is familiar, goes with the first and second persons who in this case discuss a third party. The objects of these discussions are excluded from them, and that is not what is implied by the participation on equal terms which we pride ourselves on (Clifford 1983; Fabian 1983: 80–7). That moral objection is sometimes extended: the discussions colour our fieldwork since, however much we participate, we know that sooner or later we will discuss the natives with our colleagues, in the present, using 'them' to refer to people who are now 'you'. We prospect our performance in our other environment and that introduces duplicity into our participation in the field. Of course, that would apply whatever tense we wrote in: and if the choice really were between distancing

the participants and collaborators in our work, and involving extraneous readers in the issues, it does not seem an easy matter to make a blanket decision.

2 Here is an interesting phenomenon: when anthropologists summarise myths they *re-write them in the present tense*, like the synopsis of an opera or play. Lévi-Strauss's Asdiwal (present tense) (1967) is based on Boas's text (past tense). In fact, Boas translated and published all the texts he had taken by dictation in the past tense, which perhaps approximates to the sense of the original. He also published summaries of those stories he had heard but which were not authentic dictations, in the present tenses. Leach's *Genesis* is present tense; the original is past. His *gumlao* myth is also present tense, but I have not been able to check the original (Kawla Ma Nawng 1942; Leach 1954/1964: 200–1). It all appears quite unself-conscious: that is the voice we do myths in. Or you might say, the voice we do myths in with. For the force of the past tense is to suggest that something did in fact happen: God did make Eve out of a bone; the Beaver was tricked to his death. That force is discarded when the text is represented: it becomes an item of performance, something which is not real but which is told. Representing makes the past tense object amenable to abstract discussion because it relieves the critic from the necessity of discussing whether the events and movement of the spirit described really did happen, and what their significance to the people concerned might be: the critic is then free to discuss the hidden meanings. But I agree it would be odd to discuss whether Figaro really did measure his bedroom.

3 The Book of Common Prayer mixes the present tense and the future imperative 'shall'. Roman Catholic texts use the present: '*Als het lijk de kerk wordt binnengedragen, zingt men...*' (from a Dutch missal, 'De Begrafenisplechtigheid').

4 (Evans-Pritchard 1940: 2–13). And – always at the margins – you may note Peter Brook's production *The Ik* in 1976, based on Colin Turnbull's ethnography; and the 1979 play *Sergeant Ola and his Followers*, which acknowledges (p. 7) Professors Peter Lawrence and Peter Worsley (Lan 1980).

5 The exceptions are those medieval paintings which show a history or biography, tell a story, in a series of episodes. And movies. But these too are discussed in the present tense.

6 The original, and still the most sensitive, is Clifford (1983). He gives a sympathetic review of experimental attempts to share authorship, and hence 'authority', between anthropologists and their informants.

7 The other, much discussed, is Malinowski's 'Introduction' (1922: 1–25).

8 'The first act is ... the driving into the ground of a tethering peg and the tethering of the animal to it ... Sometimes after the victim has been staked, a libation of milk, beer or water is poured over, or at the foot, of the peg' (Evans-Pritchard 1956: 208).

REFERENCES

Barthes, R. (1982) The Photographic Message. In S. Sontag (ed.) *A Barthes Reader*. London: Jonathan Cape, 196–210.

Behnke Jr, R. H. (1980) *The Herders of Cyrenaica. Ecology, Economy and Kinship Among the Bedouin of Eastern Libya*. Urbana, Ill.: University of Illinois Press.

Clifford, J. (1983) On Ethnographic Authority. *Representations* 2: 118–46.

Evans-Pritchard, E. (1937) *Witchcraft, Oracles and Magic among the Azande*. Oxford: Oxford University Press.

—— (1940) *The Nuer. A Description of the Modes of Livelihood and Political Institutions of a Nilotic People*. Oxford: Clarendon.

—— (1956) *Nuer Religion*. Oxford: Clarendon.

Fabian, J. (1983) *Time and the Other*. New York: Colombia University Press.

Fernea, R. (1989) Book Review. *American Anthropologist* **90**: 1012–13.

Freedman, M. (1966) *Chinese Lineage and Society: Fukien and Kwantung* (LSE Monographs on Social Anthropology 33). London: Athlone Press.

Geertz, H. (1979) The Meaning of Family Ties. In C. Geertz, H. Geertz and L. Rosen (eds) *Meaning and Order in Moroccan Society: Three Essays in Cultural Analysis*. Cambridge: Cambridge University Press, 315–91.

Gellner, E. A. (1969) *Saints of the Atlas* (Nature of Human Society Series). London: Weidenfeld and Nicholson.

Hubert, H. and Mauss, M. (1964/1899) *Sacrifice: Its Nature and Function*. London: Cohen and West.

Jamous, R. (1981) *Honneur et Baraka*. Cambridge and Paris: Cambridge University Press and Éditions de la Maison des Sciences de l'Homme.

Kawla Ma Nawng (1942) *The History of the Kachins of the Hukawng Valley* (trs. J. L. Leyden). Bombay: privately printed.

King's College (1989) *Order of Service for the Funeral of Professor Sir Edmund Leach*. Cambridge: King's College.

Lan, D. (1980) *Sergeant Ola and his Followers* (Methuen's New Theatrescripts). London: Eyre Methuen.

Leach, E. R. (1964/1954) *Political Systems of Highland Burma. A Study of Kachin Social Structure*. London: Bell, for the London School of Economics.

Lévi-Strauss, C. (1967) The Story of Asdiwal. In E. R. Leach (ed.) *The Structural Study of Myth and Totemism* (ASA Monographs 5). London: Tavistock, 1–48.

Lewis, I. M. (1973) *The Anthropologist's Muse*. An Inaugural Lecture. London: Athlone Press.

Loizos, P. (1975) *The Greek Gift. Politics in a Cypriot Village*. Oxford: Blackwell.

—— (1981) *The Heart Grown Bitter. A Chronicle of Cypriot War Refugees*. Cambridge: Cambridge University Press.

Luca da Tena, C. and Mena, M. (1987) *Guide to the Prado*. Madrid: Silex.

Malinowski, B. (1922) *Argonauts of the Western Pacific. An Account of Native Enterprise and Adventures in the Archipelagoes of Melanesian New Guinea* (Studies in Economics and Political Science). London: Routledge & Kegan Paul.

—— (1926) *Crime and Custom in Savage Society* (International Library of Psychology, Philosophy and Scientific Method). London: Kegan Paul, Trench, Trubner and Co.

—— (1965/1935) *Coral Gardens and their Magic, vol. 1: Soil-tilling and Agricultural Rites in the Trobriand Islands* (Indiana University Studies in the History and Theory of Linguistics). Bloomington: Indiana University Press.

Okely, J. (1983) *The Traveller-Gypsies*. Cambridge: Cambridge University Press.

Peters, E. L. (1960) The Proliferation of Segments in the Lineage of the Bedouin of Cyrenaica. *Journal of the Royal Anthropological Institute* **90**: 29–53.

—— (1967) Some Structural Aspects of the Feud Among the Camel-herding Bedouin of Cyrenaica. *Africa* **37**: 261–82.

—— (1970) The Proliferation of Segments in the Lineage of the Bedouin of Cyrenaica. In L. E. Sweet (ed.) *Peoples and Cultures of the Middle East* **1**. New York: Natural History Press, 363–98

Rabinow, P. (1986) Representations are Social Facts. Modernity and Postmodernity in Anthropology. In J. Clifford and G. E. Marcus (eds) *Writing Culture. The Poetics and Politics of Ethnography* (A School of American Research Advanced Seminar) Berkeley, Calif.: University of California Press, 234–61.

Rosaldo, R. (1986) From the Door of his Tent. In J. Clifford and G. E. Marcus (eds) *Writing Culture. The Poetics and Politics of Ethnography* (A School of American

Research Advanced Seminar) Berkeley, Calif.: University of California Press, 75–97.

Salter, L. (undated) Synopsis. In *Don Giovanni*. London: Phillips.

Strindberg, A. (1960) The Ghost Sonata. In *Miss Julie and Other Plays*, trs. Max Faber. London: William Heinemann Ltd, 95–136.

Chapter 14

Self-conscious anthropology[1]

Anthony P. Cohen

... an anthropology that makes an ethnographic problem of itself offers pragmatic insight into the social worlds it examines and to which it belongs. (Herzfeld 1987: x)

SOME BIOGRAPHICAL OBSERVATIONS

Many anthropologists with fieldwork experience will recall the uncertainty with which they actually, or mentally, answered the question put to them by people whom they were 'in the field' to study: 'Who are you?'. The uncertainty is composed of a number of factors: What *should* I say? (i.e. what would it be politic to say?) What *can* I say? (i.e. what could I say that would be intelligible? Is there an answer which is at once comprehensive and faithful? Do I even know who I am?). We cope with this aggravated sense of self-consciousness by resorting to all sorts of more or less honourable devices. But the problem should be seen as one of self-instruction as well as of strategy. It ought also (but seldom does) put us on our guard when we reciprocate with the same question. So anxious are we for information that we often fail to see just how perplexing the question can be. Evans-Pritchard famously recalled his Nuerosis in regarding the unforthcoming Nuer as bloody-minded, rather than as stumped (1940: 12–13). I was impressed by the disinclination of Whalsay islanders to offer introductions when we first met. I supposed that, since they all know each other and knew of my existence it did not occur to them that I would not know who they were. After all, on their own territory how could anyone *not* know? When I would enquire of a friend about the identity of a third party to whom I had just spoken, the answer would usually be given in terms of genealogical referents. Genealogy is rarely a neutral account in Whalsay, if anywhere, but is perhaps the most neutral, least complicated answer available. In public discourse in Whalsay, who a person is depends upon *who* is being asked and *by* whom.

In the summer of 1986 I took with me to Whalsay the first draft of the book I was then writing about the community, intending to show it to some of the people who appeared in the book (Cohen 1987). One man who looms large in it is a controversial figure, well known for the single-mindedness and vigour with which he pursues his campaigns. His presence locally is such that he might reasonably be described as 'universally known'. Notwithstanding the regard and affection I have for him, I had tried to write about him 'warts and all', reporting his somewhat ambivalent standing in the estimations of the islanders. I made reference to various anecdotes which are invariably offered locally as evidence of his idiosyncratic behaviour. He did not object to any of this – although his own explanations of these anecdotal incidents were notably more prosaic than the versions which circulated throughout Whalsay – nor of my account of the extremely contentious manner in which he had campaigned thirty years previously for a harbour development, an argument which caused considerable strife within the community and which still evokes painful memories. He made only one objection: to my description of his brief fishing career as 'inglorious', the judgement of it which was certainly made by the many people who had commented about it to me. Far from being inglorious, he said, it had been 'da maist glorious' time of his life.

All the stories elicited by mention of his name are of things 'known' about Henry: 'everybody knew' them, 'Oh, aye, we aa' ken wir Hendry'. Yet, what was known 'about' him was clearly not known *by* him, or was known in a quite different way. Indeed, he would not recognise himself in other people's versions of him. Self-knowledge and social knowledge of persons are incongruent. Anthropologists tend to privilege the second over the first, in spite of their personal experience of the fallacies with which the Other constructs the Self.

Many years ago, at a conference in Scotland, I presented a paper which contrasted strategic modes of public identity among political activists in rural Newfoundland. I contrasted them as, respectively, over- and under-communicating the *bayman* archetype of the Newfoundland outporter: as, on the one hand, emphasising, and on the other as masking the stigmas popularly regarded as inhering in Newfoundlander identity within Canada (Cohen 1975).[2] A member of the audience who had known me slightly ten years earlier during my undergraduate days told me later that the paper was only incidentally about Newfoundlanders: it was obviously an autobiographical statement. I was sufficiently shaken by his observation not to want to pursue the discussion, but assumed that he was referring to my Jewishness, lapsed entirely in religious observance, supposedly betrayed in my committed anti-Zionism, but nevertheless evident in my name. I did not think then that he was correct (nor do I now): I was writing about Newfoundlanders, rather than about myself. However, his comment did persuade me that, as an anthropologist, my concern with identity had its source in my personal experience; more than that, that my construction of identity as 'a problem' or dilemma, though hardly original, was a reflection of my own struggles. It would not be contentious to suggest that many anthropologists are motivated by a personal problematic as well as by mere intellectual curiosity (an issue raised in several contributions to the 1989 ASA Conference, *Anthropology and Autobiography*, and to this volume). Fabian tersely remarks that, 'our past is present in us as a project' (1983: 93).

There is nothing very novel in this. If we accept that anthropology is an essentially interpretive exercise, it must be clear that interpretation cannot begin from a *tabula rasa*. Rather, it must use all the resources of sense-making that are available to us. Further, it would be impractical, tedious and a denigration of our expertise to have to provide an autobiography as the interpretive key to our ethnographies. If we are really saying that the only paths to the Yanomamo or to the Whalsay islanders are through the life-histories and self-analyses of their ethnographers, we clearly call into question the scholarly integrity of the entire ethnographic record. Knowing that Leach was a mathematically-inspired engineer (Leach 1961: 6, 1984: 9–10) may enable me to appreciate some nuance in *Political Systems of Highland Burma* (1954) which I had previously missed; but I do not need to know his background in order either to read his account of the Kachin, nor to make a judgement about its authenticity. By the same token, *Nuer Religion* (Evans-Pritchard 1956) and *The Drums of Affliction* (Turner 1968) must both be comprehensible as accounts of, respectively, Nuer and Ndembu, rather than as records of their authors' conversion to Catholicism. But that is not to say that they can or should be regarded as ethnographic and interpretive documents which somehow stand independently of their authors' religious experiences and convictions.

So, what importance should we impute to the anthropologist's self? Where should it fit into the equation, if at all? It is a commonplace of fieldwork experience that we learn a good deal about ourselves while struggling to understand others. This self-discovery does not concern only our hitherto unsuspected resourcefulness, durability and ingenuity; it is also that, by struggling to understand other people's complexities, we are brought face-to-face with our own. Thus, Jean Briggs's 'discovery' of the emotional discipline displayed by Utku Inuit prompts her also into frustration with her own emotional self-indulgence (1970). Southwold's doubts about God and Buddha are re-energised by the confrontations of 'theological' and 'village' Buddhism in Sri Lanka (1983). There is here a transposition of self and other. Indeed, in anthropological discourse we are accustomed to making instrumental use of the Other in our self-discovery. But we have been educated to the contrary view: that using the self to discover the other offends the fundamental canons of anthropological science. How curious that we should have succumbed to this rigid discrimination. Needham argues that it arises from anthropologists' assumptions about psychological universality: that we suppose we can recognise others' states of mind because we assume they must be like our own, or can be linguistically constituted as such (1981: 57, 60). He goes on to castigate such assumptions. However, I would suggest that our dogmatic segregation of Self and Other has had the *contrary* consequence of constituting us (self) as qualitatively *different* from the Other, depicting this qualitative difference in terms of our complexity and uniqueness, and *their* simplicity and generalisability. As Wendy James puts it, we impute to ourselves a 'potent ego', but to them a lack of 'moral personhood' (1988: 143; 1987: 57). This is the discrimination which Hannerz satirises as the 'Great Divide' (1983: 350). We do not avoid egocentricity, ethnocentricity (nor Eurocentricity for that matter (Needham op. cit.: 71; Herzfeld 1987: 7) by supposing we can, or should, neutralise the self until the completion of the day's research work. To the contrary. The inevitable conjunction of self and other has been noted by Stein as one of the processes of 'counter-transference' characteristic of medical diagnosis (Stein 1985) where self insinuates itself as an 'explanatory model' (Kleinman 1980). As an anthropologist, I cannot escape myself; nor should I try. In studying others I do not regard myself as merely studying my self; but rather, as using my self to study others.

ANOTHER BIOGRAPHICAL OBSERVATION

Recently, three of us, schoolfriends since the ages of nine or ten, were talking about the efforts of our ex-headmaster to contact former pupils of the school (which no longer exists) all over the world. It had been a very small, predominantly Jewish school which, after the Second World War, had mostly recruited foreign pupils, particularly from the Middle East. My two friends, both lawyers, were reflecting on the disproportionate number of our former associates who seemed to have achieved professional or financial success, or have risen to positions of prominence in their own countries. They surmised that our Jewishness, that is, our membership of an historically disadvantaged minority group, motivated us to impress ourselves on our host societies, and suggested that this applied to each of us.[3] Again, I disagreed. First, it did not explain the absence of such motivation among many – most? – Jews, nor among other minority ethnic groups. Second, it did not address my awareness of my own motivation since, in most circumstances, I am not conscious of myself as a Jew.

I said as much – as, indeed, I have for as long as I can remember, but my friends demurred, figuratively tapping the sides of their noses: 'we know better'. Do they? I read my own conduct and life in one set of terms; they construct them in another. Are they not doing to me, like the Whalsay islanders do to Henry, what we do as anthropologists (a) to those whom we study, when we subordinate their individuality as members of society X or as bearers of culture Y (cf. Needham op. cit.: 56); and (b) when we insist on reading our colleagues' works biographically as well as, or instead of, ethnographically (Geertz 1988)? Incidentally, our disagreement about me is an interesting refutation of Fortes's contention that self-knowledge is only knowledge if it is externalised:

> How does one know one is a Jew ...? One can only know it, obviously, by showing it in some way; to sit back in your armchair and know gets you nowhere; it is meaningless. So if you want to know who you are, you have got to show it ... (1983: 395–6)

In the past we blithely referred to our self-consciousness as fieldworkers. But we have barely begun to plumb the depths of that consciousness, nor of its implications, for anthropological research and writing. For years we were instructed to eliminate it from our processed anthropology. We now acknowledge that self-consciousness is a useful learning device through which we test on ourselves our perceptions of the cultures we study. Moreover, many of us would accept that, by its very nature, ethnography is an ethnographer-focused art. 'The magician', says Hastrup, 'is part of the plot' (1989), a sentiment echoed in many of the papers at the 1989 conference. But how do we avoid writing just about the magician, or so positioning her/him that the trick is obscured?

A further complication is our ingrained and correct fear of ethnocentrism which inhibits us from recognising qualitative similarities between the self of the anthropologist and that of the anthropologist's 'subject'. This would be defensible if it was due only to a determination to avoid constructing others in one's own image. But it is not defensible if it results in the axiomatic denial of such similarity *when this has the consequence of denying to others the complexity which we impute to ourselves*. By and large, we do not regard ourselves as generalisable. Yet, the categorical techniques of our discipline, indeed the conventional definition of our task as the discovery of 'culture', implies our generalisation of others. We have reserved the Self as the province of mysticism, of artistic expression or psychology. Anthropologists' concerns with it have been denigrated as self-indulgence (Friedman 1987) or worse (Sangren 1988), or have been confined to the elaboration of putative cultural theories. Perhaps this is because we do not know how to reconcile the notion of the unique self with a generalisation such as culture. We (anthropologists) have 'method'; they (those whom we purport to observe) have culture. We have strings to our bows besides anthropology; that is, beyond our method there lie our selves (which we may confide to our diaries, even to novels or to poetry). What could lie beyond *their* culture, assuming we exclude biology? It has been a peculiarly inhumane approach to ethnography (cf. Okely 1975) and one for whose exposure the 'reflexivists' and experimental ethnographers can claim some credit.

Let us determine to avoid trying to reinvent the wheel. The purpose of this discussion is not to rehearse the weary old truism that the ethnographer's self intrudes upon the ethnography; nor that social theory should address the relationship of the individual and society – for it, and anthropology, have always done so. Indeed, anthropology has long acknowledged its difficulty with the self. Our present object is to so formulate the problem that we might begin to exploit the intrusive self as an ethnographic resource rather than suffer it as a methodological hindrance. I suggest three ways in which this expedient use of the self may help us. We can use our experience of the complexity of our selves to contain the anthropologist's temptation to generalise and simplify others. We may recognise that self-hood, the sense of personal identity, is not merely contingent or relative, but has a certain absoluteness, or a 'self-driven' element. Finally, with these points in mind, we might make sense of concepts in other cultures which approximate to our notion of 'personhood', but without rendering them egocentrically, ethnocentrically or Eurocentrically, as analogues of our concept of self.

AN HISTORICAL SKETCH OF THE ANTHROPOLOGY OF THE SELF

I suggest that we will not be much assisted in this exercise by recent musings of experimental psychologists, nor of some philosophers (while Luhmann is elegantly sceptical about the help available from sociology (1986: 313–14)). The philosophers seem strangely absorbed by the problem of whether a person at different moments may be properly spoken of as the 'same' person (Williams 1973; Swinburne 1984), and with distinguishing among the body, the person and the self. Psychologists pursue their own semantic puzzles over discriminations between person or self, and 'personality' (not to be confused with Mauss's struggle with *personne*, person*age*, and *moi*); and clearly tend towards relativism: to a view of the self as 'other-directed' (Gergen 1977). In this, they resemble early psychological anthropologists like Hallowell, Lee and Florence Kluckhohn. Lee added a Buberesque ideological dimension to her view of the socialness of the self, arguing that its autonomy can only be realised in a person's 'relatedness' with others, the degree to which such relatedness is achieved being an expression of 'cultural value' (e.g. Lee 1976). Hsu pursued the point, with some sophistication, distinguishing among gross cultural types – Chinese, Japanese and western – on the basis of the extent to which the individual's 'psychosocial homeostasis' (the essential self?) is rooted in relationships of her/his own making, the Chinese being at the minimal extreme, the western at the maximal (e.g. 1985). The spectre at this feast, often curiously unacknowledged by British anthropologists (with Fortes an honourable exception (e.g. 1973)), is G.H. Mead. Mead went beyond a recognition that individuals cannot be regarded as cultural automata, to consider in some detail the question of how the individual symbolises her/himself in interaction, a concern from which the tradition of symbolic interactionism sprang.

Mead distinguished between the 'Me' – the unthinking being, the enduring product of experience – and the 'I', the consciousness of being, the being
which, through its competence to symbolise, is capable of behavioural
control, precisely because it conceptualises the self. The 'I', the active agency
of being, has to be continuously creative to keep the person (including the
'Me') viable, a view of the 'self' which has had recent anthropological echoes
(e.g. Heelas 1981a: 13–14; Lock 1981: 32). Much of Mead's work elaborated
this creative aspect of the individual, dealing, for example, with the human's
unique power to 'manipulate', to intercede, through 'mind', between means
and ends; to intervene, say through language, in the process between
perception and 'consummation'. It is in this mediating phase that individuality inheres in the form of reflective thinking. Mead's individual, both in its
reactive and proactive modes, is permeated by the Other; but, to the extent
that reflexivity is retained and nurtured, is not determined by it (see, e.g.
Mead 1934).

Such influence as Mead had on anthropology was largely through the
interactionists and phenomenologists, surfacing later among theorists of
strategy, game and transaction. It seems to have missed most British
scholars, at least until after the 'discovery of mind' and the demise of the
deterministic paradigms. That Mead is still not routinely taught to British
undergraduates is an expression of this historical neglect, but the omission
has become even more curious with the accession to our reading lists of
contemporary 'reflexive' anthropology. For Mead of course, as, earlier, for
Cooley, social interaction is at the very foundation of self-conception: both
are accomplished by 'taking the role of the other' – viewing oneself and one's
behaviour from what is imagined to be the perspective of an Other,
anticipating the Other's reaction. The 'I' component of the self is the analyst
of this self-'observation' who modifies or plans behaviour on the basis of the
analysis. The conceptual material for the analysis is partially derived from
'culture' (which accounts for the similarities among members of a society);
but is mediated through the individual consciousness in ways which reflect
cultural theories of the relation of individual to society.

This all sounds rather dated in the context of recent symbolic theory and
developments in linguistics and semiotics. However, another curiosity of
recent anthropology is that our conceptualisation of the self, the symbol*iser*,
has not kept pace with our ever more complex and refined approaches to
symbol*ism* itself. In his book on ethnic identity, Epstein (1978) quotes the
Leach of a decade earlier sounding even more relativistic than Mead himself:
'*I* identify myself with a collective *we* which is then contrasted with some
other. What *we* are, or what *other* is will depend upon context' (Epstein
1978: 100, quoting Leach 1967: 34). By contrast, Epstein also quotes Rabbi
Mendel of Kotsk – and one could be forgiven for wondering who, of Leach
and the Sage, is the modern and who the medieval: 'If I am I, simply because
I am I, and thou are thou simply because thou art thou, then I am I, and thou

art thou. But if I am I because thou art thou, and thou are thou because I am I then I am not I and thou art not thou' (Epstein 1978: 1).

The reluctance to address the issue of the essential self may have been the product of a tradition of social theory which, since the late nineteenth century, had treated self-consciousness as an aberration. For Marx, in capitalist society it was a false consciousness, a manifestation of the individual's alienation; for Durkheim, it signified the inadequate subordination of the individual by society. Mauss's concern with the person or self took the form of a cross-cultural review of the degrees of licence afforded by cultures (and their legal and religious institutions) to individuals and individualism. His was still, and not surprisingly, a structural rather than an 'experiential' approach to the self (Mauss 1938; Carrithers *et al.* (eds) 1985). Throughout the traditions of structural functionalism and British structuralism, the individual was analytically consigned to membership of groups and categories, and perceived as refracting their collective conditions and characteristics. This was entirely consistent with a theoretical model in which the parts of society were conceptually identified by reference to their unique functions. In this kind of schema, individuals were regarded as significant as structures in themselves or as related to structure in identifiable ways, a view which is still propounded by Dumont (1986).[4] Even in structural*isme*, individuality is subordinated to the uniformities of cognitive structures. In all these approaches, the individual is depicted as determined by culture, society, psychology or environment, or by a combination of any of these. Hence, individuals were regarded as generalisable. Individuality was thus portrayed as a theoretical problem: as a deviation from a putative norm, it was something to be explained – as wilful deviance, a failure of socialisation, or as the breakdown of the normal constraints of life.

Whatever the particular theoretical variety of anthropological positivism, individuals were displayed as almost incidental. This posture did not change appreciably until we began to recognise 'meaning' as a problem; to see social differentiation *within* cultures in every respect as normal; to push the problem of generalisation to the centre of the methodological stage.

The relationship between this general paradigm shift and the conceptualisation of the individual is obvious. We belatedly recognised 'meaning' as a matter of interpretation, rather than of stipulation, and then also had to revise our view of symbolism accordingly. Not only were symbols acknowledged as saying many things in many voices, but as being *heard* in quite different registers. Hence, the idea of culture integrating its individual members by their sharing of its symbols required some qualification. Further, we came to recognise that this variability of meaning might not be susceptible to ethnographic 'documentation', precisely because the very nature of symbolism locates it, at least partly, in a non-observable realm. Symbols are thus perceived by people through their *individual* (rather than culturally-cloned) consciousnesses. We cannot hope to make sense of *their* perception of symbols – that is, of their 'membership' of society – without acknowledging their individuality; and cannot do that without recognising the character of our own. I see no more of myself in Leach's statement of contingency than I do in my friend's version of me as a replicate of *their* experience as Jews, or than Henry does in his friends' accounts of him as laughably eccentric and seasick. Rabbi Mendel tells me who I am not; but neither he, nor anyone else, can tell me who I am.

WHO AM I?

If I am not necessarily the person that others see, and if I am not necessarily the person who I *imagine* that others see, and if I am not merely the persona whom I present to others (for whatever reason), who am I, and how might I discover the answer? As I suggested at the outset, posing the question is instructive because it alerts us to the enormity of the task we assume in describing other people - and to the immensity of our misrepresentations of them when we treat them categorically ('as typical examples of a genus' (Watson 1989)); or when we confuse them with our and others' *perceptions* of them. I do not suggest that ethnographers should become psychoanalysts, searching for the irreducible essence of a person buried so deeply that the person may be unaware of it: simply, that we should allow the intractability of the problem to discipline our pens. Hywel Lewis described the difficulty eloquently, but succinctly, in his Gifford lectures:

> (If I am asked) what is this 'I' that has these thoughts and this pain, how is it in turn to be described over and above describing the thoughts or the pain, or noting them, what is the self or subject over and above there being the pain etc.?' – I am wholly nonplussed. There is nothing I can begin to say in reply, not because it is exceptionally difficult to give a correct description, but just because there is no description that can be offered. My distinctness, my being me, is quite unmistakable to me, there can be nothing like a rare vase or painting where we can indicate the properties that make it unique, but unique in a final sense of just being itself. (1982: 55).

This irreducibility and elusiveness of our own selves should be an invaluable mnemonic. If we do not do descriptive justice to individuals, it is hard to see how we could do it for societies. If the substance of 'self' is indescribable, and if (as I trust) (*pace* Douglas 1983: 43) we accept that there is no more mileage in trying to use the self to discriminate between types of society, how, then, can we use the self ethnographically? A tentative answer is 'experientially', for this is the only way to avoid the fictional abstractions that inevitably emerge from sociological theories of individualism or of the self, and from taxonomies of society and individualism. How is self-hood experienced?

ETHNOGRAPHY AND SELF-HOOD

Commenting on this chapter at the ASA Conference, my colleague Ladislav Holy remarked that, in practical terms, only *social* knowledge is accessible to us; and asked whether people's self-knowledge should be an issue for anthropology if it is not available to the ethnographer. The ethnographer can only guess at it with the experience of her/his own self-knowledge (which, in itself, is relational in source and nature, especially when the 'discovery' of the anthropologist's self is so heavily influenced by fieldwork and literary encounters with the Other). In this respect, he observed, anthropological accounts are necessarily reflexive and autobiographical.[5] But, he concluded, this suggests the danger, all too manifest in contemporary anthropology, of 'too much self, too little other.'

My response to these cogent arguments is that, although people's self-knowledge is not easily available to the ethnographer, anthropology cannot continue to be written as if it does not exist, or is immaterial, or, even, is less important than 'social' knowledge. People's knowledge of themselves is of *critical* importance to us for without it we misunderstand them. Its availability does certainly present us with profound methodological difficulties, for which we may have only the very imperfect device of our own experience – and here I hasten to distance myself from any suggestion that anthropology should be 'about the anthropologist's self': rather, it must be *informed* by it.

It is with such self-experience in mind that I argue that anthropology may have exhausted the usefulness of contingency and relativism as means of revealing theoretically how people experience self-hood. Relativism has spanned diverse theoretical traditions in anthropology and is based on views of the individual as plastic, as capable of reformulation by society through various processes of socialisation and initiation. Some exponents of such views defend them with the assertion that in the societies with which they are concerned there is no 'asocial' concept of self and, therefore, no experience of self-apart-from-society (e.g. Lienhardt 1985). John Mbiti remarks, 'I am because we are, and because we are therefore I am' (1970: 141). I am not convinced. My sense of self does not only become crucial when I experience contradictory social demands made of me; or social constructions made of me from which I dissent. It is to be found also in my solitary, Cartesian soliloquy; in my experience of personal space; in the increasing proficiency with which I learn the use of the concept which mediates between the absoluteness and the contingency of self: 'us'. When 'I' becomes 'we', one does not necessarily contradict self but, rather limits it. One says, in effect, there are aspects of 'I' which are not relevant to 'we' and which must be, or can be left out of consideration for the moment. The self that is taken into 'we' is a particularistic, but not a contradictory, version of self.

I will now attempt to illustrate these various points with something of a

Cook's tour of the comparative ethnographic record. Several critics have called this excursion into question. Quite apart from its presupposition of the comparability of extremely diverse cultures, and the generalisability of any one of them (which I have been to some lengths to criticise), it has been suggested that it privileges anthropological over indigenous knowledge (Rapport: personal communication). Further, ethnographic examples cannot, of themselves, do anything to establish the integrity of my claim for a 'self-driven self', as opposed to a 'society-driven self', which can only be axiomatic (Campbell: personal communication).

My critics' reservations would certainly be justified except, I think, that my reasons for introducing these ethnographic accounts are somewhat different. I wish to suggest that a person's consciousness of self and of social membership are not merely reconcilable, or complementary, but that the second may be built on the first (rather than vice versa). Further, it seems to me that this relationship *cannot* be appreciated without the explicit introjection and use of the anthropologist's self – and that, far from this being a weakness of a particular argument or style of anthropology, it is both the limitation and the strength of anthropology as such.

'I' AND 'WE' AS VERSIONS OF THE SELF

The first case is drawn from Hastrup's account of the Icelandic freestate, the period between settlement by the Norse in the ninth and tenth centuries until its full colonisation in the thirteenth century. Hastrup suggests that at first concepts of time and space were ego-centred. People lived in isolation. The measurement of time was material only in relation to the routine observed in the conduct of one's own subsistence activities. Moreover, since its reckoning was based on observations of the sun and moon, it would vary according to vantage point. Concepts of space were likewise related to the unique coordinates of ego's location. Space was demarcated by reference to ego conceptualised as occupying its centre.[6] As the population increased and settlements became denser, social relations obviously assumed greater prominence and the mechanisms of the state proliferated, among them absolute, rather than egocentric, standard measures of time and space. But the one did not simply dislodge the other. The two systems of reckoning coexisted, each prevailing in different spheres. So far as the individual's immediate environment was concerned (say, the farmstead), there was retained a model of space 'as a circular, multi-dimensional area with ego in the centre ...' (1985: 56). However, when the space in question was beyond the personal 'fixed' domain (for example when reference was to an area which implied the individual moving between fixed points outside his own domain) then it was divided by a scheme based on fixed, objective coordinates reflecting the socio-political sub-division of the country into quarters. Rather than being ego-centred, this model of space was society-centred (66). For so long as the two systems coexisted, the imposition of a social system for the reckoning of space did not especially compromise the former individualistic mode.

A structural-functional reading of this history would see the state displacing the self to the degree at which the individual became a mere basket of social roles or repository of social facts, the kind of picture which Wirth depicted as the fate of social actors on the urban stage (1938). A Meadian perspective would sustain the view of the more inclusive self evident in Hastrup's account. For example, Ralph Turner insists that, 'People are not just miniature reproductions of their societies'. Rather a person's experience of his/her articulation with social structure generates a 'self-conception', that is, a consistent symbolisation of self which runs through all the person's activities (Turner 1976: 989–90). This essential self may be *informed* by social engagement, but is not dependent on it: it is an expression of autonomy rather than of contingency. Consider this lesson in self-hood administered to Turnbull by an Mbuti on the banks of the River Lelo.

THE REALITY OF SELF

> Stand at the edge of the water, I was told, and look at your reflection. Who is it? It looks like you, but its head is down there, looking up at the other you. Is it thinking the same thing, wondering who you are? Then put out your foot, over the water, and gently lower it. The other foot will come up to meet yours, and if you are very careful (not to break the surface of the water), you will feel that other foot touch yours. You are getting to know your other self. Then as you lower your foot further into the water the other foot comes up, passes through your foot, and disappears into your leg. The deeper you go into the water the more of your other self enters into you. Just before you go right down into that other world, look down, and see yourself down there, all but your head. Only your other self's head is there. And then look upward as you go right under the surface, and you see nothing. Your other self has passed into the world you left behind, taking your place. Now walk across the bottom of the river, and slowly come out on the far side. If you look up from under the water you will see nobody, just the forest, but as you emerge into that world something will leave you, passing through your body down into the water. Now who is the real self, and which is the real world? (Turnbull 1983: 122)

It is possible to read into this probing of the apparent a number of themes which are prominent in Mbuti culture. The one to which I would draw attention here is a notion of balance. Not only does this seem to embrace many features of Mbuti life, but also expresses a resolution of the dialectic of self and society. The Mbuti live nomadically within the Ituri forest, speaking a wide variety of languages and revealing a plethora of extraneous cultural influences. They live in and on the forest, have a very fluid kin structure, moving from band to band, and from place to place, as they judge expedient. Around them, on the edge of the forest, live Mbira villagers who contrast with them in most respects: they are tribal, sedentary, non-pygmy, cultivators, who are incompetent in the forest, depend on the Mbuti to supply them with its produce, but play the roles of patron to the Mbuti's client. The villagers are *alter* to the Mbuti *ego*.

Here we have the Mbuti, contemplating his reflection in the river and talking about his two selves. Who or what might they be? They could be a metaphorical statement of this curious opposition between the forest nomad and sedentary villager, but this is improbable: ethnic encounters do not often seem to be conceptualised in terms of mirror images – at least, not unless we think in terms of distorting mirrors. Rather, the very idea of the reflection of two images may be a paradigm for the reconciliation of contradictory themes which are perceived as inherent in the human social condition, among which is the opposition between self and society. So far as the Mbuti are specifically concerned, the existence of oppositions and of their resolution is a constant refrain in the culture (Turnbull 1965). There is the obvious distinction betweenn the Mbuti and the villagers: distinct tribally and ethnically; in terms of modes of subsistence and social organisa- tion; physically and topographically different; believing in different gods and spirits. Yet, they live in a degree of symbiosis, the Mbuti supplying the villagers with forest foods (roots, berries, meat and honey) and build- ing materials: the villagers, probably unwittingly, certainly unwillingly, providing the Mbuti with lootable cultivated foodstuffs. Their 'contra- definition' is reconciled through the great circumcision festival of *Nkumbi*, held approximately every three years, through which many of the locally- dwelling peoples are federated.

There are a host of other oppositions: for example, between biological and classificatory kinship. The latter suggests a pronounced egalitarianism, all the women of one's mother's generation being one's mother; all the children of your child's generation being your children. The equality is ruptured by marriage but this contradiction is itself at least partially resolved, by the licence to resume unrestricted sexual relations during the three years following the birth of a child. There is the contradiction between the ideals of non-aggression, of passivity, of freedom and the sanctity of life; and, the necessity for adults to hunt and kill game and meat, a contradiction resolved by the ritual purification of adults, thus polluted, by uncontaminated children. There is the contrast between the ideal of peace, *ekimi*, and noise or crisis, *akami*, resolved through the mediation of youths bringing the crisis out into the open and music-ing it away with the sacred *molimo-made*.

The metaphor of reflections and reconciliation might itself be metaphorised as weights on either side of a scales. If they are unresolved, one pan will outweigh the other. The ideal of resolution is to bring them into balance.

Being out of balance, *waziwazi*, does not imply movement from the individualistic to the collective modes of self. It just means being disoriented. When the Mbuti refers to the 'real self', he/she can have in mind both the individual and the member of the collectivity. In this view, then, the mere fact of sociality does not compromise the idea of self.

SOCIETY, SELF, OTHER

Why might it be that the Mbuti seem to have achieved a reconciliation of self and society which has eluded most of us? The answer might be that they accord greater value to the self than to the social: the individual is not permanently tied to kin or hunting groups, and enjoys a mobility which suggests an avoidance of the social impingement of self (and, incidentally, provides a marked contrast to the individualism which Riviere describes among potentially mobile Guianan peoples (1984: 94 ff)). But this view bears all the hallmarks of that 'society-driven' view of the individual which has dominated anthropology and which still directs us to limit our interpretation of 'inner states' to what can be documented in terms of 'social facts' (cf. Needham op. cit.) or of generalised cultural models of the constitution of personhood (e.g. White and Kirkpatrick 1985; Heelas 1981b). If, instead, we were to allow the possibility of the *self*-driven individual the Mbuti case would not look so discrepant.

The society-driven view sees the self being tugged in different directions by the competing claims and allegiances of the individual's social ties, each of which entails a role with appropriate script. But for too long anthropology has simply tended to accept the social psychologists' axiom that we *are* so subordinated – indeed, that we may even connive at such self-subordination strategically and tactically: that is, we attempt to make ourselves appear as we believe others would wish them to, or in ways in which we would wish others to perceive them. In this tradition, the self confronted by society is merely Performance. What lies beneath the script and the make-up is indiscernable. This kind of analysis threatens to eliminate the self as a real entity altogether. For example, in his book, *The Tactical Uses of Passion*, Bailey analyses displays of emotion, the very antitheses of self-control, in terms of their tactical potency (1983). It is a theory of self with no null-hypothesis – just as, in his earlier exhibition of political masks, he precludes logically the possibility of a person claiming truthfully not to be masked (1977). This may be an especially explicit attack on the saliency of self-motivation, but it is not much more exaggerated than the mainstream social anthropology which persists with the use of general categories from which the self is excluded on the grounds of irrelevancy or methodological inaccessibility or is treated as culturally defined.

The contrary, self-driven view may be less exciting theoretically, but may be closer to our experience. It is certainly true that we suffer from a contemporary idiom which assumes our passive conformity and complicity, which treats us as reflecting, even parroting the social influences which are brought to bear on us. 'The self', says Lock, 'is constituted by culture' (1981: 22). By extension, this would suggest that we wear designer-selves by courtesy of the advertising copy-writers and market manipulators; indeed, even allow the 'rights' which we rhetorically express as inalienable from ourselves, to be defined, and increasingly curtailed by the sophistry of our political leaders.

This view of the self-as-clone should not satisfy us. Our own theoretical approaches to symbolism and meaning contradict it. We do not merely ingest stimuli, whether these are symbols or directives. We *interpret* them; *we* make sense of them, and the stimulus does not dictate what sense we shall make of it. Of course those who direct them at us try to contrive in us particular interpretations, or attempt to limit the kinds of interpretation we might make. But there is evidence to suggest that we are still left with plenty of interpretive (or misinterpretive) space. The 'self-driven' view does not deny the reality of the pressure exerted on individuals to conform to normative role definitions, nor that many, even most people do succumb. There is no suggestion here of the individual compulsively fighting a war of resistance against society. But *experientially* most of us would feel ourselves to be in control – that is, in control of our selves. Indeed, the contrary feeling is defined as pathological and may be diagnosed as 'a breakdown'. Nor should we dismiss the claim to self-control as self-delusion for, in organising our time and space, our social relationships, our self-definition and presentation, we are struggling to keep ourselves in balance, to keep ourselves, as the Mbuti would have it, in the centres of our spheres. In this struggle, the self speaks in the active voice as 'idealist' rather than as *passiones* (see Douglas 1982; Heelas 1981b: 39 ff). Fortes might not have wished to go quite as far as my own over-stated suggestion, but he nevertheless points us in the direction: 'The individual is not a passive bearer of personhood; he must appropriate the qualities and capacities, and the norms governing its expression to himself' (1973: 287). The public expression or presentation of an identity may be very different from its private experience. It is not merely a matter of making the implicit explicit (to borrow a phrase from Crick (1989)); nor, as Hastrup laments, of turning oneself 'inside out' (1989). Marilyn Strathern has recently showed that this assumption is one of the curses of our time (1989). Public identity is a transformation of the self, not an equivalent expression of it. To mistake the two is to make a fundamental error about self-perception. So far as anthropology is concerned, the active self is present again (and again) when the selves of the anthropologist ('personal' and 'anthropological') contrive an interpretation of what is said and heard in the field (Rosaldo 1980: 233; Cohen 1987: 94; 1989: 47–9).

This does not dispute the existence of cultural theories of the self, nor of indigenous theories both of the constitution of the individual and of personhood. Rather, it complements them. For example, take the idea, reported both in Morocco and Andalucia, that a person's moral credibility (and, therefore, social visibility) is based less upon identity (who the person *is*), than upon acknowledged moral accomplishment – or, at least, conformity with an ideology of accomplishment. Writing about Sefrou, Morocco, Rosen observes,

> It is a world – and hence a self – in which people are known by their situated obligations and by the impact their actions have on the entire chain of obligations by which they and their society are known. Human beings do not create themselves but they do place themselves in those contexts ... (1984: 179)

Pitt-Rivers describes reputation in Alcalá de la Sierra in similar terms (1972). Notwithstanding the putative doctrine of Moroccan Islam, Rosen subtly shows that self-hood, like most other variable things in Sefrou life, *is* negotiable and, therefore, *is* created by the power and ingenuity with which the individual deploys and exploits available resources.

There may be tensions between the society's dominant ideology of personhood and the individual's concept of self. There are societies which apparently attempt to impose complete control over the definition and experience of self: Goffman's asylum and Campbell's Sarakatsani (1964) (at least with respect to in-marrying brides) are examples. Goffman himself, like other 'total institutions' theorists (1964) (but not Campbell), acknowledges the difference between imposed role behaviour and self-perception, a distinction manifested in the resilience of self both in 'total institutions' and, *pace* Campbell, in rural Greek marriages (Du Boulay 1974). There are societies in which these tensions are resolved, but without sanctions; Hastrup's medieval Iceland (above) is a case in point. And there are societies which theorise the constitution of personhood, but in a way which may be tantamount merely to providing terms of reference for the self, while *appearing* to do rather more. That is the sense with which I read Wendy James's account of Uduk personhood (1988). The characteristics attributed to stomach and liver constitute physiological explanations of personal psychology, but in a quite impersonal way: really, they map out explanatory space within which the individual can find a unique niche. They leave intact the individual's essential moral autonomy and self-motivation. The individual is 'singular', possessed of a personal Genius (88): 'The human being is the creature of no ruling god, no inner passion, nor are persons mere puppets of an external order' (91; and cf. Beattie 1980: 313–14). Individuals are mostly free to contrive their own relationships (94). All of this is consistent with the idea of *arum* as the driving force, for *arum* is 'inside' the person (133) and, even having in mind Needham's strictures regarding the translation of psychological states, might reasonably be viewed as an approximation to the concept 'self'.

This requires some qualification, for *arum* has multiple meanings: spirit, or ghost (8) or spiritual power (11), 'timeless things of myth' and pre-civilised people (142); animating personal force (7) or 'vital being' (100). *Arum* is certainly not simply assimilable to the concept of self, not only because of the multi-referential nature of the term, but because one could not properly speak of a person as being in control of *arum* in the way in which we talk about 'self-control'. *Arum* is force, vital essence, and therefore cannot be forced. But we do not need to suggest that *arum* and 'self' are equivalents. The beauty of James's exposition is that, without succumbing to the temptations of translation, she shows how the non-equivalent concepts of *arum* and self nevertheless inform our understanding of each. Our own experience of the difficulty of encapsulating the concept of self, not to mention the confusion which arises from the plethora of theories of the self, helps us to an appreciation of the elusiveness of *arum* – and vice-versa. This is an intellectual exercise, but one built on personal, subjective experience. That is to say, it is a different kind of interpretation than might be involved in the juggling of mathematical formulae, or the documentation of 'social facts'. It is largely the product of introspection, of a scrutiny of the self as a '... touchstone for understanding the world of others ...' (James 1988: 144). Hence her conclusion, and one which I share, that 'Self-knowledge is intimately linked with the possibility of understanding others ...' (156).

What, then, of the difficulty with which we began, of the inaccessibility of 'inner states' or self-knowledge? This is not just a problem of eliciting 'indigenous psychology', but arises whenever we impute a state and product of mind to other people (within or across cultural boundaries). It is evoked by questions of 'symbolism', of 'meaning', of 'interpretation', of intention and so forth. To declare these out of bounds because of the difficulties of conceptual or verbal equivalence would be to paralyse anthropology. It would be the academic 'equivalent' of retreating from society because your closest associates interpret your own behaviour and biography in ways which differ from yours. There is no option for us as social members or as social anthropologists but to proceed from the premise of self. It does not have to be a flabby procedure. Its virtue lies in more than its logical inevitability: it also replicates the process of ordinary interaction, of our lay assumptions that we have understood each other, that we have achieved 'intersubjectivity'. '... [E]very version of an other', says Clifford, 'wherever found, is also the construction of a "self" ...' (1986: 23). We have long recognised this as a characteristic of social life. It has taken us longer to recognise it as a necessary condition of anthropology. Now we should celebrate it as our most potent interpretive resource.

NOTES

1 This is the second of a three-part project which examines anthropological constructions of self and other. The first paper compared some uses of these categories in the British and French traditions (Cohen 1989). The present chapter explores ethnographic implications of 'the Self': how we, as anthropologists, conceptualise self-hood among those whom we study, and how our concepts relating to 'the self' derive from, and/or contribute to our own self-knowledge. The final instalment will relate consciousness of self to the idea of personal identity, and will argue that this sense of personhood must be acknowledged as the fundamental human right in order that it may be protected from subversion and abuse by political, economic and other sources of power (Cohen, in press).

   For their careful reading and criticism of an earlier draft of this chapter, I am indebted to Paul Baxter, Alan Campbell, Jim Fernandez, Ladislav Holy, Robert Paine and Nigel Rapport.

2 During the 1960s, Newfoundland generally, and rural Newfoundland in particular, was stigmatised in mainland Canada by the cult of 'humour' known as the 'Newfie joke'. This was a vicious and racist depiction of a backwardness, an exaggerated form of the Polish and Irish jokes which flourish elsewhere. Newfoundland only joined the Confederation of Canada in 1949. For many years thereafter it retained the characteristic features of underdevelopment: unemployment and underemployment; high rates of outmigration, infant mortality, and tuberculosis; a rudimentary infrastructure, shortage of capital, meagre educational provision, intense sectarianism, and so forth.

3 An eminent Jewish scholar, Rabbi Jonathan Sacks, recently echoed this sentiment: 'If Judaism no longer unites Jews, over-achieving does' (Sacks 1989).

4 Interestingly, Dumont's own taxonomy of 'individualism' as a cultural mode in India has been challenged recently (Mines 1988).

5 See, e.g. Paul Spencer's sensitive illustration (1989) and this volume.

6 Lock notes that self-awareness is necessarily anchored in time and place (1981: 24).

REFERENCES

Bailey, F.G. (1977) *Morality and Expediency: the Folklore of Academic Politics.* Oxford: Blackwell.

—— (1983) *The Tactical Uses of Passion: an Essay on Power, Reason and Reality.* Ithaca: Cornell University Press.

Beattie, J, (1980) Representations of the self in traditional Africa. *Africa*, **5**(3): 313–20.

Briggs, J. (1970) *Never in Anger: Portrait of an Eskimo Family.* Cambridge, Mass.: Harvard University Press.

Campbell, J. (1964) *Honour, Family and Patronage.* Oxford: Oxford University Press.

Carrithers, M., Collins, S and Lukes, S. (eds) (1985) *The Category of the Person: Anthropology, Philosophy, History.* Cambridge: Cambridge University Press.

Clifford, J. (1986) Introduction: Partial Truths. In J. Clifford and G. E. Marcus (eds). *Writing Culture: The Poetics and Politics of Ethnography.* Berkeley, Calif.: University of California Press: 1–26.

Cohen, A. P. (1975) *The Management of Myths: The Politics of Legitimation in a Newfoundland Community.* Manchester: Manchester University Press.

—— (1987) *Whalsay: Symbol, Segment and Boundary in a Shetland Island Community.* Manchester: Manchester University Press.

—— (1989) La Tradition Britannique, et la Question de l'Autre. In M. Segalen (ed.) *L'Autre et le Semblable: Regards sur l'Ethnologie des Sociétés Contemporaines.* Paris: Presses du CNRS: 35–51.

—— (in press) The Future of the Self: Anthropology, and the City. In A. P. Cohen and K. Fukui (eds) *The Age of the City: Urbanism and Social Life at the Turn of the Millenium.* Edinburgh: Edinburgh University Press.

Crick, M. (1989) Ali and Me: An Essay in Street-corner Anthropology. ASA Conference on Anthropology and Autobiography, York; this volume.

Douglas, M. (1982) *In the Active Voice.* London: Routledge & Kegan Paul.

—— (1983) How Identity Problems Disappear. In A. Jacobsen-Widding (ed.) *Identity, Personal and Socio-cultural: A Symposium.* Uppsala: Acta Universitatis Uppsaliensis: 35–46.

Du Boulay, J. (1974) *Portrait of a Greek Mountain Village.* Oxford: Clarendon Press.

Dumont, L. (1986) *Essays on Individualism: Modern Ideology in Anthropological Perspective.* Chicago: University of Chicago Press.

Epstein, A. L. (1978) *Ethos and Identity: Three Studies in Ethnicity,* London: Tavistock.

Evans-Pritchard, E. E. (1940) *The Nuer. A Description of the Modes of Liveliehood and Political Institutions of a Nilotic People.* Oxford: Clarendon.

—— (1956) *Nuer Religion.* Oxford: Clarendon.

Fabian, J. (1983) *Time and the Other: How Anthropology makes its Object.* New York: Columbia University Press.

Fortes, M. (1973) The Concept of the Person among the Tallensi. In G. Dieterlen (ed.) *La Notion de la Personne en Afrique Noir.* Paris: Editions du CNRS: 283–319.

—— (1983) Problems of Identity and Person. In A. Jacobsen-Widding (ed.) *Identity, Personal and Socio-cultural: A Symposium.* Uppsala: Acta Universitatis Uppsaliensis: 389–60.

Friedman, J. (1987) Comment on Keesing, 'Anthropology as Interpretive Quest'. *Current Anthropology,* **28**(2).

Geertz, C. (1988) *Works and Lives: The Anthropologist as Author.* Oxford: Polity Press.

Gergen, K. J. (1977) The Social Construction of Self-knowledge. In T. Mischel (ed.) *The Self: Psychological and Philosophical Issues.* Oxford: Blackwell: 139–169.

Goffman, E. (1964) *Asylums.* Harmondsworth: Penguin.

Hannerz, U. (1983) Tools of Identity and Imagination. In A. Jacobsen-Widding (ed.) *Identity, Personal and Socio-cultural: A Symposium,* Uppsala: Acta Universitatis Uppsaliensis: 348–60.

Hastrup, K. (1985) *Culture and History in Medieval Iceland.* Oxford: Clarendon.

—— (1989) Writing Ethnography: State of the Art. ASA Conference on Anthropology and Autobiography, York; this volume.

Heelas, P. (1981a) Introduction: Indigenous Psychologies. In P. Heelas and A. Lock (eds) *Indigenous Psychologies: The Anthropology of the Self.* London: Academic Press: 3–18.

—— (1981b) The Model Applied: Anthropology and Indigenous Psychologies. In P. Heelas and A. Lock (eds) *Indigenous Psychologies: The Anthropology of the Self.* London: Academic Press: 39–63.

Herzfeld, M. (1987) *Anthropology Through the Looking Glass: Critical Ethnography in the Margins of Europe.* Cambridge: Cambridge University Press.

Hsu, F. L. K. (1985) The Self in Cross-cultural Perspective. In A. Marsella, G. De Vos and F. L. K. Hsu (eds) *Culture and Self: Asian and Western Perspectives.* London: Tavistock: 24–55.

James, W. (1987) Mauss and the Tortoise's Predicament. *Journal of the Anthropology Society of Oxford* **XVIII**(1): 49–57.
—— (1988) *The Listening Ebony: Moral Knowledge, Religion and Power among the Uduk of Sudan*. Oxford: Clarendon Press.
Kleinman, A. (1980) *Patients and Healers in the Context of Culture*. Berkeley, Calif.: University of California Press.
Leach, E. R. (1954) *Political Systems of Highland Burma. A Study of Kachin Social Structure*. London: G. Bell for the London School of Economics.
—— (1961) *Rethinking Anthropology*. London: Athlone Press.
—— (1967) *A Runaway World*. London: Oxford University Press.
—— (1984) Glimpses of the Unmentionable in the History of British Social Anthropology. *Annual Review of Anthropology*, **13**: 1–23.
Lee, D. (1976) *Valuing the Self: What we Can Learn from Other Cultures*. Prospect Heights, Ill.: Waveland Press Inc.
Lewis, H. D. (1982) *The Elusive Self*. London: Macmillan.
Lienhardt, R. G. (1985) Self: Public, Private. Some African Representations. In M. Carrithers, S. Collins and S. Lukes (eds) *The Category of the Person: Anthropology, Philosophy, History*. Cambridge: Cambridge University Press.
Lock, A. (1981) Universals in Human Conception. In P. Heelas and A. Lock (eds) *Indigenous Psychologies: The Anthropology of the Self*. London: Academic Press: 19–36.
Luhmann, N. (1986) The Individuality of the Individual: Historical Meanings and Contemporary Problems. In T. C. Heller, M. Sosna and D. E. Wellbery (eds) *Reconstructing Individualism: Autonomy, Individuality, and the Self in Western Thought*. Stanford: University Press: 313–25.
Mauss, M. (1938) Une Catégorie de l'Esprit Humain: La Notion de Personne, celle de 'Moi'. *Journal of the Royal Anthropological Institute* **68**.
Mbiti, J. (1970) *African Religions and Philosophy*. New York: Doubleday.
Mead, G. H. (1934) *Mind, Self and Society: From the Standpoint of a Social Behaviorist*. Chicago: University of Chicago Press.
Mines, M. (1988) Conceptualising the Person: Hierarchical Society and Individual Autonomy in India. *American Anthropologist* **90**(3): 568–79.
Needham, R. (1981) Inner States as Universals. *Circumstantial Deliveries*. Berkeley, Calif.: University of California Press: 171–88.
Okely, J. (1975) The Self and Scientism. *Journal of the Anthropology Society of Oxford* **6**(3): 171–88.
Pitt-Rivers, J. (1972) *The People of the Sierra*. Chicago: University of Chicago Press.
Riviere, P. G. (1984) *Individual and Society in Guiana: A Comparative Study of Amerindian Social Organization*. Cambridge: Cambridge University Press.
Rosaldo, M. Z. (1980) *Knowledge and Passion: Ilongot Notions of Self and Social Life*. Cambridge: Cambridge University Press.
Rosen, L. (1984) *Bargaining for Reality: The Construction of Social Relations in a Muslim Community*. Chicago: University of Chicago Press.
Sacks, J. (1989) The Paradox of Peoplehood. Sherman Lecture, University of Manchester, 8 May.
Sangren, P. S. (1988) Rhetoric and the Authority of Ethnography: 'Postmodernism' and the Social Reproduction of Texts. *Current Anthropology* **29**(3): 405–35.
Southwold, M. (1983) *Buddhism in Life: The Anthropological Study of Religion and the Sinhalese Practice of Buddhism*. Manchester: Manchester University Press.
Spencer, P. (1989) Indulging in Automythologies. ASA Conference on Anthropology and Autobiography, York; this volume.

Stein, H. F. (1985) *Psychodynamics of Medical Practice: Unconscious Factors in Patient Care*. Berkeley, Calif.: University of California Press.

Strathern, M. (1989) *After Nature: English Kinship in the Late 20th Century*. The Morgan Lectures: University of Rochester.

Swinburne, R. (1984) Personal Identity: The Dualist Theory. In R. Swinburne and S. Shoemaker *Personal Identity*. Oxford: Blackwell.

Turnbull, C. M. (1965) *Wayward Servants: The Two Worlds of the African Pygmies*. London: Eyre and Spottiswoode.

—— (1983) *The Mbuti Pygmies: Change and Adaptation*. New York: Holt, Rinehart and Winston.

Turner, R. H. (1976) The Real Self: From Institution to Impulse. *American Journal of Sociology* 81(5): 989–1016.

Turner, V. W. (1968) *The Drums of Affliction*. Oxford: Clarendon Press for the International African Institute.

Watson, C. W. (1989) Autobiography, Anthropology and the Experience of Indonesia. ASA Conference on Anthropology and Autobiography, York; this volume.

White, G. M. and Kirkpatrick, J. (1985) Exploring Ethnopsychologies. In G. M. White and J. Kirkpatrick (eds) *Person, Self and Experience: Exploring Pacific Ethnopsychologies*. Berkeley, Calif.: University of California Press: 1–32.

Williams, B. (1973) *Problems of the Self: Philosophical Papers, 1956–1972*. Cambridge: Cambridge University Press.

Wirth, L. (1951/1938) Urbanism as a Way of Life. In P. K. Hatt and A. J. Reiss (eds) *Cities and Society*. New York: Free Press: 46–63.

Name index

Subject index